THE
PARLEMENT
OF FOULES

The Creator with His creatures

THE
PARLEMENT
OF FOULES

An Interpretation

BY

J. A. W. BENNETT

OXFORD
AT THE CLARENDON PRESS
1957

Oxford University Press, Amen House, London E.C.4

GLASGOW   NEW YORK   TORONTO   MELBOURNE   WELLINGTON
BOMBAY   CALCUTTA   MADRAS   KARACHI
CAPE TOWN   IBADAN   NAIROBI   ACCRA   SINGAPORE

PRINTED IN GREAT BRITAIN

PREFACE

THE first draft of this study (which does not pretend to be a complete exposition) was written during a sabbatical term spent by the long wash of Australasian seas, far from libraries and the accessories of learning. I have since perused most of the discussions of its subject that have appeared in the last half-century and that are now conveniently listed in Griffith's *Bibliography of Chaucer, 1908–1953*; but I have judged it neither possible nor profitable to indicate where my opinions coincide with, or differ from, those of earlier writers. 'A view of a subject,' Hazlitt remarks, 'to be connected and regular, cannot all be new'; and it is heartening rather than dispiriting to find that since I began to write at least some of the critics named in the Bibliographical Note have interpreted this poem or parts of it in ways not essentially different from those followed here. I have found it necessary to make some generalizations about medieval philosophy that may well suggest a greater ignorance or misunderstanding of this philosophy than anyone who writes about medieval poetry should have to confess. Here the excuse must be, first, that the philosophical climate—to accept the current misuse of Glanvill's phrase—in which Chaucer wrote has not hitherto been sufficiently considered, often not considered at all; and secondly that to add the desirable riders and qualifications would be to do ineptly what has been done magistrally by De Wulf, Gilson, and Van Steenberghen.

I owe thanks to Professor C. S. Lewis and Mr. C. G. Hardie for several corrections and suggestions.

J. A. W. B.

CONTENTS

LIST OF PLATES

So, knowing my youth, which was yesterday,
And my pride, which shall be gone tomorrow,
I turn my face to the sun, remembering gardens
Planted by others—Longinus, Guillaume de Lorris,
And all Love's gardeners in an early May.

SIDNEY KEYES

Prologue

Who was hier in philosophie
To Aristotle in our tonge but thou?

HOCCLEVE, *Lament for Chaucer*

CONJECTURE about the poem that Chaucer called 'the book of seint Valentynes day of the Parlement of Briddes' and that copyists labelled *tractatus de congregacione volucrum*, or 'The Temple of Bras', bulks large in the lumber of learned articles and theses piled up in half a century of *Chaucer-Forschungen* and university expansion. For some four hundred years the poem, though included in all editions of Chaucer pretending to completeness, received little attention save from poets or plagiarists. Thus Lydgate, Chaucer's most diligent disciple, owed to it the conceit in the presentation-verses that he sent with an eagle to Henry VI and Katherine his mother, 'sittyng at the mete vpon the yeris day in the Castell of Hertford':

> This foole with briddes hathe holde his parlement
> Whereas the lady which is called Nature
> Sate in hir see, lyche a presydent,
> And alle, yche oon, they dyd hir besy cure
> To sende to yowe good happe, good aventure;[1]

By 1550 Chaucer's title had been borrowed for a poem[2] and a play;[3] and T. Howells adapts several lines of the work itself in his *Devises*, 1581. But Thomas Tyrwhitt, that

---

[1] *Minor Poems*, E.E.T.S. (o.s.), 192, p. 649. He refers directly to the poem in his *Falls of Princes*, ll. 311–15. [2] *v.* S.T.C. 19304.

[3] Bishop Gardiner forbade 'the players of london, as it was tolde me, to play any mo playes of Christe, but of robin hode and litle Johan, and of the

excellent eighteenth-century editor who as Clerk to the
House of Commons had a professional interest in parliaments, was the first to opine that Chaucer might have intended his bird-fable as a covert comment on a human
match; and he suggested that it was the marriage between
John of Gaunt and Blanche of Lancaster.[1] Upon similar
hypotheses modern students have built up a whole archi-
pelago of supposition, and it has come to be assumed, as
with too many other poems, that in order to divine the intention of the poet we must decide what was the occasion
that prompted his verses.

The present writer, on the contrary, would maintain
that, even if we were to discover definite evidence of such
an occasion, the discovery would illuminate this poem no
more than the knowledge of any similar origin or setting,
whether in historical fact or local feature, helps us to
understand the inner force of any work of genius. As Henry
James ruefully allowed when he made pilgrimage to New
Bedford in search of the House of the Seven Gables, such
a work repudiates its historical or local connexions as soon
as they are retraced: 'they are a ladder which genius kicks
back from the top of its wall'. Whatever one is to say about
topical allusions—and it would be foolish to deny their
existence out of hand—must be said after we have considered what is manifestly the writer's main intent, and the
scheme of his book or poem as a whole; we are likely to find
that the more sure and satisfying the imaginative work, the

Parlament of byrdes and suche other trifles': William Turner, *The Seconde
Course of the Hunter At the romishe fox* . . . [? Zürich], 1545, sig. G, fol. ii.

[1] *The Canterbury Tales* (1775), i, p. xxvii, n.e. Tyrwhitt's position as a civil
servant lends piquancy to his remark that 'notwithstanding the petrifying quality
with which Custom-House accounts might be expected to operate upon
Chaucer's genius, he probably wrote his *House of Fame* while he was in that
office' (ibid.).

less important will become the topical references, or auto﹥
biographical scaffolding. The kind of criticism perfected
by the late Professor Manly and Professor Rickert, valuable
as its results may be for the historian, puts such a pre﹥
mium on documentary research that it gives scant oppor﹥
tunity, or none, for literary judgement. It puts a study of the
Wardrobe Accounts before perusal of the books that we
know Chaucer pored over 'til fully daswed was his look'.
It leads graduates in search of a thesis﹥subject painstakingly
to edit the daybook of Wordsworth's carpenter. It makes
the precise date of a poem seem more important than the
meaning of the text.

The *Assemble of Fowles*—to use de Worde's title—has
suffered more than any other poem of Chaucer's from this
misdirection of energy. Yet to describe as wearisome and
wasteful the controversy over its date and supposed allu﹥
sions that began with Koch and Emerson is not to pose as
an exquisite with a fine scorn of dryasdusts and the dull
duty of an editor; still less is it to denigrate Manly, whose
early findings may still be read with profit.[1] It is not less
learning than one pleads for, but a new perspective. We
must avail ourselves

> Of all that industry can reach
> Or stiff grammarians quaintly teach;

Thus we may have to reconsider the vogue for similar
poems—some of them anagrammatic—in fourteenth﹥century
France: a vogue evidenced by poems known to Chaucer
and now accessible in such scholarly works as M. Piaget's
edition of Graunson; if the poem is a cryptogram, as
some critics have urged, we are most likely to learn the
clue by comparing it with others of like pattern. But even

---

[1] v. *Festschrift für L. Morsbach* (Niemeyer, 1913), pp. 279–90.

though they provide analogue or model, they will not explain why Chaucer chose such a model, or such themes. Thanks to investigations of modern scholars we now know more, perhaps, than many of Chaucer's contemporary readers did about the court that these critics take to be the setting for the poem. Yet nothing that the most minute study of this court has detected throws light on the structure of the poem as a whole. When Chaucer introduces topical or personal allusions into his other poems they are usually explicit enough—as in the Prologue to the *Legend of Good Women*, or the Epilogue to *Troilus and Criseyde*. Not only are such explicit allusions absent from the *Parlement*, but the Proem indicates at once that we are to be concerned with themes and issues that are timeless. We cannot treat the rest of the poem as a *pièce d'occasion* without implying that Chaucer could be diverted from his initial speculations about love and human felicity by rumours of an aristocratic or royal marriage: whereas the whole bent of his poetical training would incline him to plan the work in its entirety before lifting his pen. He had been brought up on the 'modern' theory of poetry, as set forth in Geoffroi de Vinsauf's *Poetria Nova*; and a passage in *Troilus and Criseyde* shows that he had taken to heart these lines of Geoffroi's:

> Si quis habet fundare domum, non currit ad actum
> Impetuosa manus; intrinseca linea cordis
> Praemetitur opus, seriemque sub ordine certo
> Interior praescribit homo, totamque figurat
> Ante manus cordis quam corporis; et status ejus
> Est prius archetypus quam sensilis . . .
>
> . . . .
>
> Mentis in arcano cum rem digesserit ordo,
> Materiam verbis veniat vestire poesis.[1]

[1] See opposite for note.

To claim this degree of premeditation is not to imply that the architectonics of the poem are grand or complex. Our English genius, whether in poetry or building, is most at ease in comparatively simple forms—in Royal Crescent or Salisbury Cathedral, in Henry King's Elegy, or Gray's; its best attempts at the elaborate—*The Canterbury Tales, The Faerie Queene*—remain unfinished. And in its finest achievements there is a hint of the homely, and—as in the *Parlement*—the 'commonsensible', the everyday; it is there in 'Prithee, undo this button'—and in the shops that Oxford squeezes into the curve of the High between All Souls and Queen's. But if Chaucer's poem is modest in scale and often familiar in tone, its structure is sure, and even deft; and through the timehonoured formulas of humility that preface it we glimpse what Mr. Coghill justly calls 'an acute and questioning intelligence'. This critical curiosity, and this sense of form, will surprise no one familiar with

Note 1 to previous page.

¹ *Poetria Nova*, ed. E. Faral, *Les Arts poétiques du XIIe et du XIIIe siècle* (1923), p. 198 :

> The hand that seeks a proper house to raise
> Turns to the task with care; the measured line
> Of th'inmost heart lays out the work to do,
> The order is prescribed by the inner man,
> The mind sees all before a stone is laid,
> Prepares an archetype . . .
>
> . . . .
> So in the poet's secret mind the plan
> Unwitting grows, and only when 'tis grown
> Comes poetry to deck the frame with words.

Cf. *Troilus and Criseyde*, i. ll. 1065 ff., and Boccaccio's *De Genealogia Deorum Gentilium*, xiv. vii: [Poesis] fervoris sunt sublimes effectus . . . peregrinas et inauditas inventiones excogitare, meditatas ordine certo componere, ornare compositum inusitato quodam verborum atque sententiarum contextu, velamento fabuloso atque decenti veritatem contegere. (Trans. on p. 39 of C. G. Osgood's version of this section, entitled *Boccaccio on Poetry*, Princeton, 1930.)

the Chaucer canon; the surprise would be if we did *not*
find them.

As to form, it will be enough for the moment to indicate
the main lines of the poem's development:

1. A preliminary statement, or overture, on the miraculous
   power and mysterious paradox of love, as revealed by
   the poet's reading (ll. 1–14).

2. A thesis: the other-worldly doctrine of Cicero's *Somnium Scipionis* as interpreted by Macrobius, with its
   emphasis on love of the common weal as the sole earthly
   good (ll. 29–84).

3. An antithesis, likewise given a dream-form, and embodying in the image of a double gate (ll. 127–52) the
   preliminary paradox of ll. 1 f.; behind this double gate
   the dreamer finds

   (*a*) A paradisal park of vernal innocence and birdsong
         (ll. 170–210).

   (*b*) A garden, surrounding a Temple of Venus—the
         setting for a display of the stages of human passion
         (ll. 211–94).

   (*c*) An open-air assembly of birds of every kind, pre-
         sided over by Nature; in this assembly, and in the
         debates that it proceeds to hold, we perceive cor-
         relatives to the themes of the earlier passages; love
         and mating are the main concern, but they are
         shown as related to, not as irreconcilable with, the
         common weal (ll. 295–658).

4. A synthesis, or at least the suggestion of a synthesis:
   Nature, in accordance with her divine function, knits
   the whole diverse assembly 'in even accord', and offers
   consolation to unsuccessful lovers. The dream closes
   with a gay roundel that voices the birds' adoration of
   the goddess Nature, and the dreamer's—which is here

to say the reader's—sense of a dilemma diminished, if not resolved. (Chaucer is not writing a textbook on ethics and we must not expect to find explicit formulas, neat and simple.)

Coda: Thus the poet's devotion to the 'olde bokes' of Cicero and Macrobius has led him, despite an un-propitious beginning, to a happy conclusion; he can now turn back to his other books with hopeful con-fidence (ll. 695–9).

As to the acute and questioning intelligence, it is in-dicated by Chaucer's very decision to assess the apparently conflicting claims of personal love, love of heavenly things, and love of the public weal, and to consider what Nature, as vicegerent of God, has to do with Venus. If Deschamps's praise of Chaucer as 'Socrates, pleins de philosophie', smacks of rhetorical flamboyance, it was not out of flat-tery that Chaucer's first follower, Thomas Usk, called him a 'noble philosophical poet'. Usk, himself a sensitive analyst of love, uses the phrase in respect of *Troilus and Criseyde*; and in that poem, as in most of Chaucer's, all the philosophical passages are occasioned by climaxes or crises in a love-relation.[1] It is as a poet who is for ever pondering the nature and effects of love that he introduces himself at the very beginning of the *Parlement*: 'Love . . . my feling Astonyeth with his wonderful worching.' If there be a humorous flicker in the lines immediately following, there is certainly no hint that love can be smiled away. And if, adapting a common formula, he confesses 'I knowe not love in dede', this does not mean that the poem is in any sense second-hand, or superficial. By 'philosophical poet' Usk meant more than a skilful versifier of current doctrine.

[1] Cf., e.g., *Troilus and Criseyde*, iv, ll. 960 ff., *Canterbury Tales*, A. ll. 1251 ff.

In his day (and long after) the epithet, which Chaucer was
the first to use in English, implied learning in natural even
more than in metaphysical science; and his *Astrolabe*—
to say nothing of the new-found *Equatorie of the Planetes*
—testifies to the poet's scientific interests, kindled perhaps
by Oxford friends at the college of Walter de Merton, the
centre of English science in the mid-century. Of natural
philosophy there is, to be sure, little direct trace in our
poem—though the power and dignity accorded to the
Empress Nature is itself indicative of the admiring mind
with which Chaucer surveyed the visible world. But there
is much more than a trace of that speculative curiosity
about the relation of men and women to each other and to
this visible world, which in the two preceding centuries
had issued in works as diverse as Bernardus Silvestris's *De
Mundi Universitate*, Jean de Meun's continuation of the
Roman de la Rose, and Dante's *Commedia*. Behind them all
lay the christianized Platonism of Chartres or the christianized Aristotelianism of St. Thomas. The two movements had produced not only a sharpened sense of wonder
(a sense far more characteristic of this earlier Renaissance
than of the Romantic Revival to which Watts-Dunton
attached the phrase), but a passion for understanding the
world, for finding causes and natural laws: hence Dante's
concern with the spots on the moon, de Meun's with the
rainbow, Chaucer's (in the *Hous of Fame*) with the nature
of sound—and of dreams. By this all-embracing curiosity
their poetry is linked with the interpretations of Vincent of
Beauvais and the speculations of Roger Bacon and William Ockham—and distinguished from the poetry of the
sixteenth-century Renaissance, where we might expect, according to received ideas, to find a like interest; nothing in
this later poetry has the encyclopaedic range of Dante, de

Meun, or even of the Seventh Book of the *Confessio Amantis*;
we may find in *The Faerie Queene* a vision of Nature that
resembles Chaucer's in its universality; but that is because,
as we shall see, Spenser, almost alone among the Eliza-
bethans, drank deeply from Chaucer's poetry and shared
his vision.

The emergence of Nature as a fully rounded allegorical
character in the medieval poetry of the vernaculars is in
part a result of the Aristotelian renaissance and the new
view of the universe that it made possible. But this Nature
is conceived of as the vicegerent of God. However daring
the speculations of the poet-philosophers, they never doubted
that the prime cause of the phenomenal world was the
same Creator who had fashioned man in His own likeness.
Both religious orthodoxy and poetic speculation built much
on the scripture that is central in Langland's thought (for
example), as it was in St. Bernard's: 'Faciamus hominem
ad imaginem et similitudinem nostram';[1] when Chaucer,
on his way to the House of Fame, beholds the operations
of Nature in the upper air—

> the eyrish bestes,
> Cloudes, mistes, and tempestes,
> Snowes, hailes, reines, windes,
> And th'engendring in hir kindes—

it is in an exclamation upon this divine fashioning of man
that his ecstasy expresses itself:

> O God, quod I, *that made Adam,*
> Muche is thy might, and thy noblesse![2]

This way of characterizing the Deity is not, of course,
unique; but Chaucer's use of even commonplace phrases is

---

[1] For the scholastic interpretation of the verse *v. Summa Theologica*, i, Q. 93.
[2] *Hous of Fame*, ll. 965–71.

deliberate. That 'Man to Gods image, Eve to mans was made' was likewise to become a commonplace: 'Tritum est in scholis', wrote Pico della Mirandola, 'esse hominem minorem mundum, in quo mixtum ex elementis corpus et spiritus caelestis et plantarum anima vegetalis et brutorum sensus et ratio et angelica mens *et Dei similitudo* conspicitur.'[1] 'It is an adage of the schools that man is a little world in which one sees . . . the likeness of God.' But Pico was not the first to give it fresh significance. And not till Hamlet's 'what a piece of work is a man . . .' were these 'common-places' given a context of personal disillusion.

The greatest medieval poets, then, 'accept the universe', in a sense somewhat more profound than Margaret Fuller's; and their acceptance was quite concordant with current orthodoxy. For all the Lucretian majesty of Nature as she appears in Alain of Lille, in Jean de Meun, in the *Parle-ment*, she is for each poet but 'the vicar of the Almighty Lord'. Yet the poets, deliberately or no, take us a stage further than the schoolmen—and come near to perilous places. Anyone accepting the full implications of the prin-ciple of plenitude, says Lovejoy, 'would have summoned men to participate, in some finite measure, in the creative passion of God . . . would have found the beatific vision in the disinterested joy of beholding the splendour of crea-tion . . .'[2] But this is precisely what Jean de Meun did (and

---

[1] Pater cites the passage in *The Renaissance* (ed. of 1912, p. 42). 'But perhaps', he adds, 'it had some new significance and authority, when men heard one like Pico reiterate it. . . . The proclamation of it was a counterpoise to the increasing tendency of medieval religion to depreciate man's nature.' With his mind on certain late medieval books of devotion, Pater ignores works more truly repre-sentative of medieval thought.

[2] A. O. Lovejoy, *The Great Chain of Being* (Cambridge, Mass., 1936), p. 84. He claims that even Dante approaches heresy when giving this doctrine a Christian colour: ibid., p. 69.

precisely why he was condemned by Gerson). Even in its most abstract form the doctrine of plenitude and continuity in Nature verges upon heresy. It was all very well to re‑ cognize sexual desire as the force by which this Nature continuates society, and propagation as a duty imposed by God. But sexual love, or Venus, seemed to stand at the opposite pole to Christian Agape, or Charitas. The doc‑ trine of *amour courtois* had changed somewhat since the days of the troubadours: it had long since admitted that love was possible within marriage; but it still placed on love between men and women a supreme value which the Church could never allow. The story of Héloïse and Abélard had added new names to love's martyrology; but its monument was a correspondence (whether authentic or not hardly matters for our purpose) which, drawing largely on the language of Cicero's *De Amicitia*, spiritualized affec‑ tion without in any way relating it to sexual love.[1] St. Thomas, like Abélard himself, had incorporated a prin‑ ciple of plenitude into his teaching; and his conception of Christian society involved a recognition of the virtues of the married state such as not all patristic writers had been willing to give; but his doctrines did not win universal acceptance; and nowhere does St. Thomas, or any other schoolman, attempt an analysis of what Monsignor D'Arcy calls 'The Mind and Heart of Love'.[2]

None the less, the developments in philosophic and re‑ ligious thought throughout the twelfth and thirteenth cen‑

[1] *v.* E. Gilson, *Héloïse and Abélard* (1953; French ed., 1948), and *The Mystical Theology of St. Bernard* (1955; French ed., 1947), App. IV. It was doubtless the prestige which the *De Amicitia* acquired from its use by ascetical writers that led to its being reprinted and translated so often in the Renaissance.

[2] Not, of course, that he is silent on *amor* and *amicitia* (his teaching on which has been discussed by P. Geiger *et al.*); his belief in the unity of body and soul inevitably affects his view of marriage (and *v.* p. 145 below).

turies did conduce to a new evaluation of human love,
which inevitably affected poetry. Christian, Platonic, and
Aristotelian concepts formed fresh combinations, and their
impact on each other resulted in a release of poetic as well
as of intellectual energy. 'The master of the Art of Love',
wrote William of St. Thierry, 'is [not Ovid, but] Nature, and
God, who is the author of Nature.' Within the boundaries
of such a doctrine a Christian poet might work with some
freedom, if with few guides. And it is as a poet delighting
in this freedom that we can picture Chaucer. He knew, if
only from the *Roman*, the varieties of speculation that the
more unorthodox Paris schoolmen had indulged in; yet
he nowhere indicates adherence to its more daring doctrines.
He knew Alain's *Anticlaudianus* and *De Planctu Naturae*;
yet shows no trace of allegiance to the neo-platonism that is
suffused throughout these works. He knew and admired
the 'grete poete of Ytaille'; but the figure of Beatrice, in
which Dante imaged his own synthesis of divine and
human love, never crosses his pages; he is perhaps even
now listening respectfully above the crystalline spheres to
Charles Williams's exposition of Dante's Romanticism—
but perhaps, also, confessing that 'I ne can not bulte it to
the bren.' Dante, Alain, de Meun were among the writers
that, as he puts it at the very beginning of our poem, 'Of
usage, what for luste, what for lore', he often read. But the
poem would hardly have taken the form it did if his purpose had been simply to rephrase doctrines culled from
them. Indeed, his introductory stanzas show that he is here
approaching the problems of human love *ab initio*. He will
take from 'olde bokes' what help he can, but he will make
a fresh and individual assessment of their doctrines and
their stories. He proffers, in the end, no definitive, certainly no
doctrinaire, solution. Rather, he sets conflicting attitudes in

delicate equipoise, and moves almost imperceptibly towards a position that comes nearest to being explicit in
Theseus' noble conclusion to the Knight's Tale, and in the
firmly measured *exordium* of the Franklin's.

If nothing revolutionary by way of doctrine emerges from
these poems, their value is none the less for that. 'The
grand work of literary genius', wrote Arnold, 'is a work of
synthesis and exposition, not of analysis and discovery. Its
gift lies in the faculty of being happily inspired by a certain
intellectual and spiritual atmosphere, by a certain order of
ideas. . . . The grand power of poetry is not a power of
drawing out in black and white an explanation of the
mystery of the universe, but of so dealing with things as to
awake in us a wonderfully new, full, and intimate sense of
them.' To the *Parlement* more than to any other of Chaucer's
poems does this dictum apply, and it deserves more attention than Arnold's much-quoted and misphrased judgement that the poet 'lacked high seriousness'. Most of all in
the Golden Middle Ages was synthesis and reconciliation
of apparently conflicting authorities the preoccupation of
literature. 'A comprehension of the world', says Curtius,
'was not regarded as a *creative* function, but as an assimila-
tion and retracing of given facts. . . .'[1] Chaucer, as it
happens, by accepting the doctrine of plenitude, took the
only possible way of putting in its proper place the view of
the body as the prison of the soul, to which Cicero's *Somnium* gives classic expression; and thus provided us with an
epitome of the philosophic development of the entire
Middle Ages.

This synthesis of doctrine is aptly displayed in a work
that in technique shows a synthesis of modes. If Chaucer

---

[1] E. R. Curtius, *European Literature and the Latin Middle Ages* (1953; German
ed., 1948), p. 326.

did not owe to any single predecessor the love-doctrine
emergent in the *Parlement* he was certainly indebted to
Alain, Dante, the *Roman*—and Boccaccio—for scenes,
images, phrases that, in Livingston Lowes's metaphor
(which we may properly borrow, since Lowes set out on
the Road to Xanadu from this very poem), had sunk into
the well between Conscious and Unconscious. But scenes,
images, phrases, patterns are the very least of his debts to
them. What these masters in the art poetical chiefly gave
him was the precedent of dealing freely with topics as vast
as the universe itself, of disdaining petty textbook boundaries on form and subject, of providing paths or pointers
from one philosophy to another—Alain, for instance, provides a bridge from the Platonism of the twelfth century to
the Aristotelianism of the thirteenth. He showed his awareness and appreciation of this freedom in the most practical
way: by himself enlarging the limits of poetry still further,
so that in his verse the comic and the gay can rub elbows
with the scientific and the philosophical, the eternal find a
place beside the everyday. How far Chaucer's predecessors
and contemporaries succeeded in giving organic unity to
their miscellaneous themes—and, in the *Roman* at least,
to shifting points of view—is still debated; the passion for
mirroring the infinite variety of the universe in a *speculum*
certainly left little room for classical concepts of form. But
the achievement of unity in miscellaneity in the *Parlement*,
as in the final glory of the *Tales*, scarcely abides our question. Doubtless he learnt his literary economy, and his
boldness of treatment, unconsciously; reading his poets
and his 'auctoritees' at least as much in search of 'sentence'
as of rhetorical models. But he may well have found
encouragement for his speculative freedom, for his interest
in the varieties of human behaviour, in such philosophers

as Oxford's William Ockham—who at this very time,
following where several Englishmen (Bacon, Robert Kil-
wardby, Daniel of Morley) and Albert the Great himself
had led, was turning away from metaphysics to study the
actual behaviour of things, as Chaucer in our poem turns
from the doctrines of Macrobius to the goings-on of birds.
And he may well have learnt something of pattern from
schoolmen too. The frame of fourteenth-century scholastic
discussion was the *disputatio*; and some of his birds speak
as though taking part in a clerkly disputation. In a larger
sense, as already suggested, the poem reflects the great debate
of the age between the philosophy of plenitude and the
philosophy of other-worldliness. Elsewhere this debate is
carried on by learned clerks in the Latin of the Schools;
Chaucer, profiting in this most of all by de Meun's boldness, ventures as a layman to discuss these themes in the
vulgar tongue.

But nowhere has Chaucer's relish for poetic freedom
more striking result than in the fusion of the 'solace' that
he created by his own artistry out of the materials of his
fellow poets, with 'al this newe science that men lere'. A
Gower or a Henryson, like a medieval preacher using
exempla to stir a torpid audience, keeps 'lust' and 'lore'
formally distinct; and if Harry Bailly can be taken as a
typical listener, audiences were well content with a tale 'In
which ther be som mirthe or som doctrine'—some pleasure
or some profit. The pleasure of the *Parlement* comes, at least
in part, from the embodying of 'doctrine' in birds whom we
recognize as our fellow creatures under their feathers. If
with a recent writer we regard the poem as no more than a
'pretty little *jeu d'esprit*'; if we assume that it has no organic
unity, that the proem and the paradisal park are, equally,
merely decorative—then we had better close our Chaucer

and open our *Reader's Digest*. For it is in the fusing of
'sentence' with 'solace' that Chaucer's whole art consists.

The critic just quoted sensed, perhaps, that her appraisal
of the poem was not altogether adequate, for she follows it
up with the metaphor that has been a boon to many a
modern Chaucerian. 'There are signs in the *Parlement of
Foules*', she says, 'that in spite of his success in handling the
French conventions, Chaucer was already growing restless
within the pretty confines of the garden of the *Rose*.'
The image seems apt enough until we remember that the
Roman contains much else besides a pretty garden: it includes discussions of every kind of love—'charite' and 'love
of frendship' as well as *amour courtois*; a picture of the little
world of man and the great world of Nature; statements
on destiny and free will. If one were required to search the
Parlement for signs of discontent with 'the French conventions', it would be the treatment of the 'conventional' dream
of the paradisal park that one would first consider. In this
dream, as Chaucer describes it, Nature holds the central,
the commanding place; but in assigning her this place
Chaucer, so far from discarding the French poem, was
following Jean de Meun himself, on a track marked out
long before by Alain of Lille. It is Alain—in contrast, he
says, to poets who had contrived 'fictitious distortions'—
who first presents Nature as the true source of knowledge
of love; and the further one goes in the *Roman*, the clearer
becomes the community of philosophic ideas that de Meun
shared with Alain. In reading the *Roman* Chaucer ex-
posed himself not so much to soft poetical breezes wafted
from the garden of the Rose as to the strong winds of
thirteenth-century philosophy. If he was not over-shaken

by them it is perhaps because, like Alain, Dante, and Jean
himself (who not only translated but also glossed the *Consolatio Philosophiae*),[1] he was firmly rooted in the far older
philosophy of Boethius; the ground he had in common
with these poets throughout his life was Boethian ground;
each of them drew from it such constituents as were as-
similable to their own pattern of thought—unless it would
be truer to say that each found it possible to accommodate
the new philosophy within the old Boethian boundaries:
for of impatience with these boundaries none of them show
any sign.

As for the conventions, allegorical and other, that critics
have taught us to associate with the *Roman*, Chaucer seems
to have accepted them as easily as a modern writer accepts
the conventional terms of Freudian or Jungian psychology:
terms invented, as it happens, to describe some of the very
conditions and paradoxes that perplexed and fascinated
Chaucer. In the *Parlement* the most obvious conventional
devices are the dream-setting, the paradisal park, the per-
sonifying of the accompaniments of love, the assembly of
birds, the love-*débat*. For all of these precedent can be found
in French poetry, and for some of them in Italian.[2] Yet the
total effect in Chaucer is far from that of a pastiche or a
poetic exercise. For one thing, he does not pick up these
devices casually. The dream-setting, for example, sorts

---

[1] Alain gives an honourable place to Boethius in his *Anticlaudianus* (iii. 135),
and draws on him constantly. Dante places him in Paradise (*Par.* x. 124-9).
De Meun's version (in the preface to which he says that he had also translated,
inter alia, 'le livre Aeldred de Espirituel Amistie'—a work still further removed
from the *Roman* than is the *Consolatio*) has been edited in *Medieval Studies*
(Toronto), xiv, 1952. The question of Chaucer's acquaintance with it is discussed in *English Literary History*, iii (1936) pp. 170-81.

[2] *v.* J. M. Manly, loc. cit., and (for love-visions) W. O. Sypherd. *Studies
in the Hous of Fame* (1907); and p. 135 below.

perfectly with both the opening account of a *somnium* and
the paradisal scene that soon entrances dreamer and us.
And to these scenes and figures he has added an indefinable
unifying and fortifying colouring of his own, compounded
of grave and gay, of intellect and imagination; it 'crepeth
subtilly' into all parts of the poem, and makes of the adapted
elements something homogeneous, and new. Merely the
fresh juxtaposition of these elements accounts for some of
the novelty. Thus (to anticipate), the paradisal garden at
the beginning of the dream—which at first sight is but a
variant of the meadow‑scene of birdsong and crystal river
at the opening of the *Roman*, but which also shares some
features with the 'good' timeless park that we enter towards
the close of that poem—this garden assumes a new signifi‑
cance when we find set in the midst of it a Temple of
Venus with attendant worshippers, all, or almost all, taken
from a somewhat different context in Boccaccio's *Teseida*.
Again, in the enthronement of Nature we shall find some‑
thing of Alain, in the bird‑assembly something, possibly, of
another French poet. But in arraying the birds as Nature's
subjects, and in presenting three of them as courtly suitors,
Chaucer is not simply varying the usual pattern of a St.
Valentine's Day poem: he is relating the world of Nature
to the smaller world of *courtoisie*. And if the dichotomy
between the bird‑suitors and the human lovers, between
the environs of Venus' Temple and Nature's 'place so
swote and grene', is not absolute, this very indeterminacy
provides a hint that some—the ennobling, the unequivocal—
aspects of human love are reconcilable with Nature's divine
purpose. Beneath the interwoven literary patterns we detect
the development of a viable philosophy of love itself, neither
wholly original nor wholly eclectic, but growing unforcedly
out of a soil blended of romance and scholasticism and

sifted experience of mankind. In assessing this philosophy
we should remember that the courtoisie out of which it
partly grew was never a completely static creed.[1] Always it
retained some relation to the conditions of contemporary
society. No one knew better than Chaucer that

> for to winne love in sondry ages,
> In sondry londes, sondry been usages;

and we shall be in slighter danger of taking this courtoisie
as part of a vast literary conspiracy if we remember that not
all its assumptions were peculiar to medieval Europe: the
dilemmas of Troilus and Criseyde reappear as far away in
space and time as the Long Island of Scott Fitzgerald's
Gatsby: the suitors of the *Parlement* would find sympathy
amongst Polynesian tribes.[2]

The presentation of birds with human attributes is not,
of course, a normal concomitant of the poetry of courtoisie
—though more than one instance can be found in it:
Chaucer himself does not surpass in verve and artistry the
twelfth-century debate between an owl and a nightingale
that provides the first treatment of love-topics in English
medieval verse. Talking birds are also to be found in the

[1] Special reasons for its stiff and static quality in the fifteenth century are
adduced by J. Huizinga, *The Waning of the Middle Ages*, 1924, chap. viii.

[2] Cf. the description of Maori betrothal ceremonies in William Satchell's
attractive tale, *The Greenstone Door*: Once a year the girls dance before the young
men; the lover names the maiden of his choice, who may or may not accept
him. In Satchell's story one rejects a suitor because he is not of sufficiently high
social standing, another (like Gower's Rosiphelee) refuses any engagement, a
third (like the formel in the *Parlement*) shyly demurs: 'Perhaps next year I shall
reply to you, but this time I am too young.' Polynesian legend, again, suggests
certain qualifications to Mr. Lewis's theory of the origins of romantic love. On
the other hand, a novel like Whyte-Melville's *White Rose* strikingly bears out
his claims for the 'survival-value' of courtoisie: not only does it include a
rose motif, but its main scenes are so many enactments of the various encounters
allegorized in the *Roman*.

story of St. Brendan as narrated in the early South English Legendary: the saint and his followers visit 'þe foulen parays', a paradise of birds singing melodiously (like those in the paradisal park that Chaucer enters in his dream) but also (like those of Chaucer's *parlement* proper) gifted with speech—they adjure the travellers to 'thank our lord Christ' who has provided a resting-place on a whale's back.[1] Such birds—witness the voluble eagle in the *Hous of Fame*, or Chauntecleer and Pertelote in the *Tales*—are, one might almost say, Chaucer's liveliest characters. And in our poem he enriches the Aesopian tradition by using it to give dramatic life to the principles of plenitude and natural law as the Middle Ages conceived them. 'The perfection of the universe', Aquinas had declared, 'consists in the orderly variety of things';[2] variety and order characterize the bird-assembly over which Chaucer's Empress Nature presides. Such a view of the universe, as modern commentators on St. Thomas recognize, makes it a supreme work of art, and God the supreme artist; and to the poet as well as to the philosopher in Chaucer such a view would quickly commend itself. His bird- or animal-scenes, 'frequent and full', have their artistic no less than their philosophic justification, reminding us of those vivid, crowded pages of the Pepys sketchbook that rival Uccello or Audubon, or of those forty very English birds so lovingly drawn and coloured in the Sherborne Missal.[3] His busy conies,

[1] *South English Legendary*, ed. C. Horstmann, E.E.T.S. (o.s.), 87, p. 230.

[2] *v.* p. 141 below.

[3] The Pepys sketchbook is reproduced in vol. xiii of the Walpole Society's publications (1924–5). It is usually treated as English work, but Mr. David Lack informs me that some of the birds depicted belong to southern Europe; and Professor Wormald sees Lombard influences in the drawing (*Journal of the Warburg and Courtauld Institutes*, xvii, 1954, p. 195). On the other hand, the late-thirteenth-century 'Bird Psalter' recently acquired by the Fitzwilliam

quacking geese, and insistent cuckoo seem cousins to the creatures that frolic on the margins of Queen Mary's Psalter or peer through the winding leaf-patterns of the Luttrell Manuscript. Nor is the resemblance fortuitous. Chaucer's poetry, like these minor masterpieces, is part of the four-teenth-century flowering of East Anglian culture; the artists, like the poet, combine a loving devotion to Nature (if hardly in the Wordsworthian sense, or even Gilbert White's) with an irrepressible liveliness, a keen sense of delight in the incidental. But it is the crowdedness of their scenes that is distinctive. Earlier poets had written about owls and nightin-gales, earlier artists—in particular Cluniac sculptors—had used ducks and other birds for ornament; but rarely before the fourteenth century do we find these assemblies of birds of all sorts in one single manuscript or poem.

The bird motif allows Chaucer both to distance and to isolate the particular conditions of human love with which the poem is concerned—to free himself of the complica-

Museum is undoubtedly English, as is the fourteenth-century Holkham Bible (reproduced in full by W. O. Hassall, 1954), which was perhaps painted in London, and which includes in its creation scene (*v.* Frontispiece), an owl, hawk, heron, swift or swallow, woodpecker, blackbird, magpie, peacock, peregrine falcon, and wren; and Dr. Hassall notes that 'the best falconry manu-scripts are Anglo-Norman'. The Sherborne Missal (*c.* 1400) is likewise un-doubtedly English. Almost all the birds occurring on pp. 363–93 of this manuscript bear their vernacular names—including Chaucer's 'stork', 'gai', 'cormeraunt', 'roddoke', 'heyrun', 'uelduare', 'fesaunt hen' 'throstilcok' (*sic*: in fact a blackbird). Some of the illustrations are reproduced in colour as the frontispiece to the Roxburghe Club edition of the Missal (Oxford, 1920). East Anglian motifs have been detected in the decoration. The birds on the early-fourteenth-century murals at Longthorpe, near Peterborough, have been related to East Anglian illumination in *Archaeologia*, xcvi (1955), pp. 21–22. For representations of birds in English medieval glass *v.* C. Woodforde, *Journal of the British Archaeological Association*, 3rd ser., ix (1944) pp. 1–11.

Pages from the Pepys MS. are reproduced on Pl. 4.

tions attending a human story while making capital out
of the minor incongruities involved in giving the birds
human attitudes and anxieties. Thus their impatient
'Have done, and let us wende' transports us for the moment
to a modern House of Commons with back-benchers
anxious to be off for the Easter Recess—or to that other
animal-parliament which a poet of different art and purpose had sketched only a little earlier in the Prologue to
Piers Plowman. The duck swears 'by my hat'—but this is as
much part of our pleasure (and Chaucer's) as is Brer Rab-
bit's 'ceegyar'. The goddess Nature raps out a sharp 'Hold
your tongues!'; but it does not make the birds less birdlike,
or Nature less divine: she speaks and acts, indeed, as all
Chaucer's anthropomorphic deities act and speak. The
dialogue, like the dramatic tension, grows in the most
natural way out of a conventional setting; there is no 'break-
ing loose from the conventions' except—and it is a notable
exception—that Chaucer avoids the prolix monologues of
French fable and romance. And here lies perhaps the
cardinal difference between him and his predecessors. The
very length of the *Roman* prevents us from grasping its *sen*;
and nowhere in the course of its 22,000 lines does it come
near such telling imaginative statement of the relation of
Nature to human love as Chaucer here achieves in one-
thirtieth of the space. He keeps the *disputatio* pattern of the
Roman, but he compresses and enlivens it by variety;[1] even

---

[1] The presence of this pattern in the *Roman* has been ably argued by Alan
M. F. Gunn, *The Mirror of Love* (Lubbock, Texas, 1952). He concludes:
'The poem is to be described as a disputation because the various personages
who discourse within it upon the subject of love show a consciousness of the
differences between their own views and those of the other speakers, and attempt
a more or less systematic exposition of their own doctrines and a refutation of the
theories and precepts of their opponents' (p. 321). *Mutatis mutandis*, this might
be said with equal truth of the disputants in the *Parlement*.

as, when he turns to Boccaccio's ten-thousand-line *Teseida*, he reduces it by three-quarters, whilst yet finding room to make of Theseus a complex and likeable character, at once more human and more godlike than the Italian Teseo. 'To th'effect' is his motto, and it indicates his briskness as well as his empiricism. Like his own Nature, and his own Knight, he knows exactly when 'ther is namoore to sey'.

Some thirty years ago an anonymous reviewer of Mr. Eliot's *Tradition and the Individual Talent* remarked that a poet makes the best use of tradition when he continues the exploration both of what may be said in terms of poetry, and of the manner of saying it, beyond the point to which the exploration has been carried before: 'he poeticises complex experiences that have never been poeticized before'. This is precisely what Chaucer attempts, however modestly, in the *Parlement of Foules*; the complex experience being that of the poet himself when he ponders the problems and paradoxes of love, and in particular the relation of personal love to the common weal and to the laws set in the universe by Nature, vicar of God. The poem differs in scope from earlier explorations of a similar kind partly, at least, because some of it concerns the relation of men and women not only to each other but to society: a concern that is ultimately to issue in the collective pilgrimage to Canterbury foreshadowed at the close of the *Hous of Fame*, where the poet begins to turn from his books to those 'neyghebores that dwellen almost at thi doores', and where the 'tidings of love' are to be sought amongst the crowd of shipmen, pilgrims, and pardoners that is to crystallize into the company at the Tabard.

The exegesis that follows makes no claim to be definitive. So long as it leads to a closer scanning of this carefully wrought poem, and to a better understanding of the medieval poet's craft, it will have fulfilled its purpose. If the expositor errs, he can plead that perhaps he errs with Spenser, who for all his differences, for all his cloudiness, was closer to Chaucer in spirit and tradition than any academic interpreters of the poem. It was professedly from Chaucer that Spenser learnt of Alain, and it was from the Fowls' Parley that he derived the doctrine of the great Mutability Cantos. On Chaucer's poem these and other passages of *The Faerie Queene* will prove to be an extended and sometimes an enlightening commentary.

CHAPTER I

The Proem

To what fyn made the god that sit so hye,
Benethen him, love other companye,
And streyneth folk to love, malgre hir hede?
And then hir joye, for oght I can espye,
Ne lasteth not the twinkeling of an eye,
And somme han never joye til they be dede.
What meneth this? what is this mistihede?
Wherto constreyneth he his folk so faste
Thing to desyre, but hit shulde laste?

The Compleynt of Mars

He suddenly struck in and quoted Macrobius; and thus gave the
first impression of that more extensive reading in which he had
indulged himself.

BOSWELL, *Life of Johnson*

[In the Middle Ages] advances were made not through any
grandeur of intention, but because the men who actually studied
the classical authors were always led by their immediate interests
further than they had originally intended.

R. R. BOLGAR

IF modern Chaucerian criticism has established one thing
more firmly than another, it is the poet's knowledge and
mastery of the rhetorical modes as promulgated by half a
dozen earlier writers, French and English, and as practised
by the poets in whom he was deeply read and by whom
he was greatly influenced.[1] No one will nowadays be sur-
prised to find the Chaucer whom the nineteenth century

---

[1] Cf. Gunn, op. cit., chap. v, *passim*: D. Everett, *Essays in Medieval Literature* (1955), p. 154.

liked to regard as the artless 'poet of the dawn' beginning
the *Parlement* with an elaborate *circumlocutio*:

> The lyf so short, the craft so long to lerne,
> Th'assay so hard, so sharp the conquerynge,
> The dredful joy, that alwey slit so yerne:
> Al this mene I by love . . .

—where *contentio, oxymoron, sententia, chiasmus, suspensio*, all
play their parts. But it is more conducive to an understanding of the nature and development of the poem to
realize that here we have a variant of a common literary
topos: the instability and duality of love. Just as much as the
employment of figures of speech, the appropriation of such
a traditional theme on which variations could be played at
will indicates Chaucer's familiarity with the *artes rhetoricae*;
and gives us the more reason to think that the poem will
show such ordonnance as poets skilled in developing *topoi*
would display. Pattern, in fact, is apparent from the outset—and more apparent later than in the long and elaborate
poems of which this is to some extent a miniature. The
whole work could be analysed in rhetorical terms, much as
Professor Gunn has analysed the great *Roman de la Rose*
itself; the primary difference between the *Roman* and the
Parlement being that de Lorris takes some 3,000 lines to
reach the point where Chaucer begins: 'The peyne is
hard', says Resoun (in the Chaucerian rendering), 'out of
mesure,

> The Joye may eek no whyl endure:
> And in the possessioun
> Is much tribulacioun;
> The Joye it is so short-lasting,
> And but in happe is the geting;'[1]

---

[1] *Romaunt of the Rose*, ll. 3279–84; *Roman de la Rose* (henceforth cited as
RR), ll. 3051–4.

Like many *topoi*, this of 'love's good and evil gift'—so
Euripides phrases it in the *Medea*—is as old as the Greeks;
and like many others it was repointed by the *clerici vagantes*:

> An amor dolor sit,
> An dolor amor sit,
> Utrumque nescio;
> Hoc nimis sentio,
> Jucundum dolor est
> Si dolor amor est;

whilst one of our earliest English lyrics begins:

> Loue is sofft, loue is swet, loue is goed sware.
> Loue is muche tene, loue is muchel kare . . .[1]

And Chaucer had lately found a highflown variant of it in
Alain's *De Planctu Naturae*.[2] By Shakespeare's time the
two loves of comfort and despair have become the theme
of any Romeo who remembered his grammar school rhetoric;

> What is it else? [he concludes] A madness most discreet,
> A choking gall—and a preserving sweet.

But these paradoxes do not persist in literature unless they
bear some relation to life. If 'd|aruryes greme and grace' is the
topic to which the Green Knight's lady draws Sir Gawain
it was because the fourteenth-century reader felt 'unsely
jolif wo' to be the lot of lovers: and the travail and dis-
quietude that love involves are voiced throughout a work
as different in spirit from *Sir Gawain* as *El libro de Buen
Amor*. 'Ever', says Criseyde, in the same poem that includes
Chaucer's supreme paean on the 'pleasaunce of love'—

[1] *English Lyrics of the Thirteenth Century*, ed. Carleton Brown (Oxford,
1932), no. 53.
[2] p. 472 in T. Wright's edition (*Satirical Poets of the Twelfth Century*, ii,
1872).

> Ever som mistrust, or nice stryf,
> Ther is in love, som cloud is over that sonne.[1]

It is an unease shared by Troilus—who uses the very phrase 'dredful joy'—though hardly by Boccaccio's lovers. If either Criseyde or Troilus could rationalize this unease there might be no tragedy; but it takes a Donne to be objective about love while still in its toils. Chaucer's immediate avowal, 'I knowe not love in dede', is not to be dismissed as a tag or trick, though to be sure many a French poet, including his admired Graunson, speaks of love 'par devinaille' ('by conjecture'). Like the slow measure, the cumulation of metaphors, the careful suspension and balance of the opening stanza—and in contrast to that from the *Compleynt of Mars*, cited above—it helps to prepare us for a full, impersonal treatment of an ancient theme.

An ancient theme; but one that in the century before Chaucer had been pondered with a special intensity. As first the troubadours and then the romancers and the poets of *il dolce stil nuovo* sang the praises and enhanced the value of human love, the question of reconciling their assump, tions with everyday experience on the one hand or eternal Christian verities on the other, had grown the more acute. At one time Averroes, with his doctrine of different levels of truth, may have seemed to offer an answer. But Averro, ism had been roundly condemned in 1277—at the very same time as Andreas Capellanus's *De Arte Honeste Aman, di*. To the orthodox this simultaneous condemnation may well have suggested that *any* discussion of human love was likely to be hazardous: especially since it was likely to in, volve the notion of free choice, which would lead on to free will, which—witness the history of Averroism itself— might bring one close to heresy. At another time another

---

[1] *Troilus and Criseyde*, ii. 780–1.

Arab philosopher, Avicenna, had attempted a solution by means of Plato's ideal ladder. But by the thirteenth century Plato was no longer deemed an adequate guide; and to us Avicenna is relevant chiefly as a reminder that in Arab no less than in Christian countries philosophic develop-ment went along with developing speculations about love;[1] whilst textbooks of love (themselves sometimes showing the influence of the schools) vied in popularity with textbooks of philosophy. Yet nowhere outside Dante or before Chaucer were the paradoxes glanced at in this first stanza resolved any more satisfactorily than in the French literature of courtoisie. Chaucer may well have felt as he turned from 'the bokes (that) rede I ofte, as I yow tolde' that none of them gave much hope of a clue to the mystery.

As with many a medieval poem, the main development of the *Parlement* is implicit in the opening verses. These balanced lines and phrases foreshadow the double gate, symbol of love's duality, through which we are later to accompany the poet; the couplet

> So sore, iwis, that whan I on hym thynke
> Nat wote I wel wher that I wake or wynke[2]

prepares us, by its note of anxiety and its mention of sleep, for the uneasiness with which the poet is to turn to his bed and dream; whilst the god of love who 'wol be lorde and sire' (l. 12) we are to meet in the dream as 'Cupide our Lorde', at the entrance to Love's garden.

The theme as announced, with its incidental reference to

[1] Cf., e.g., *The Ring of the Dove* (trans. A. J. Arberry, 1952).
[2] ll. 6–7. It recalls Deschamps's *balade* beginning

> Pris m'a Amour, et si soudainement
> Que je ne say se je dors ou je veille,

to the second line of which Chaucer has given his own twist, just as in the first line he has adapted Hippocrates' *Ars longa, vita brevis est.*

'Love's folk', is hardly different from that of the *Hous of Fame*, which was probably written within a few years of the *Parlement*. There the avowed purpose of his journey was to learn 'tidinges of Loves folke, If they ben glade'; and there too we find him poring over his books in search of such tidings. From the time of the *Book of the Duchesse* onwards it is to the 'olde clerkes' that he directs these inquiries about the nature of love. The *Hous of Fame* breaks off just as he seems about to learn the truth of the mystery from 'a man of gret auctoritee'. Now the *Parlement*, another dream-poem, is to begin by introducing just such a man of 'auctoritee' in the person of Scipio Africanus, as he figures in Cicero's *Somnium Scipionis*. We are in the fourteenth century, which had the traditional respect for accepted authorities—in the technical sense of authors (Cicero being one) who could be cited and appealed to in scholastic disputation. For reasons that have lately been set forth by E. R. Curtius and R. R. Bolgar, this respect was accorded to pagan as well as to patristic writers. But it was not a mere superstitious regard for antiquity and tradition. As Chaucer himself puts it in the Prologue to his 'book of the XIX Ladies':

> Wel ought us thanne on olde bokes leve
> *There as ther is non other assay by preve.*[1]

The doctrine of these 'olde wyse', as found in their 'olde apreved stories' (he there remarks) bears on 'holinesse, regnes, victories', but also teaches 'of love, of hate . . .'. To such authorities he turns, therefore, quite naturally, in our poem, when he wishes to learn 'a certeyn thing' that the context suggests is concerning love. From 'olde bokes', he goes on, 'Cometh al this newe science'. We must beware

---

[1] *Legend of Good Women*, Prol. G. 27-28.

PLATE I

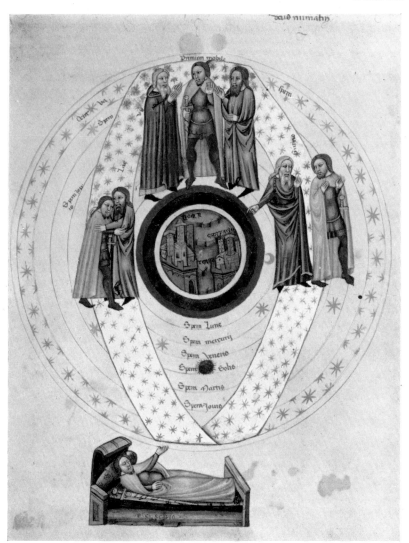

The dream of Scipio

of giving these lines too modern a meaning: they reflect, if distantly and obliquely, the enthusiasm of the medieval humanists as they expounded the rediscovered philosophy of Aristotle and other thinkers who, in de Meun's phrase, 'les anciens livres firent'; the enthusiasm that is still alive in Chaucer's Oxford Clerk, who would sooner have twenty books of Aristotle 'than robes riche, or fithele, or gay sautrye'. The 'newe science' of scholasticism had made it possible to reinterpret Aristotle without jettisoning either St. Augustine or the neoplatonists; and so had produced a fuller view of Nature, of human society, and, in certain writers, of human love.

If Cicero seems an odd authority for Chaucer to turn to when perplexed by the duality of love, we must remember that a still more profound poet, Dante, ranks the pagan orator with Boethius as a philosopher (and in the Middle Ages that was to rank him very high indeed); that the *De Amicitia*, surprisingly platonic as it is in form and content, was the only classical discourse on human affection that had proved acceptable to the twelfth-century ascetical writers —through whom it may have had some influence on the development of *courtoisie* itself; that the book which the poet chose was enshrined in and inseparable from the Commentary by Macrobius which for the Middle Ages constituted a veritable cyclopedia of philosophy, natural and moral: and, finally, that from the viewpoint of the fourteenth century both Macrobius and Cicero were worthy of equal respect as *veteres*—goodly writers of the antique times—whether pagan or Christian hardly mattered: distance in time lent reverence to the view. It is hardly surprising, then, to find the *Somnium Scipionis* on the shelf of a poet who translated Boethius, wrote the *Astrolabe*, and read deeply in the *Divina Commedia*. Manuscripts including the

Commentary had been accessible in England since the
time of Bede; the opening lines of the *Roman* testify to the
prestige it enjoyed in the thirteenth century; and Chauntecleer's appeal to

> Macrobeus, that writ the avisioun
> In Affrike of the worthy Scipioun,

as one who

> Affermeth dremes, and seith that they been
> Warninge of thinges that men after seen,[1]

if inexact, provides a sufficient indication why the poet who
pondered so much on dreams and cast other poems beside
the *Parlement* into the dream-form, should show respect for
the work. Its appeal, like that of many books we now dub
'typically medieval', outlasted the Middle Ages and in fact
increased with the increasing interest in cosmology.[2] The
tendency in Chaucer's day was to identify the work as a
whole with Macrobius; but a careful reading of the Commentary would make it clear that the basic text was

---

[1] C.T.B. 4313–6. Cf. *English Poems of Charles of Orleans*, E.E.T.S. (o.s.),
215, 1941, ll. 4744 ff.; *RR*.

[2] The 'worthiness' of Scipio Africanus is accepted by medieval writers from
John of Salisbury onwards; and Petrarch is as much 'medieval' as 'humanistic'
in writing *Africa* as a memorial to him. Indeed, that poem shows him doing
what Chaucer attempted, in part, in the *Parlement*: reconciling the Ciceronian
virtues and the Christian; cf. R. R. Bolgar, *The Classical Heritage* (1954), p.
255. Sigismondo's interest in Scipio as his honoured ancestor led to the
Somnium providing imagery for his Tempio Malatestiano at Rimini (*c.* 1450):
cf. Charles Mitchell in *Studi Romagnoli*, ii (1951), pp. 83 ff.

Some thirty-five editions of Macrobius were printed between 1472 and 1628.
For Skelton he is still the authority 'that did treat of Scipiouns dream what was
the true probate'; and Ben Jonson refers to the Commentary in his Notes to the
Hymenaei, 137 ff.: *v. Works*, (ed. Herford and Simpson), vii, pp. 214, 216, 221.
Neither Boswell nor Malone thought it necessary to explicate the reference at the
passage in the *Life of Johnson* cited at the head of this chapter.

Cicero's; and to Cicero he assigns it in l. 31, as if to em⁄phasize that it was a thoroughly reputable work.

We need not here repeat 'the grete of his sentence' (l. 35)—by which Chaucer means the essence of its teaching—especially as a new translation of both *Somnium* and *Com⁄mentarium* is to hand.[1] It will be enough to note that Chaucer, like King Ælfred rendering Pope Gregory's Latin *Pastoralis*, follows Cicero 'hwilum word be worde, hwilum andgit of andgiete'. ('Now word for word, now accord⁄ing to the general sense.') Sometimes he glances at Macro⁄bius' gloss, sometimes he summarizes. Thus ll. 43–48 compress a long passage of *oratio recta*, including a prophecy of the younger Scipio's fortunes and a hint that he is to die at the hands of his kinsmen. To one phrase in the Latin here Chaucer gives an interesting contemporary cast: where Cicero writes *patriam* or *rem publicam* Chaucer puts 'the comune profyt'. The philosophy of the Roman politician and patriot had inevitably a political flavour: and 'comune profyt' has exactly the political connotations required. But the radius of the phrase had extended until it included the suggestion of peace and general harmony: thus Chaucer's Parson avers that if God had not ordained degree 'the comune profit might not han be kept, ne pees ne rest on erthe'; and the Clerk says of Griselda, when Petrarch has simply *publica obibat officia*, and the French version of his tale 'la chose publique adrescoit';

> The comune profyt koude she redresse.
> Ther nas discord, rancour, ne hevinesse
> In al the land that she ne koude apese;[2]

---

[1] *Macrobius's Commentary on the Dream of Scipio* (trans. William H. Stahl, New York, 1952). For a French version of the *Somnium* and an assessment of its philosophy *v.* Pierre Boyancé, *Études sur le Songe de Scipion* (Bordeaux and Paris, 1936); and for an account of its influence *v.* Bolgar, op. cit., pp. 43–44.

[2] C.T.E. 431–2. In his translation of Boethius, i, Pr. iv. 9—where again the

For this virtuous lady, to seek the common good is to follow 'pees' and 'charite'. In marked contrast is the complaint of Dido in the *Hous of Fame*, that men seem often to love 'for singuler profite'[1] which is the opposite to 'charite'; and there is a like antithesis between 'charite' and self-regarding passion at the end of the *Confessio Amantis*, where a Venus who is something more than the pagan goddess of that name decrees

> That thou nomore of love sieche,
> But my wil is that thou besieche
> And pray hereafter for the *pes*.[2]

All this gives an ironical significance to the phrase 'comune spede' in the context in which we shall find it later in the *Parlement*. For the present we may note the association of the concepts of concord and degree, and the implied dichotomy between passionate love and the common weal. In an hierarchical society lovers of rank 'may not, as unvalued persons do, carve for themselves'. So the Marquis of the Clerk's Tale plausibly excuses himself to Griselda: 'I may not doon as every plowman may.' More than their own happiness hung upon their attachments; and if they ignored the common profit, the outcome was likely to be the tragedy of a Lancelot, as acknowledged by

context is political—Chaucer renders *commune commodum* as 'commune profyt'. The phrase, or its French antecedent, recurs often in the proceedings of the Plantagenet parliaments; and Langland uses it concerning his parliamentary rats (*P. Pl. Prol.* B, l. 148). St. Thomas uses it of marriage: loc. cit., p. 11, n. 2.

[1] l. 310. For 'singular' as opposed to 'common' profit, cf. Dunbar, 'To the Merchantis of Edinburgh', ll. 71–72.

[2] viii. 2911–13. Venus seems here to be associated with the planetary Venus (*v.* p. 56 below): cf.

> Out of my sihte al sodeynly,
> Enclosed in a sterred sky,
> Up to the hevene Venus straghte (ll. 2961–3*).

Guinevere in her poignant cry: 'Through this same man and me hath al this warre be wrought.' The conflict of values is as old as the stories of Aeneas and Dido, Cleopatra and Antony—and as contemporary as the House of Windsor. We do not need a topical key to the *Parlement* in order to see that Chaucer had the conflict in mind as he wrote this poem. But we may need to re-read *Troilus and Criseyde* if we think that he or his contemporaries would, or could, ever count the world—in the sense of the *res publica*—well lost for love. Troilus himself (in marked contrast to Boccaccio's Troilo), when tempted to elope with Criseyde, recognizes that

> I sholde han also blame of every wight
> My fadres graunte if that I so withstode,
> Sin she is chaunged *for the tounes gode*.[1]

Certainly for Cicero, platonist as he was—or as he was whilst writing the *Somnium*—any judgement that placed a premium on passion would have been incomprehensible. The only happiness he thinks worth considering is that of heaven 'ther as joy is that last withouten ende' (l. 49), the only means of attaining it, pursuit of the common good. Chaucer could have found no stronger contrast to the 'dredful joy' of the unstable human love that he considers in his opening lines—where 'slit' evokes all the associations of the Troilus story: Criseyde was 'sliding of corage'. And Africanus' next sentences, with their platonic insistence that death is a release from the trammels of the body, that 'our present worldes lives space' is the real death, offers a still sharper astringent for love. Chaucer summarizes his doctrine, neither shunning it nor glossing it over. It was, after all, as familiar to him as it was to the Donne of the

---

[1] *Troilus and Criseyde*, iv. 551–3.

Anniversaries; and he was to put it into the mouth of his Theseus, as cheerful and extrovert a character as could be desired. Like African's assurance that 'rightful folk shal gon, after they dye, To hevene' (ll. 55–56), it easily took on an orthodox Christian colour: St. Paul's 'who shall deliver me from the body of this death?' provided an obvious parallel, just as Plato's teaching that the good will occupy themselves with 'the things that are above' would seem to anticipate the Epistle to the Colossians.[1] On the other hand, Cicero's location of these righteous souls specifically in the Milky Way Chaucer may have found as novel as it was irrelevant to his purpose; he keeps the barest reference, and is careful not to commit himself, saying simply that Scipio was shown 'the galaxye'—a word of Chaucer's adoption, and derived, not from the *Somnium* itself, but from Macrobius' Greek gloss on Cicero's *orbis lacteus* 'qui γαλαξίας vocatur.'

Whilst in no way perverting his sources, Chaucer is imperceptibly shaping them to his own purpose. To Scipio, looking down from his 'sterry place', the earth seemed so small 'ut me imperii nostri, quo quasi punctum eius attingimus, poeniteret'; But Chaucer abandons the imperial reference, choosing to emphasize in a more general way the littleness of earth 'At regard of the hevenes quantite' (l. 58): a line that not only echoes Boccaccio's account of Arcita, as the dying knight looked down from the spheres,

> . . . ogni cosa da nulla stimare
> a rispetto del ciel;[2]

---

[1] Cf. *Republic*, vii. 517 C. A conscious adaptation of Pauline phrase to twelfth-century semi-platonic philosophy may be detected in the Gloss to chap. vi of Alain's *Anticlaudianus* (*v.* p. 127 below): '[Natura] dicit ego intendo . . . dominum hominem, cujus conversatio in coelo existat.' (Wright's edition, p. 280, n. 6; with which cf. Phil. iii. 20.)

[2] *Teseida*, xi. 2. Boccaccio, who certainly read Macrobius with attention,

but also brings to mind the use which Chaucer made of that account in describing Troilus' death. Indeed, all of Chaucer's poems about the state and fate of lovers involve us in cosmology—from Theseus' picture of the universe as linked by the chain of love, to the *Hous of Fame*, with its contrast between the Temple of Venus, set in a sterile desert, and the aerial regions from which the whole world 'no more semed than a prikke'; and always the cosmology is used to point the littleness or transience of man: 'Thanne may ye see that all this thing hath ende'; 'The grete tounes' (we may think of Troilus' Troy, or Scipio's Rome) 'wane and wende . . . He moot ben deed, the king as shal a page.'[1] And in the *Hous of Fame* the poet makes specific allusion to the Ciceronian cosmos:

> half so high as this
> Nas Alexander Macedo,
> Ne the king, dan Scipio,
> That saw in dreme, at point devys,
> Helle and erthe and paradys.[2]

The likeness of Troilus' situation and perspective to Scipio's strengthens our sense that the pattern of the *Parlement* is in

may have owed to the *Somnium* his treatment of Arcita's transmigration; though it is even more like *Pharsalia*, ix. 1 ff. But his insistence on Man's littleness in comparison with the heavens is a medieval commonplace, partly deriving from Ps. viii, partly from Boethius II, Pr. vii. 3, which Chaucer renders: '. . . the resoun of *a prikke at regard of the gretnesse of hevene*': cf. *Parlement*, l. 58.

[1] C.T.A. 3025–30.

[2] ll. 914–18. Those who follow Livingston Lowes in search of 'hooks and eyes' may find in Alexander the hook that Chaucer's poetic memory provided between the theme of his proem (the earth *sub specie aeternitatis*) and the immediately following scene of a paradisal garden: the Alexander of romance not only flew far above the earth (cf. *Hous of Fame*, loc. cit.) but also visited the earthly paradise; *v.* p. 71 below. The story of his flight was known in England from the eleventh century (cf. the carving on the tympanum at Charney Bassett); and it has an analogue in the delightful Irish folk-tale of Daniel O'Rourke: W. B. Yeats, *Folk Tales of the Irish Peasantry* [n.d.], p. 97.

some sort the inverse of that of the *liber Troili*. And in the
next few lines, penned, like the rest, with one eye on
Macrobius, this impression grows firmer:

> And after shewed he hym the nyne speres,
> And after that the melodye herde he
> That cometh of thilke speres thryes thre,
> That welle is of musik and melodye
> In this worlde here, and cause of armonye.[1]

Just so Troilus, like Arcita, saw from 'the holughnesse of
the eighthe spere'

> The erratik sterres, herkenynge armonye,
> With sounes full of hevenysshe melodye.[2]

Someone may here object that though the music of the
spheres has its place in Macrobius, and lends grandeur
to the apotheoses of Troilus and Arcita, this pedagogic
passage might have been spared at this point in a poem
ostensibly about love; just as it is spared by the Knight,
who passes over quickly the fate of Arcite's soul. It is perhaps
time to reiterate that the medieval love-poet could be as
wide-ranging as Donne; not because he lacked a sense of
direction, or liked to display his learning, but because his
theme was often nothing less than the relation of human
love to the universe itself:

> In hevene, and helle, in erthe and salte see
> Is felt thy might, if that I wel descerne;
> As man, brid, best, fishe, herbe and grene tree
> Thee fele in tymes with vapoure eterne:

So Chaucer hymns this love, blissfully echoing Boccaccio, in his proem to the third book of *Troilus*. And just as
there the proem sets the tone for the description of love's

---

[1] ll. 59–63. For a correction of Skeat's note on these lines *v.* E. P. Anderson, *Trans. Amer. Philol. Ass.* xxxiii (1902).   [2] *Troilus and Criseyde*, v. 1811–12.

'grete worthinesse' that is to follow, so here the lines that speak of music, melody, and harmony provide the very key-words of the dream to come, in which birds are to sing 'with voys of aungel in hir harmonye'. To question the relevance of these earlier lines is like reproaching Dante for taking us through the heavenly bodies in the *Paradiso*, or Lorenzo for reading Jessica the lesson in heavenly music from the night-sky at Belmont:

> There's not the smallest orb which thou beholdest
> But in his motion like an angel sings,
> Still quiring to the young-eyed cherubims.
> Such harmony is in immortal souls.
> But whilst this muddy vesture of decay
> Doth grossly close us it, we cannot hear it.[1]

The ensuing reference to the great or platonic year would seem no more out of place to contemporary readers (or, for that matter, to the Yeats of *Michael Robartes*) than would Jean de Meun's more specific mention, in words that Chaucer's somewhat resemble, of the

> trente e sis mile anz
> Pour venir au point dreitement
> Ou Deus le fist prumierement;[2]

but Chaucer, 'short and quik', like his own Clerk, even in

---

[1] *The Merchant of Venice*, v. i. 60–65. Dr. Tillyard has an interesting comment on part of the passage in *The Elizabethan World Picture* (1943), p. 38. For the transference of the theme of the harmony of the spheres from medieval art (in which the harmony is usually represented by angels making music) to Renaissance art *v*. Charles de Tolnay, *Journal of the Walters Art Gallery*, vi (Baltimore, 1943), pp. 83 ff.

[2] *RR*, ll. 16816–18. Jean is referring to Hipparchus' precessional period, often confused with the great year. To Skeat's note on estimates of the periodic year may be added the references in Sir John Davies's *Orchestra* (st. 36). The classical sources are discussed by Boyancé, op. cit., c. iv.

things of 'hie sentence,' reaches this point in sixty-seven lines; the *Roman* takes precisely 16,750 more.

As he compresses, Chaucer continues to remould. Lines 65 to 70 represent some four paragraphs of the *Somnium*, whilst finding room—if we follow the majority of the manuscripts—for a reference to earth's 'torment' which has no place in Cicero (or even in Macrobius)[1] but which will acquire significance when we come to the tormented lovers soon to appear in the poet's own dream; Cicero dwells instead on the vanity of earthly glory and the difference between the platonic and the ordinary year. Again, the lines

> and al shulde out of minde
> That in this world is don of al mankynde[2]

represent a passage that in Cicero occurs in another context (c. vii. 1, 5) with no implication that the memory of all human activity and achievement will fade when the great year is accomplished.

That Chaucer is not at the mercy of his source is evident from the rest of his précis. African's bold injunction that man should recognize his own divinity—*Deum te igitur scito esse*—is modified to read 'Know thyself firste immortale'; and that the modification is not fortuitous is clear if we consult, as Chaucer at this point surely did, Macrobius' gloss on the passage: 'Haec sit praesentis operis consummatio, ut animam non solum immortalem sed deum esse clarescat.'[3] By eliminating the statement that the man who

---

[1] Except inasmuch as he discusses the view that the tortures of the infernal regions represent sufferings produced in the present life by a bad conscience, greed, &c. E. P. Hammond argues against the reading 'torment': *Manual*, p. 109.

[2] ll. 69–70.

[3] *Comm.* II. xii. 5: 'la hardiesse de "tu es un dieu" peut sembler aller plus loin que Platon' (Boyancé, op. cit., p. 124).

most withdraws from the body whilst on earth reaches
heavenly bliss *velocius* (which yields only the 'swiftely' of
l. 76), and by rendering *de salute patriae* as 'comune profit',
to echo l. 47, Chaucer underlines his purpose of represent‑
ing his 'olde boke' as one concerned with the public weal,
and not with human love.

But if Cicero has nothing to say about love, he gives
Africanus something to say about *libido*, and that at the very
close of the dream:

eorum animi, qui se corporis voluptatibus dediderunt, earumque
se quasi ministros praebuerunt, impulsuque libidinum volupta‑
tibus obedientium, deorum et hominum iura violaverunt,
corporibus elapsi, circa terram ipsam volutantur; nec hunc in
locum, nisi multis exagitati saeculis, revertuntur;[1]

words to which Chaucer adds a prayer of partly Christian
colour that has no equivalent in the *Somnium*:

> But brekers of the lawe, soth to seyne,
> And likerous folk, after that they ben dede,
> Shul alwey whirle about th'erthe in peyne,
> Til many a world be passed, out of drede,
> And than, *forgeven alle hir wikked dede*
> *Than shul they come into this blisful place,*
> *To which to comen, God the sende his grace.*[2]

Whether Chaucer gave *libido* the classical meaning of 'sen‑
sual passion' is a nice question. By the time of Prudentius
the word denoted 'sodomy'; and nothing in the context—
or in Macrobius, who practically ignores the passage—
would prevent a medieval reader from taking this as

---

[1] c. ix. 2: 'the souls of those who have given themselves up to bodily pleasures
and become their slaves, and who, being driven by their passions in obedience
to these pleasures, have violated the laws both divine and human, when they
are freed from the body, revolve round the earth and return hither only after
long ages of torment.' [2] ll. 78–84.

Cicero's meaning; whilst anyone familiar with Alain's *De Planctu Naturae* would certainly be inclined to identify the transgressors of human and divine law with the perverts there castigated for hindering the perpetuation of the species and the operation of the principle of plenitude. The only hint that Chaucer gives of his manner of interpreting the passage is in his use of 'likerous': likerousness = *luxuria*, which, though its medieval connotations might include sodomy, is usually contrasted with the chaste love that leads to marriage, and for Chaucer, well read in the *Inferno* as he was, Scipio's words (and in particular *volutantur*) would inevitably evoke the doom of Francesca and Paolo, confined in that circle of the *lussuriosi* where

> La bufera infernal, che mai non resta,
>   mena gli spirti con la sua rapina;
>   *voltando* e percotendo li molesta;[1]

whilst twenty lines later comes Dante's allusion to Semiramis, 'Che *libito* fe' *licito*'. That Chaucer should think of Dante as he pondered Macrobius is in no way surprising: Africanus' journey through the spheres being a probable exemplar for the *Paradiso*. From this fifth canto (as Livingston Lowes noted) he was to draw further before he finished the next two hundred lines; and perhaps as he turned to it, his eye was caught by the opening lines of Canto ii:

> Lo giorno se n'andava, e l'aer bruno
>   toglieva gli animai, che sono in terra,
>   dalle fatiche loro . . .

---

[1] *Inferno*, v. 31–33. I leave it to students of Dante to decide whether he owed his image to the *Somnium*, i.e. to Macrobius' edition of it; and to Shakespearians to consider whether Claudio's fear of being 'blown with restless violence round about the pendant world' arises from his lechery and infraction of the 'just but severe law'. Chaucer's reference to 'hell' (l. 31) is, strictly, unwarranted; but *v.* p. 43.

Certain it is that they provide the beginning for his very next stanza:

> The day gan fallen, and the derke nyght,
> That reveth bestes from hir besinesse,
> Berefte me my boke for lakke of lyght.[1]

But there is no word in Dante, of course, and only a phrase in the *Somnium*, to suggest that the torments of those 'peccator carnali, Che la ragion sommettono al talento', will ever cease, that they will come at length to a 'blisful place' (nor are the heavens so described anywhere in Cicero). This consolation Chaucer has extracted chiefly from Macrobius' gloss, whilst ignoring the neoplatonism and necessitarianism on which that gloss is based:

> Saecula infinita dinumerans, quibus nocentium animae in easdem poenas saepe revolutae, sero de Tartaris emergere permittuntur, et ad naturae suae principia, quod est caelum, tandem impetrata purgatione, remeare. Necesse est enim omnem animam ad originis suae sedem reverti . . .[2]

This is the only passage in our texts where, as in the *Republic* (x. 615 A B), the torments are described as purgatorial. The explanation would enable Chaucer to give the passage a meaning consistent with Christian orthodoxy; whilst *impetrata purgatione* may have reminded him that elsewhere in the *Commedia*—in *Purgatorio*, xxvi—we are shown the lecherous who have repented of their lust and

---

[1] ll. 85–87.

[2] 'After infinite ages the souls of the guilty who have been whirled about ceaselessly in the same torments, are permitted at length to emerge from their tortures and having obtained purgation to return to the primal cause of their being, namely heaven. For it is necessary that every soul return to the place of its origin.' John Scotus Eriugena also conceived of a cosmic return to God (*De Divisione Naturae*, 5. 25 ff.), but it is hardly likely that Chaucer was familiar with his view.

who will attain at length to heavenly bliss. Chaucer is ostensibly doing no more than summarize the *Somnium*, and can hardly be accused of any universalist heresy; rather, he is tentatively approaching that doctrine of mutability which Spenser, with some avowed reliance on the *Parlement*, was to set forth in his finest, if unfinished, cantos.

Night has fallen, and Chaucer has reached the end of the *Somnium*—or more precisely, of the *Commentarium*: for Cicero he could have read in an hour, it is Macrobius who would take 'al the day' (l. 28); and that he read to the end of this commentary is suggested by his later reference to the 'olde booke totorne Of which Macroby roghte noght a lyte' (ll. 110–11)—with the smiling allusion, perhaps to the poet's inability to find, or afford, an elegant copy, and certainly to Macrobius' closing words: 'nihil hoc opere perfectius quo universa philosophiae continetur integritas.' He is anxious and depressed, for he has been all day long studying a work of elaborate and elevated but essentially dualistic philosophy without finding aught of that 'certeyn thing' which he had hoped to learn. The antithesis of

> For both I hadde thynge which that I nolde,
> And eke I ne hadde thynge that I wolde[1]

is as old as Boethius; Chaucer himself makes it in his *Compleynt to Pite* ('What so I desire . . . that have I not': ll. 99–100), in *Troilus* (iii. 445), in *Anelida and Arcite* ('what he may not gete, that wolde he have': l. 203); Gower, characteristically, makes the 'thing' explicit: 'He which hath of love his make . . . He hath that he wolde have';[2] and earlier romances, French and English, provide such precedents as

---

[1] ll. 90–91, cf. *De Consolatione Philosophiae*, iii, Pr. 3. 5.
[2] *Confessio Amantis*, viii. 3078–83*.

> Il ha dolur de ce qu'il a
> E plus se deut de ce qu'il n'a,

in Thomas's *Tristan*. But it is the contexts of these formulas, rather than the formulas themselves, that are of interest. For they all occur in love-poetry; an indication that it is love-doctrine which Chaucer has sought and not found. The couplet, then, is not here merely ornamental: it concludes the first movement of the poem, recalls its purpose, and indicates what import Chaucer attaches to the *Somnium*. In effect, all that Cicero could say to the poet was that felicity was attained by love of the common weal, and that this earth must be considered the prison-house of the soul; into his strongly dualistic thinking human passion entered only inasmuch as he emphasized the penalty for 'unlawful' pleasures. This was an attitude that could be and had been reconciled with Christian doctrine. In so far as the dualism was platonic it had been largely assimilated to Christian philosophy before St. Augustine; in so far as chapter and verse could be cited for it from St. Paul, it could be made to sort well enough with the austere ascetical teaching of the Fathers. Abundant early manuscripts of, and references to, the Macrobian text, indicate that it was considered a proper book for monastic libraries.[1]

But on this dualism the twelfth-century Renaissance and its Aristotelian aftermath had exercised their modifying and corrective if sometimes confusing influences. To speak of the movements in question as a rebirth of knowledge is almost as misleading as to apply the same metaphor to the fifteenth century; men's knowledge and ideas did not change overnight; nor was it simply a question of access to the *Physics* of Aristotle. Chaucer, in any event, did not look

[1] Manitius lists manuscripts from eleven English monasteries alone: *Zentralblatt für Bibliothekswesen*, Beiheft 67, p. 230.

at these intellectual movements through our spectacles, or
in the perspective that time gives us. Indeed, it might be
urged that he did not look at them at all, knowing them
only by results that were still fructifying in his century. It is
doubtful whether he had read a line of Bernard of Chartres
or St. Bonaventure, Albert the Great, or even St. Thomas
himself;[1] but he was steeped in poets who had absorbed or
adapted many of the new doctrines and who felt that there
were more things in heaven and earth than were dreamt
of in Africanus' philosophy. To be sure, neoplatonic and
'other-worldly' elements were present in most of the new
syntheses: Van Steenberghen has recently pointed out that
the eclectic 'Latin' Aristotelianism of the earlier thirteenth
century was strongly influenced by neo-platonism; on the
other hand many a schoolman, not to say many a priest,
must have looked askance at the thinly veiled naturalism
that was born in Paris from the unsanctioned union of
scholastic thought and *amour courtois*, and that is mirrored
in parts of the *Roman*.[2] But for our present purpose we do
not need to ask to which scholastic party Chaucer may
have inclined (though his affinities are just as surely with
St. Thomas, the philosopher of the concrete and existent, as
Langland's are with St. Bonaventure); all we need to remember is that he must have read the poets of the new
movements with something of the same intellectual thrill
that they themselves had felt when the new speculations
first spread through the ruelles and lecture-rooms of Italy
and France. No phrase but Miranda's 'brave new world',

[1] It is worth noting that the two last-named, along with Vincent of Beauvais,
were critical of the Pythagorean notion of heavenly music adopted by Macrobius and Boethius.

[2] For scholastic influences on the *Roman*, *v*. G. Paré, *Les Idées et les lettres
au XIIIe siècle* (Montreal, 1947). For a criticism of Paré's views *v*. Helmutz
Hatfield's review: *Symposium* (Syracuse, N.Y.), May 1948.

however tarnished it be by Mr. Huxley's satiric touch, will convey the wonder with which poets and schoolmen alike had gazed on the universe through Aristotle's glass, when St. Thomas had polished and refocused it. A new view of Man's relation to Nature and to society now became possible—indeed became necessary as society became stabilized and christianized. Alain of Lille, to whom Chaucer is to turn in the *Parlement*, wrote before the adjustments in question had taken place. But he anticipates some of their effects. His *Anticlaudianus*, platonic as much of it is, involves a very different view of the relation between body and soul from that expressed in the *Somnium*: Alain can envisage a man who

> In terris humanus erit, divinus in astris.
> Sic homo, sicque deus fiet. . . .[1]

A century later a Beatrice of human birth can draw a poet up to a paradisal height from which the earth still looked as little as it had seemed to Scipio, but from which, also, divine and human love were seen as counterparts, not contraries. Like Scipio, Dante had in his dream-journey through the celestial spheres a virtuous pagan for guide; if the *Commedia* embraces so much more of human life and feeling as well as of human learning, that is in part because Dante could benefit from both the achievements of scholasticism, and the new sensibility that had grown up alongside scholasticism, manifesting itself in Italian poetry even before it appeared in that of France.

The English poet, then, feeling the need of solace and refreshment after finishing the dualistic *Somnium*, 'write with lettres olde', might well look hopefully at the *Commedia*, with its 'newe science' and its Christian cosmology.

---

[1] *Anticlaudianus*, ed. R. Bossuat (Paris, 1955), i. 239-40. Alain seems to be echoing Bernardus Silvestris, *De Mundi Universitate*, II. x. 19: cf. p. 197 below.

We shall find evidence that Dante was not far from his
mind as he approached the centre of this poem, whilst of two
works by the Alain aforementioned he was to make liberal
use. Chaucer, it would appear, so far from being the 'fore-
runner' of the next renaissance, is in some ways the belated
English representative of poetic and philosophic movements that had begun nearly two centuries before. The
only feature of the poem 'pointing forward' to the Renaissance that we associate with Italy (with the doubtful exception of the Boccaccian figures soon to be considered) is the
theme of the *Somnium* itself, which was to attract Raphael;
yet more than one medieval artist had chosen this subject
before Raphael; and his painting provides but another
instance of the debt of Renaissance classicism to medieval
exemplars.[1]

Essentially a movement towards a comprehensive and
catholic rationalism, this earlier renaissance did not involve deposing old authorities in favour of new. The
platonists and the patristic writers were still respected, Aristotle was sometimes (and at first, often) questioned, and de
Meun read his Macrobius and his Boethius (who had
hoped to translate the *Physics*) along with his St. Thomas
and his Albert. The antithesis between Christian and
pagan philosophy—as distinct from pagan religion—had
never been absolute; and the value that Cicero set on the
res publica was not altogether different from that which
St. Thomas accorded to *commune bonum*, when he said that
it should be the criterion of political action. Inasmuch
as western Christendom inherited and adapted to its own
purposes the conception of the *imperium Romanum*, it in-

---

[1] *v.* Pl. 1. The MS. from which this illustration is taken was written at Rome
in 1383. Raphael's painting and the sketch for it are reproduced in *One Hundred
Masterpieces from the National Gallery* (p. 49, no. 213).

herited and converted—if belatedly—this conception of the
common weal. Chaucer can very properly accommodate it
within his poem, and very properly add the Christian reference to divine grace just noted. The author of *Troilus*
was not the man to reject out of hand the implication that
pursuit of the common weal might exclude the pursuit of
love; nor must one be either a platonist or a disillusioned
romantic to be conscious of 'the abortive sorrows and
shortwinded elations of men'—and in especial of lovers.

We shall shortly see that the themes Chaucer singled out
for emphasis in his summary of the *Somnium* recur in his
own dream, providing recurring motifs that are clearly not
accidental. But this is not the only sort of influence the
Somnium had: other themes or statements lodged in his
mind without finding a place in the précis, whilst apparently yielding motifs of a different kind as the poem
developed. Certain phrases of the Latin texts seem to have
suggested images or set off trains of thought: Cicero, for
example, in accordance with the religious value that he
attaches to *caelum*, speaks of the skyey regions as *templa*
(c. iv. 1), and this use is striking enough for Macrobius to
attempt an explanation:

bene autem universi mundus dei templum vocatur propter
illos, qui aestimant, nihil esse aliud deum nisi caelum ipsum
et caelestia ista, quae cernimus. Ideo ut summi omnipotentiam
dei ostenderet posse vix intelligi, numquam videri, quicquid
humano subicitur aspectui, templum eius vocavit, qui sola
mente concipitur, ut qui haec veneratur ut templa, cultum
tamen maximum debeat conditori, sciatque quisquis in usum
templi huius inducitur, ritu sibi vivendum sacerdotis.[1]

[1] *Lib.* I, c. xiv. 2: 'Yet the world is properly called the temple of the universal
God as regards those who think that there is no other god but that heaven and
those celestial objects that we can see. In order to show, therefore, that the
omnipotence of the supreme God can scarcely be comprehended, and never be

With this *templum* (accessible, says Cicero, when God
releases us from the fetters of the flesh) poetic memory
might easily link a very different temple, with very different
acolytes: the Temple of Venus that Chaucer had read of in
the *Teseida* and that figures in his coming dream. Again,
Macrobius more than once introduces into his commentary
the figure of personified Nature: notably in his second
chapter, where he explains that philosophers make use of
fabulous narratives

quia sciunt inimicam esse Naturae apertam nudamque
expositionem sui, quae sicut vulgaribus hominum sensibus
intellectum sui vario rerum tegmine operimentoque subtraxit,
ita a prudentibus arcana sua voluit per fabulosa tractari: sic
ipsa mysteria figurarum cuniculis operiuntur, ne vel haec
adeptis nudam rerum talium se Natura praebeat . . .[1]

This passage, which may well have given to Alain the hint
for attiring Natura in the robe that she wears in his *Planctus*, may equally well have reminded Chaucer of her appearance in that poem, wearing this robe, on which he is
soon to bestow, almost literally, a life of its own. It is hardly
less likely that the passage, and the immediately succeeding
references to mysterious rites and lascivious practices—

beheld, he called whatever can be seen by human eye the temple of Him who is
apprehended by the mind alone, so that whoever venerates these objects as
temples may yet owe the greatest worship to the Creator, and whoever is led to
use this temple may know it his duty to live as a priest.' Boyancé comments:
'Chez Platon, nous avons le cosmos, l'univers organisé qui frappe le savant
d'admiration; chez Cicéron, nous avons le Ciel, qu'il faut écrire avec une maju-
scule, pour en bien définir la valeur religieuse, le Ciel, séjour de tout ce qui est
éternel, et récompense promise aux élus . . .'; op. cit., p. 58; *v.* also p. 116.

[1] *Lib.* I, c. ii. 17: 'For they realise that an open and naked exhibition of herself is distasteful to Nature, who, just as she has withheld an understanding of
herself from the vulgar senses of men by veiling herself with a variegated covering,
has also wished to have her secrets handled by the wise through fables. Thus her
rites are veiled in mysterious labyrinths so that she may not show herself stripped
of such coverings even to initiates.'

Numenius, we are told, dreamt that he saw 'ipsas Eleusinias deas habitu meretricio ante apertum lupanar prostantes'— prompted his imagination to juxtapose, in the dream narrative to follow, the temple in which it is Venus that shows herself as almost naked, and Nature is decked 'right as Alayne in the Pleynte of Kinde deviseth' (ll. 316–17).

Finally: in describing the power of musical sounds, Macrobius asks:

et quid mirum, si inter homines musicae tanta dominatio est, cum aves quoque, ut lusciniae et cygni aliaeve id genus, cantum veluti quadam disciplina artis exerceant . . .?[1]

The sequence of thought here is not obvious; but that may be the very reason why Chaucer would dwell on the lines. From them may have been born the first suggestion that, as Scipio's heavenly dream had been to the accompaniment of the music of the spheres, the consolatory dream of an earthly paradise that now follows should be accompanied by birdsong; it is a fact that of the birds listed in Nature's array the swan and the nightingale are almost the only ones particularized by their song.

The agnostic reservation that in the stanza beginning at l. 106 accompanies comments on the nature of dreams, derived from Claudian, is in accord with the opening of the *Hous of Fame*, if not as forthright as the scepticism of the Pertelot who boldly urges 'Do ye no fors of dremes.' There is nothing remarkable about this agnosticism, nothing anticipatory of Renaissance doubt, though critics have tried to find it: Langland likewise quotes 'Cato's' *Ne somnia cures*, and we do not think of Langland as an *esprit fort*.

[1] Ibid. iii. 10: 'And is it at all strange if music has such power over men when birds like the nightingale and the swan and others of that kind practise song with almost the technique of an art?'

The interest of the comments on the causes of dreams lies not in their 'frigid interpretations' but in the appeal that they would have for Chaucer's first readers: an appeal not unlike that which attracts modern readers to Freud—whose classifications medieval categories occasionally foreshadow. Something of this same appeal attached to any poem cast, as the body of the *Parlement* is, into the dream-form. It was the sheer excitement of dreams and their interpretation that made this form popular, and that accounts for the rise of what we glibly call a convention. Chaucer himself would read his Macrobius attentively, not only because it interpreted the work of an 'auctorite' but also because that work was a *somnium*—the special kind of dream that veils with ambiguity the true meaning of the information offered. Macrobius, moreover, in the third chapter of his first book, classifies and transmits all the Greco-Roman dream lore that goes back at least as far as the gates of ivory and horn in Book XIX of the *Odyssey*, and that Claudian had adapted from Lucretius.[1] Macrobius' chapter early became the *locus classicus* for dream-typology; and would make it easy for Chaucer to take Africanus as an example of the 'parent, or some other respected personage' who appears in an *oraculum* (*chrematismos*) to instruct, to warn, or to reveal the future; whilst Cicero himself had mentioned a not dis-similar example at the beginning of the *Somnium*, where he says that it often happens

ut cogitationes sermonesque nostri pariant aliquid in somno tale quod de Homero scribit Ennius de quo videlicet saepissime vigilans solebat cogitare et loqui.[2]

---

[1] *De Rer. Nat.* iv. 962 ff. For the relevant references, including Herodotus, vii. 16. 2, *v.* E. R. Dodds, *The Greeks and the Irrational* (Berkeley and Los Angeles, 1951), c. iv, and Boyancé, op. cit., p. 51, n. 2.

[2] *Lib.* I, c. 1. 4: 'the things that we have been thinking and talking about

Both Cicero's text and Macrobius' would yield precedent and suggestion for the dream that Chaucer is about to
describe. Chaucer presents it as his own *somnium* ('sweven'),
in which the same Africanus plays (at the beginning) a like
oracular role and so lends some weight to its 'sentence'.
The dream will give bodily semblance to certain aspects of
love that come closer to Chaucer's own ideal, but it will
be flecked, naturalistically enough, with some of the hard
doctrine that he had just been pondering. From Cicero's
version of Scipio's dream he takes hints for the description
of his own, in which, 'forwery of my labour al the day'
(just as Scipio is fatigued by his journey and his talk with
Masinissa in the small hours) he dreams

> How Affrikan, *right in that selve array*
> *That Scipioun hym say byfore that tyde,*
> Was come, and stod right at my beddes syde:[1]

this is clearly a reshaping of Cicero's account of how, as
a result of Masinissa's talk about Africanus, that worthy 'se
ostendit ea forma quae mihi ex imagine eius quam ex ipso
erat notior'—i.e. the younger Scipio, dreaming about the
elder, his grandfather by adoption, recognizes him from his
statue.[1] Dreams such as Chaucer now gives examples of:
dreams coloured by our day-time preoccupations—wish-
or fear-fulfilments—and induced by physical or mental
exertion, Macrobius dismisses as *insomnia*, not worth the

---

appear in our dreams, just as Ennius says of Homer, about whom he was constantly thinking and speaking in his waking hours'. Cf. *De Divinatione I*, 22. 45:
'quae in vita usurpant homines cogitant, curant, vident, quaeque agunt vigilantes
agitantque, ea si cui in somno accidunt, minus mirandumist.'

[1] ll. 96–98. Cf. *Somnium*, 1. 4. Stahl, properly enough, renders *imago* in this
passage by 'portrait-mask'; but to Chaucer the Latin word would doubtless
denote a full-length statue.

labour of interpreting: and if Chaucer's own dream (regard﹣
ing it for the moment as 'real') could confidently have been
so classified, it would not have been worth considering.
But Chaucer is careful not to commit himself in regard to
the value of his dream as such: perhaps because he does not
wish to imply that any solution emerging from it will be
complete and apodeictic. Similarly, he reduces to a mini﹣
mum Africanus' oracular function: the latter becomes a
benevolent compère rather than the embodiment of divine
wisdom; whilst retaining enough of the patience that he
showed in answering Scipio's almost otiose question about
the future life, to bear with the poet who presents himself
at the beginning—'on bokes rede I ofte, *as I yow tolde*'—as
slightly repetitious.

Speculation on Chaucer's views about Macrobius' cate﹣
gories and conclusions need not detain us. What stirred in
his mind as he considered the chapter was probably not
scientific doubt but the recollection of an array of dreams
and dreamers in the verses of Macrobius' contemporary,
Claudian—verses that the poet may have read at school and
that remained well known till the seventeenth century.[1]
Claudian himself may have been familiar not only with
Lucretius' lines noted above, but with Macrobius' cate﹣
gories—though he does not use Macrobius' label *insomnia*
for the dreams he describes in the stanza that Chaucer now
translates almost word for word:

[1] Owen Feltham quotes and translates them in his *Resolves*, no. lii (11th ed.,
1696, p. 75); Skeat cites the original in his notes. For Chaucer's acquaintance
with Claudian *v.* R. A. Pratt, *Speculum*, xxii (1947), pp. 419 ff., where he
suggests that Chaucer knew the *Praefatio* in the form in which it appeared in
the *Liber Catonianus*, the standard medieval school reader, viz. as part of the *De
Raptu Proserpinae* (for which *v.* p. 61). Pratt cites medieval glosses to the lines
such as Chaucer may have noticed, e.g. l. 3 *sompniando*, l. 5 *de chareta* (cf.
Chaucer's 'cartes'), l. 7 *furto*—'*id est tuto coitu*'.

The wery hunter, slepinge in his bed,
To wode ayein his minde goth anoon;
The iuge dremeth how his plees ben sped,
The carter dremeth how his cartes goon;
The riche, of gold; the knight fight with his foon,
The seke met he drinketh of the tonne,
The lover met he hath his lady wonne.[1]

Here the only variations from Claudian (except a few changes in order) consist in the replacement of a shipman (*permutat navita merces*) by a medieval knight, and in the phrase added to the description of the lover, who in Claudian *furto gaudet* but in Chaucer comes a shade closer to Macrobius' instance of the results of *cura animi*: 'amator deliciis suis aut fruentem se [videt] aut carentem.' Chaucer has so rearranged the sequence that the lover comes last in the file, and this mention of a lover's happiness (without any of the condemnatory implication of Claudian's *furto*) brings us gently back to the theme of the overture: namely, the nature of this happiness.

And now at last the poet's quest for a clue to this mystery is to have some reward. 'Thou hast thee so wel borne', says African, 'That some del of thy labour wolde I quyte'; it is the same word, expressing the same promise, that the eagle uses in the *Hous of Fame*:

> And thus this god, thorgh his meryte,
> Wol with some maner thing thee quyte;[2]

and in a poem of such tight verbal texture as the *Parlement* the half-heard echo of the second line of the second stanza ('ne wote how that he quyteth folke her hire') is probably deliberate.

---

[1] ll. 99-105.
[2] ll. 669-70. Cf. R. C. Goffin, *Medium Ævum*, xii (1943), pp. 40-44.

Similarly, the succeeding invocation to

> Cytherea, thou blisful lady swete,
> That with thy fyrbrond dauntest whom the lest,
> And madest me this sweven for to mete . . .,[1]

with its glance backward to Love's 'miracles and cruel ire' and forward to the dream of lovers, evidently implies that the dreamer's pleasure (communicated by this stanza's clearer tone and quicker tempo) lay in a glimpse of some positive answer to his questionings, some assurance that love was not just vanity of vanities; just so had he prayed as he proceeded to endite the dream of the *Hous of Fame*:

> Now faire blisful, O Cipris,
> So be my favour at this time![2]

Cipris and Cytherea are pagan names, but Chaucer is not here addressing a pagan goddess: the powers formerly ascribed to such deities had long since been restricted to their planets; and though sometimes—as in the *Compleynt of Mars*—the astrological and mythological *Veneres* are not easy to distinguish, here Cytherea can hardly be anything but the benevolent planet of a christianized cosmology, the cosmology that Chaucer, like Dante, accepts without question. Dante, as it happens, ascribes to this very planet a dream that bears some resemblance to Chaucer's—and prepares us for it in much the same way. He has just passed through the circle of the repentant lustful, those 'brekers of the lawe', who, like Guido Guinicelli,

> . . . non servammo umana legge,
> seguendo come bestie l'appetito;[3]

heartened by Virgil's talk of Beatrice, he has dared the pur-

---

[1] ll. 112–15. [2] ll. 518–19.
[3] *Purg.* xxvi. 83–84.

gatorial flame, and, exhausted by the ascent, lies gazing at
the stars:

> Sì ruminando, e sì mirando in quelle,
>   mi prese il sonno: il sonno che sovente,
>   anzi che il fatto sia, sa le novelle.
>
> Nell' ora, credo, che dell' oriente
>   prima raggiò nel monte Citerea,
>   che di foco d'amor par sempre ardente,
>
> Giovane e bella in sogno mi parea
>   donna vedere andar per una landa
>   cogliendo fiori . . .[1]

Thus in Dante as in Chaucer we pass from an account of
sleep after toil, to the credibility of dreams, then to the sight
of the planet of love burning in the sky, and finally to the
vision of an earthly paradise, whither Dante has been led
by Virgil and Statius, even as Chaucer is now led into
such a paradise by the great African. Not the least of the
arts that Chaucer learnt from Dante was this art of astrono-
mizing in poetry, of welding planetary allusions (compare,
for example, the opening of *Purgatorio*, ix) firmly on to a
narrative frame.

If 'Cytherea' for both poets primarily denotes the planet,
and the planet in her beneficent aspect, it is also the classical,
the Virgilian, appellation for Venus. Professor Seznec has
shown that such names were never completely depaganized;
and Chaucer was certainly not the only medieval poet to
describe the planet in terms of the goddess. In *Troilus* he is
following Boccaccio when he invokes (without naming)
this 'lady bright' as the

---

[1] Ibid. xxvii. 91–99.

> blisful light, of which the bemes clere
> Adorneth al the thridde hevene faire,
> O sonnes leef, o Joves doughter deere . . .,[1]

thus blending mythology and astrology. Troilus himself
hails first 'Citherea the swete' as mother of love and then
'Venus, the welwilly planete'; the goddess whom Palamon
addresses in her planetary hour is both Venus and 'the
blisful Citherea benigne'.[2] The power of the planet is like
that symbolized by the goddess: none, says the Knight,

> . . . may with Venus holde champartye,
> For as hir list the worlde she may gye—[3]

and as a planet, Chaucer now indicates (l. 115), she can
ordain one's dreams. The firebrand (l. 114) is a symbol
common to both goddess and planet, as appropriate to the
one burning in the sky as to the other who sets aflame the
heart of man—and, in the *Roman*, the whole world. It is
'with hir fyrbrond in hir honde' that Venus, at January's
marriage, 'aboute daunceth biforn the bride and al the
route'[4]—inciting them *all* to love; just as in the *Romaunt*

> This lady brought in hir right hond
> Of brenning fyr a blasing brond;
> Whereof the flawme and hote fyr
> Hath many a lady in desyr
> Of love brought, and sore het.[5]

Chaucer beseeches this planet for power to rhyme and to
'endyte' (a verb that he uses regularly for poems in honour

---

[1] *Troilus and Criseyde*, iii. 1–3. For Venus' parentage cf. Boccaccio, *Gen Deor. Gent.* III. xxii.

[2] Ibid., l. 1255; 'welwilly'—*benevolens*; C.T.A. 2215–16. The two aspects of Venus are fused in the 'conceit' of l. 2666—'hir teeres in the lystes fille': cf. p. 96, n. 1.   [3] C.T.A. 1949–50.

[4] C.T.E. 1727–8. For the sources of the astrology of this passage *v.* Boccaccio, loc. cit.   [5] *Romaunt of the Rose*, ll. 3705–9. RR, ll. 3424 ff.

of Venus) because she is *acute meditationis in compositionibus carminum.*[1] That he prays for this power to be given

> As wisly as I sey the north north west
> When I began my sweven for to write,

has perplexed many critics, and still perplexes. Perhaps a phrase in *Hamlet* holds the clue—though not the ironic clues that Professor Bronson and others have found there.[2] If we interpret Hamlet's 'I am but mad north north west' as part of his deliberate acceptance of Polonius' notion that the supposed madness is but 'the lovers' malady of hereos', then we may conjecture that some peculiar potency was attributed to the planet when in that corner of the sky, and in her proper 'house'. Whatever the exact reference may be, there is little doubt that the first stanza of *The Kingis Quair* contains a confused recollection of the phrase: James (who had drunk in Chaucer's poetry to the point of inebriety) there describes how

> In Aquary Citherea the clere
> Rinsed her tressis like the goldyn wyre.
> North northward approchyd the midnyght.

What this 'north northward' means no editor can tell us,

[1] Boccaccio, loc. cit.
For 'endyte' cf. *Legend of Good Women*, F. 414; *Hous of Fame*, 634, &c.

[2] The invocations cited above from Troilus make it difficult to interpret this one in ll. 113 ff. as Bronson does (*University of California Publications in English*, iii (1935), pp. 193 ff.): he thinks that Chaucer 'hardly saw Venus at all'; whilst Gardiner Stillwell's contention (*J.E.G.P.* xlix, 1950, p. 481) that 'the reference is humorous, for the poet, when he began to write, did not fix his gaze steadfastly upon Venus . . .', seems to ignore the fact that Chaucer is here referring primarily to the writing down of his dream, not of his opening stanzas; so, for that matter, does Manly's comment that north-north-west is an exact enough description of the extreme northerly position of Venus as an *evening* star. Koch's suggestion that we should read 'north *nor* west' (=S.E.) is far-fetched.

and it is doubtful whether James or his copyist could; but
we can be reasonably sure that he is following Chaucer (as
best he can) in this mention of Cytherea, since like Chaucer,
whose *Parlement* he draws on constantly, he is to tell of a
love-vision, of a garden that is a setting for love, and of
a park symbolic, like Chaucer's, of Nature's plenitude.
Neither poet would have inserted so prominent a mention
of the 'welwilly' planet except to indicate that the matter of
which he is to write will concern love, and will have good
import.

In Chaucer the invocation of the planet has its own apt-
ness. African had directed Scipio to turn his eyes to the
planets and the stars (ll. 56, 59), and after reading the
Somnium the poet would gaze at them with a new intensity; but he thinks too of their influence on mankind; and
so, by this invocation, we return from the starry spheres to
the world of men, which is the poet's prime concern. If we
take l. 118 at its face value, it must have been when he woke
that he saw Venus—and Venus is a propitious morning
star not only in the *Purgatorio*, but also in the *Compleynt of
Mars*. The stanza as a whole implies that she was shining
throughout his dream.

As if to confirm the suggestion that it was a dream worth
dreaming, the tempo of this last stanza of the Proem shows
the change above noted. Hitherto the verse-movement has
been slow, deliberate, in accord with the seriousness of the
theme: 'Of bokes rede I ofte, as I yow tolde . . . First telleth
hit . . . Than telleth hit . . . Than asked he . . . Than bad
he him . . .'; this is the pace of an expositor, and the poem
would easily 'run down' (as the Squire's Tale trails off into
similar formulas) if kept at this speed. But now, with the
sudden, dramatic appeal to Cytherea, we are brought to
the alert; and the structure of the rest of the stanza, with its

urgently repeated imperatives—'Be thou my helpe . . . So yif me might'—keeps us so. It is a signal that the first movement of the poem is over. To readers familiar with medieval composition this would be self-evident: for the commonest division of a poem was into *praefatio* and *narratio*, the *praefatio* properly consisting of a *propositio* and an *invocatio*. The invocation to Cytherea, following on the *propositio*, or statement of theme, thus fits exactly into the medieval pattern, and prepares us for the *narratio* (*sive collatio*) that now follows.

CHAPTER II

Park of Paradise and Garden of Love

> It would have tasked a landscape gardener to
> say where the policy [*scotice* 'pleasure ground']
> ended, and unpolicied Nature began.
>
> *Weir of Hermiston.*

> So I turned to the garden of love
> That so many sweet flowers bore;
> And I saw it was filled with graves.
>
> BLAKE

SCENE. *A park surrounded by 'grène stone' (which may denote emerald, or simply moss) with open double gates, each gate bearing an inscription. Enter African, leading Chaucer.*

THE park is not, *pace* J. W. Hales, Woodstock park (in its Plantagenet, pre-Marlburian form) any more than it is de Lorris's Garden of the Rose. If Chaucer had meant us to think of the former he would have said so; and the latter was entered only by a 'wiket smal'—which the dreamer in the *Roman de la Rose* found firmly shut. Nor is it the park of pleasure described in Boccaccio's *Amorosa Visione*: that carried a quite unambiguous welcome over its portal. Like all these, it exemplifies the popularity of the medieval *topos* of the ideal landscape, and Chaucer may well have remembered one or more of the earlier treatments of this theme, in which the *locus amoenus* is a park—that is, walled and gated. But the pertinent question for us is not: which model, if any, is Chaucer following? but: why does he take us into a park at all?

The answer belongs partly to the history of literature, partly to the history of art, partly to the history of western civilization itself. For in one sense, the walled park, the garden enclosed, *were* civilization; and to some medieval, even to some Renaissance painters, they were almost the whole of art. The wall enclosed the known, the beautiful, and the ordered, shutting them off from wilderness and wildness and rough weather. Eden was the more Eden when it was 'piked with a palisade'; so Milton fences it with a 'verdurous wall'. The very word *paradisus* represents the Persian 'pairidaēza', a walled enclosure. If medieval poetry is full of such paradises temporarily regained it is because they were the medieval response to the perennial human need for a Tir na n'og, a land of heart's desire, fields 'where flies no sharp nor sided hail', gardens 'set thick with lily and with rose'. They are such stuff as dreams are made on; and this *is* a dream.

The device of an inscription at the entrance was evidently suggested to Chaucer, if not to Boccaccio, by the unforgettable legend over the gates of Dante's hell; and the impress of Dante's lines is shown in the very pattern of Chaucer's: the balanced rhetorical *repetitio* in

> Thorgh me men goon into that blisful place
>
> . . . .
>
> Thorgh me men goon into the welle of grace
>
> . . . .
>
> Thorgh me men goon . . . Unto the mortale strokes
> of the pere[1]

answering unmistakably to the bell-like tolling of

[1] ll. 127–35.

> Per me si va nella città dolente;
>   per me si va nell' eterno dolore;
>   per me si va tra la perduta gente.
>
>   . . . .
>
>   lasciate ogni speranza, voi ch'entrate.[1]

—the opening lines of the canto following that whence
Chaucer had just drawn his description of the dusking
day. Dante's legend is written in black, Chaucer's in black
and gold; and Chaucer is at pains to set down in the
strongest colours the contrast between heart's-heal, good
aventure, 'grace' (which brings a flicker of association with
l. 84 of the Proem)—and mortal pain. He is here neither
parodying Dante nor improving on him—he would probably have felt attempts to do either equally presumptuous;
he is going his own quiet way. He is dealing with love,
not with mortal sin; but he knows as well as Dante did
when he wrote his fifth canto that love may lead 'al
doloroso passo'. Bial Acoil, in the *Roman*, invites not more
winningly than these golden words; but the black warning
that 'th'eschewing is the only remedye' might be from
Resoun's counsel to the lover when thwarted by Daunger—
when, that is, he finds his love disdained and unrequited:

> Daunger, that is so feloun,
> Felly purposith thee to werrey.
>
>   . . . .
>
> I rede thee Love awey to dryve,
> That makith thee recche not of thy lyve.
> The foly more fro day to day
> Shal growe, but thou it putte away.[2]

Once more we are in the presence of perplexing contraries.
But the *Roman* itself, so much of which is a like, if more

---

[1] *Inf.* iii. 1 ff. Cf. the *repetitio* at v. 100 ff.
[2] *Romaunt of the Rose*, ll. 3250-1, 3295-8; *RR* 3025-6, 3063 ff.

intricate, balance of opposites, should have prepared us for them; the difference between *Roman* and *Parlement* in this regard being chiefly that Chaucer here expresses this tension and balance in concise, pregnant imagery: the barren tree, the dry weir, succinctly symbolizing that barren and dis illusioned love which he had himself taken some hundreds of lines to describe in the *Hous of Fame*.[1]

Both legends over the entrance are true. Which a man will find true for himself, true, that is, to his own experi ence, can be learnt only by passing through it. The full statement of the contraries at this point has its structural *raison d'être*: it provides a certain suspense, provokes a cer tain curiosity, whilst reviving and confirming our earlier impression that this is a poem of paradoxes and antitheses. The promise of perpetual bliss (l. 130) might, if taken by itself, seem to imply that the dream is to repeat the pattern of the Proem, in which the 'blisful place' of ll. 48, 83 is heaven: just as the 'welle of grace' (l. 129) might seem to contrast with the 'harde grace' of earthly life (ll. 65–66). Nor are these cross weavings of phrase to be ignored. Yet 'heart's heal', 'green and lusty May', 'Disdain and Daun ger'—all *these* phrases belong to the vocabulary of earthly love, and in especial of *amour courtois*. On the other hand, again, the promise of perpetual May is to be made good, not by the revelation of a scene of happy lovers, but by a leafy landscape of everlasting spring, heavenly music, and 'gentle gales' that, as in Milton's Eden,

> Fanning their odoriferous wings dispense
> Native perfumes.

True, the Garden of the Rose, in the *Roman*, is described

---

[1] So Naxos, where Ariadne, deserted by Theseus, becomes, in the Man of Law's summary of the *Legend of Good Women*, 'the *bareyne* yle standing in the see' (C.T.B. 68).

almost as rapturously; but that is just because de Lorris
purports to present his garden as so beautiful that

> wel *wende* I ful sikerly
> Have been in paradys erthely;[1]

this is the heightened language of a poet striving for the
effect of the most picturesque earthly garden possible. If
Chaucer's description of the park, and of his delight in it
('Lord! so I was glad and wel begoon!') sometimes recalls
de Lorris (the *Roman* likewise says: 'myn hert was ful glad
of this'), we are not to conclude that they are describing
precisely the same scene or writing for precisely the same
purpose. As for the 'welle of grace': we are certainly to find
a well within the walls, yet, though in Cupid's domain, it
is given no *significacio* as a source of the grace, or mercy, that
a mistress shows to her servant in love; the only source of
grace to be mentioned will be 'the noble emperesse Nature'
(l. 319).

The ambiguities and imperfect correspondences here
noted must—if we are to take the poem seriously—be
allowed to do their own work in our minds. The most that
the critic may do at this point is to remark on their ap-
propriateness in a dream-poem and to suggest that this image
of the gate with its sharp antitheses represents a deliberate
transference—from the introductory *propositio* into the main
narratio—of African's antithesis between lasting heavenly
bliss and earthly passion leading to long-enduring pain.
This is the stark contrast that had induced the anxiety of
l. 89. The dream embodies, whilst, as often happens in
dreams, it also slightly alters, the contrast in the image of

---

[1] *Romaunt*, ll. 647–8; *RR*, ll. 635–6; 'ever', in l. 130 of the *Parlement*, seems to
point forward to ll. 173, 205, 207, 210; otherwise one might take it as merely
descriptive of a lover's sense that his joy will never cease.

the twofold gate;[1] and the anxiety is likewise duplicated, in the two stanzas that now follow (ll. 141–54), and is likewise projected in a powerful image—that of the iron bar set between two adamants 'of even might'. At first sight it is tempting to see in African's assurance that 'this wryting is nothing ment by thee, Ne by noon, but he Loves servant be' (ll. 158–9), a proof that the mortal strokes, the sorrowful weir, the barren tree, are the lot of courtly lovers; and then to go further and read the other side as speaking of a more 'natural' and wholly pleasurable love. But against this must be set the considerations that (i) 'this wryting' does not specifically refer to one side only; (ii) Disdain and Danger are not the only concomitants of courtoisie—they represent merely its unhappy aspects; (iii) African speaks of the pleasure that a *spectator* will receive; the poet would be unlikely to represent himself as deriving pleasure from watching courtly lovers in mortal anguish. African, then, must be referring to the content of the writing as a whole; and it is the more likely that the 'errour' of l. 156 is in the dreamer's thinking that *either* inscription refers to him.

   To the dreamer's doubts and hesitancy African puts an end with blunt words (though innuendo tinges his 'if thou haddest connynge for t'endyte') and a vigorous push. The incident, like the account of reader's fatigue earlier, helps to create a poetic personality, to give the 'I' of the poem and the African of the dream a life of their own. In this treatment of the relation between dreamer and guide the *Parlement* resembles—for all its differences in scale and purpose—the

---

[1] If not qualifying as archetypal, it is curiously persistent from Homer, whose twin gates of ivory and horn Chaucer would find in Macrobius, I. iii. 17, to Dr. Johnson, who, in the *Rambler*, no. 67, devises a Garden of Hope guarded by Fancy (who keeps the gate wide open) and Reason (who, acting in the spirit of her namesake in the *Roman*, keeps it shut).

Commedia rather than the *Roman.* And African's role remains not unlike that of Dante's Virgil. If his

> 'Hit stondeth writen in thy face,
> Thyn errour, though thou telle it not to me',[1]

reminiscent as it is of several remarks by Virgil to Dante,
does not precisely tally with any of them, ll. 169-70—

> With that myn hand in his he tok anon
> Of which I comforte caughte, and wente in faste—

are a clear and bold appropriation of Dante's words as
Virgil leads him through the infernal gate:

> E poichè la sua mano alla mia pose
> con lieto volto, ond' io mi confortai,
> mi mise dentro alle segrete cose;[2]

Even the down-to-earth tone of African's

> For many a man that may nat stonde a pulle
> Yet liketh him at the wrastelynge for to be,[3]

may owe something to Dante: Chaucer probably relished
as much as Miss Dorothy Sayers does the occasional chaf-
fing humour of Virgil's words, and Dante's subdued self-
mockery. Chaucer's guide, however, takes him through no
Inferno—though we have not yet done with its grim les-

---

[1] ll. 155-6. Cf., e.g., *Inf.* ii. 43 ff. (not many lines before Dante's inscribed portal, noted above), vii. 70, *Purg.* xxi. 115 ff. Cf. also Dante's confusion and fear before Beatrice, which made him say 'Yea' so imperfectly 'that to under-stand it eyes were needed' (*Purg.* xxxi. 13-15). J. L. Lowes (*Modern Philology*, xiv, 1917, pp. 705 ff.) compares *Par.* iv. 10 ff. ('il mio disir dipinto m'era nel viso'), suggesting that ll. 148-9 owe something to the opening lines of that canto, and that 'errour' represents the 'dubbi' of l. 8.

[2] *Inf.* iii. 19-22.

[3] ll. 164-5; they recall C.T.A. 2517 ff., where spectators make their guesses about the outcome of a tournament.

sons—but directly into a park resembling the Earthly Paradise that Dante does not reach until he has passed through
Purgatory. When Virgil comes to that Paradise he departs
from Dante, even as African now disappears from our
poem. This disappearance the inconsequential nature of a
dream sufficiently accounts for; and it is the kind of in-
consequence that medieval poets well knew how to exploit;
it allows Langland to ignore the Fair Field full of folk once
he has described it, or to abandon his king and knights in
a dream-church, and Chaucer (in the *Book of the Duchesse*)
to give up the search for 'th'Emperour Octavien' without
vouchsafing any reason. But in leaving African at the gate
he is perhaps following a logic not altogether unlike the
logic that required Dante to part with Virgil. Of the Earthly
Paradise and what lay beyond, Virgil, for all reverence that
the Middle Ages accorded him, could say nothing: it
would have been incongruous as well as heretical to have
him or any other pagan, however virtuous, discoursing of
paradisal mysteries. And it would have been equally in-
appropriate to retain Cicero's African as a commentator
in the park and at the *parlement* to follow: for however we
interpret the succeeding scenes we cannot establish more
than an antithetical and oblique relation between them and
African's discourse in the Proem. There the emphasis is on
the immaterial joys of heaven, here on the joys and sorrows
of a very material earth. Scipio's dream is chiefly concerned with Eternity and the life of the spirit; Chaucer's
with Nature and the impulses of the flesh. That the two
dreams have some elements in common, and that the con-
tradiction is not complete, it is part of the aim of the present
study to suggest. But African has fulfilled his function of
providing a bridge between the one dream and the other
when he thrusts the poet through the gates, and reveals the

'mater of to wryte'. He could not with poetic propriety do more.

'If we look back at Homer, Theocritus, and Virgil, and ask ourselves . . . what types of ideal landscape could late Antiquity and the Middle Ages get from these poets? we cannot but answer: the mixed forest and the *locus amoenus* (with flowery meadows *ad libitum*).'[1] Curtius' question and reply may serve to summarize the poetic history of the first part of this 'mater'—the *topographia* that occupies the ensuing forty lines. Curtius sees the origin of such landscapes in the *locos laetos et amoena virecta* of *Aeneid* VI, an Elysian scene in the strictest sense; and it happens that the same book describes the forest of pine, holm-oak, ash, and elm from which Statius and Boccaccio (in the *Teseida*) were to borrow largely. But neither *topos* might have had so long a literary history, or have appeared, in blended form, in the *Parlement*, if *amoenus* had not early been derived from *amor*; an etymology which Isidore of Seville preserved: 'Amoena loca Varro dicta ait eo quod solum amorem praestant et ad se amanda adliciant.'[2] The *topos* of a delectable region of the earth immune from the touch of time is not in origin identical with that of the *locus amoenus*, but has so much in common with it that the two easily fuse into one. Lactantius' fourth-century *Carmen de Ave Phoenice* offers one of the earliest variants of this paradisal topography in Christian verse, and had inspired an Anglo-Saxon poet to write those lambent lines that read like a rendering of Tennyson's account of the valley of Avalon into Old English.[3] From

---

[1] Curtius, loc. cit., p. 193. For an earlier, and fuller, discussion of ideal landscapes *v.* Ruskin's *Modern Painters*, IV. xiii–xvi (esp. xiv, sec. 34 ff.).

[2] *Isidori Etymologiarum Lib.* XIV. viii. 33 (ed. W. M. Lindsay).

[3] *The Phœnix*, ll. 1–84. Cf. also Prudentius, *Cathemerinon*, 3. 101.

the outset this blissful place was identified with the lost
Eden; and speculation about the seat of Eden contributed
much to the pictures of this paradise found in poems as
various as *Pearl* and the romances of Alexander.[1] De
Lorris, we saw, could describe the Garden in the *Roman*
as *seeming* to be a very 'paradis terrestre'; but this, on Mr.
Lewis's exegesis, is no more than a spurious copy of the
true Earthly Paradise, which de Meun describes towards
the end of the *Roman*. It is in the latter description that
Mr. Lewis finds de Meun to be most unlike Chaucer. Yet
the temperate breeze that

> made in the leves grene a noise softe
> Accordant to the foules songe on lofte[2]

might well have emanated from de Meun's park of good
pasture. And there are certain details in de Meun that
Chaucer seems to have remembered; his fishes resemble
those that in de Meun are depicted on the outer wall of the
park; and his *mise en scène* might have been elaborated from
de Meun's

> Erbes, arbres, bestes, oiseaus,
> E ruisselez e fonteneles

---

[1] The conjectures are found as early as Philostorgius (cf. Gibbon, Everyman
ed., ii. 243, n. 4) and are still seriously canvassed in Raleigh's *History of the
World*, Book I. III. iv, where Peter Comestor, Barcephas, and others are
cited. For some references of intermediate date, and for an account of the in-
corporation of the paradise into the romances, *v.* H. R. Patch, *The Other
World* (Harvard, 1950); M. M. Lascelles, 'Alexander and the Earthly Paradise
in Medieval English Writings', *Medium Ævum*, v (1936), pp. 31, 79, 173; and
N. Zingarelli, *Dante* (in *Storia Letteraria d'Italia*, 3rd edn., 1947), ii, p. 1168, for
studies by P. Rajna and E. Coli; and B. Nardi, 'Il mito dell'Eden', in *Saggi
di filosofia dantesca* (1930), pp. 347–74.

The description of a different kind in the legend of Sir Owain (printed in
Scott's *Minstrelsy of the Scottish Border*, 2nd edn., ii. 409) has been overlooked by
writers on the subject.

[2] ll. 202–3.

> Bruire e fremir par les graveles
> E la fontaine souz le pin.[1]

But it is folly to seek for parallels when Chaucer is evoking
Nature at her loveliest. If his verses make us think sometimes of de Lorris's mead, where

> Cleer was the water, and as colde
> As any welle is . . .
>
> . . . .
>
> The medewe softe, swote and grene,
> Beet right on the water syde,
>   (Chaucer's *river* (l. 183), i.e. river bank)

or of his garden where the birds

> songe hir song as fair and wel
> As angels doon espirituel;[2]

sometimes, again, of the green valley in the *Purgatorio*
where grass is brighter than 'fresh emerald at the moment it
is split'; and sometimes of the perpetual paradise as depicted
by de Meun or the Scots poet who described Alexander's
discovery of it: 'So temperit and sa sobir was ȝe are . . . Na
thing bot frute and flouris and spicis was . . .;

> Thare was na cloude na strublance in ȝe are,
> Bot softe and swete ȝe wedder was, and fare;'[3]

the resultant intermingled effect is no more surprising than
the ambiguity we have found in this poem at every turn.
At first sight, to be sure, the trees in Chaucer's park seem to
have been transplanted straight from de Lorris's garden,
where most of them are found growing (along with some

---

[1] *RR*, ll. 20342–5. For the precedent of the *Altercatio Phyllidis et Florae* (an
English version of which appears in J. A. Symonds's *Wine, Women and Song*) *v.*
Langlois, *Origines et sources du Roman de la Rose*, pp. 10 ff.

[2] *Romaunt of the Rose*, ll. 116 ff., 671–2; *RR*, ll. 110 ff., 663–4.

[3] B.M. MS. Add. 40732, f. 226r.

'fro the land Alexandrin')[1] But we know, as Pope knew, that such arboreal catalogues derive from a poet as much revered by Chaucer as by Dante: Statius. It is of Statius that any well-read medieval poet would first think when he came to handle this commonplace, though he might also re-call the variants in Claudian and in Joseph of Exeter, on whose version of Dares others besides Chaucer relied for certain classical lore.[2] In the hunt for such sources we must not forget the primary effect that Chaucer was aiming at—that of glades composed of noble trees (as distinct from what Gavin Douglas would call 'scroggis or ramaille') flourishing 'eche in his kinde' (l. 174); and they are characterized according to use rather than appearance: just as are the birds 'of every kinde' that we shall find in another part of the forest (311 ff.). We may think of them as illustrating Nature's 'simplicity'—in woods, says Boccac-cio, is nothing artificial, counterfeit, or obnoxious: 'sim-plicia quidem omnia sunt Naturae opera'[3]—but even more her plenitude.

[1] *Romaunt*, l. 602. Some manuscripts of *RR* read 'la terre as Sarratins' (l. 592); 'Alexandrin' conceivably refers to the Earthly Paradise as discovered by Alexander, though this form could equally well mean 'of Alexandria'.

[2] Pratt, loc. cit., quotes a gloss on Claudian's *apta fretis abies*—'id est navibus', which he suggests may have produced Chaucer's 'sayling firr' (l. 178); but *v.* below. The source in Statius is *Thebaid*, vi. 98 ff. Parallels are cited in Robinson's Notes and in those to Pope's *Iliad*, XXIII. Neckam says that the yew 'multorum artificiorum usibus accommoda est et habilis, unde et arcus taxei dicuntur': *De Natura Rerum*, lib. II, c. lxx; and that victors carried palms 'quod haec arbor oneribus quantumlibet magnis impositis non vincitur nec frangitur' (chap. lxxiv).

Chaucer knew the catalogue in *Teseida*, xi. 22–24 (and uses some of its trees at C.T.A. 2921 ff.). Cf. 'l'olmo che di viti s'innamora' with l. 177 and Boc-caccio's gloss on 'l'audace abete' in *Teseida* (ed. Roncaglia, p. 452: 'dice audace, perciò che la prima nave . . . fu fatta di tavole d'abete,' &c.) with 'sayling firr'.

[3] *Gen. Deor. Gent.* XIV. xi. The rest of the passage—which describes woods as places where the earth is covered with grass and flowers of a thousand colours;

This abundance of Nature as found in a forest had en-
thralled Chaucer from the first. In the *Book of the Duchesse*,
where there are 'many grene greves', 'thikke of trees, so
ful of leves',

> *many* an harte and *many* an hynde
> Was both before me and behynde.
> Of faunes, sowres, bukkes, does
> Was *ful* the wode, and *many* roes,
> And *many* squirrelles that sete
> Ful high upon the trees and ete
> And in her maner made festes—[1]

'Shortly, it was ful of bestes'. Squirrels and conies were as
indispensable to such scenes as they were to the margins of
an East Anglian Psalter; and Chaucer had found them
playing in de Lorris's trees. So too had Boccaccio; and as
Chaucer set about grafting into his poem the stanzas from
Boccaccio's *Teseida* that we are about to consider, he added
here and there to the forest picture a touch perhaps suggested by a phrase in the Italian (which makes no mention
of trees, beyond saying that myrtle abounded). Thus to
Boccaccio's 'molti altri carissimi bestiuoli' he probably
owes his 'bestes smale of gentil kinde'; and some of Boccaccio's birds, like some of Chaucer's, were busy 'con
diletto i nidi fare' (cf. l. 192). On the other hand, no
'smale fishes lighte', 'with finnes rede, and skales silver
brighte', swim in the 'fonti chiare' of the Italian poet:[2]
Chaucer's fishes (in their life and movement so unlike

where there are argent brooks, gay song-birds, playful little animals, and the
boughs are softly stirred by the breeze—has affinities with ll. 183-203 of the
Parlement. For Boccaccio such pleasure soothes the soul 'if it be weary'; and
Chaucer depicts himself as in that state before dreaming of the park.

[1] ll. 427-33.

[2] Skeat prints 'E fonti vive [for 'vide'] e chiare', st. 51, l. 6; and Chaucer
may have read 'vive', since the 'fonti' become 'colde welle stremes, nothing dede'

those gasping in the dried-up weir of ll. 138–40) are here as part of the scale of creatures, the chain of being in which the richness of divine creation is displayed. If we are familiar with the endless lists of trees, fishes, birds ('all the birds from here to Babylon', in Villon's phrase) that clog such poems as Alain Chartier's *Livre des Quatre Dames*, we shall be grateful for Chaucer's restraint here.

The angelic harmony of birdsong is but a prelude to still more ravishing music; and Huizinga has reminded us that in the Middle Ages music was the most vivid part and symbol of celestial joy. First there is the melody of the stringed instruments 'in accord', then a whisper of 'a little noiseless noise among the leaves', blending—as it does also in Dracontius' fifth-century account of Eden—with the birdsong. Boccaccio has:

> ogni stromento
> Le parve udire e dilettoso canto;[1]

but in Boccaccio the music proceeds clearly enough from Venus' temple; in Chaucer, we saw, it might have come from de Meun's Paradise; or Dante's. In the crystalline cantos that close the *Purgatorio* Dante had sublimated all the fine fablings of a happy land;[2] and Chaucer was never more under Dante's spell than when he endited this poem. To pluck a few of Dante's phrases from their context is not only to rob them of half their beauty but also to

(l. 187). For 'dede' =sluggish cf. A. S. Napier and W. H. Stevenson, *The Crawford Charters* (Oxford, 1895), p. 79. Chaucer's Scots admirers seized on the details: cf. *The Kingis Quair*, st. 153; Douglas, *Eneydos, Prol.* xii. 55–58.

[1] *Teseida*, vii. 53.

[2] For his treatment of the Earthly Paradise *v.* Zingarelli, op. cit., pp. 1139–70, and H. Gmelin, *Dante, Kommentar*, ii (Stuttgart, 1955), 434 ff. The earliest known representations of the paradise on any large scale is in the mosaics at S. Vitale in Ravenna. If, as is thought probable, Dante wrote part of the *Commedia* there, these may well have stirred his imagination.

allow room for the inference that Chaucer found in them
merely a series of verbal felicities; yet only by making such
a florilegium can we set forth suggestive parallels compactly,
and see at a glance the effect of Chaucer's additions to the
few lines that in the *Teseida* suffice to describe the bosky
garden.

Dante, then, in the twenty-eighth canto enters

> la divina foresta spessa e viva
> ch'agli occhi temperava il nuovo giorno;

Chaucer's forest is likewise thick and green (and sempiternal: its leaves 'ay shal laste'), and its air 'so attempre was
That never was grevance of hot ne cold'. Every wholesome
spice grew there, just as Dante's campagna gave forth
fragrance on every side. In Dante

> Un' aura dolce, sanza mutamento
> avere in sè, mi feria per la fronte
> non di più colpo che soave vento;

The branches tremble in the breeze,

> Non però dal lor esser dritto sparte
> tanto, che gli augelletti per le cime
> lasciasser d'operare ogni lor arte;
> ma con piena letizia l'ôre prime,
> cantando, ricevieno intra le foglie
> che tenevan bordone alle sue rime;[1]

In Chaucer, whilst the birds sing on every bough 'with
voys of aungel',

> Therwith a wynd, unnethe it myghte be lesse,
> Made in the leves grene a noyse softe
> Accordant to the foules song alofte.[2]

---

[1] *Purg.* xxviii. 7–9, 13–18.

[2] ll. 201–3. For 'attempre' (l. 204) cf. *Book of the Duchesse*, l. 341, and the
phrase in Boccaccio's *Chiose* noted by Pratt: 'è regione molto temperata di caldo
e di freddo'—though there it refers to Mount Cithaeron.

ERRATA

p. 77, 4 lines from bottom
for three
read trees
note 2
after 'll. 183–6'
add cf. *RR* 1413–4

In most descriptions of the Earthly Paradise, from Lactantius to the Alexander Romances, the land is separated by
water from the inhabited world. In Dante this water becomes the *bel fiume* of Lethe, which

> piegava l'erba che in sua riva uscìo;

and Chaucer likewise has water flowing in 'colde welle-
stremes, nothinge dede'; the ultimate, if forgotten, source
of all these streams being the four rivers of Paradise that
medieval writers delighted to identify and medieval sculptors, notably those of Cluny and Autun, delighted to carve.[1]
Beyond Dante's stream are 'gran variazion de' freschi mai'.
Chaucer sees a garden

> ful of blosmy blowes
> Upon a river in a grene mede,
> Ther as swetnesse evermore enow is,
> With floures, white, blew, yelwe and rede.[2]

Dante's Matilda 'volsesi in su i vermigli ed in su i gialli
fioretti' and explained the music of the forest as caused by
the motion of the pure air—

> e la percossa pianta tanto puote
> che della sua virtute l'aura impregna;

and it is by this means that the earth brings forth

> di diverse virtù diverse legna.[3]

Here Chaucer goes further, to particularize the several
virtues of the ~~three~~ mentioned. His phrase 'eche in his kinde'
goes back, and should take us back, to the *juxta genus suum*
of the first chapter of Genesis and the scriptural paradise;
which is, of course, the very place that Dante is describing:

---

[1] For the rivers of the *Hortus Deliciarum Paradisi v.* Neckam, op. cit., lib. ii,
c. ii. He notes that 'Aquae existentes in puteo aestate frigidae sunt' (cf. l. 187)
'hieme vero calidae' (ibid. c. xii).

[2] ll. 183-6.   [3] *Purg.* xxviii. 109-10, 114.

> Qui fu innocente l'umana radice;
>> qui primavera è sempre, ed ogni frutto;
>> nettare è questo di che ciascun dice;[1]

—lines that echo in Chaucer's

> Ne no man may ther wexe seek ne olde,
> Yet was ther joye more a thousande folde
> Then man can telle.[2]

So far, then, does the English poet follow the Italian. But Dante is to cross Lethe, to see the divine pageant, and the angels 'who ever attune their notes unto the melodies of the eternal spheres'. These melodies Chaucer has already de-scribed in the Proem; and it is not his purpose, as it was not African's promise, to reproduce here the lessons of the *Somnium*. Dante is now on the verge of an allegory setting forth mysteries of good and evil; Chaucer has committed himself to telling of things beneath Cytherea's sway. His park has a river-bank, to be sure, but the river is not now that 'watry sword', with which, as in *Pearl*, so in *Appleton House*, heaven guards paradise and excludes the world. Chaucer, too, mentions a tree apart from the rest ('beside a welle'); but its mysteries are not of the kind that Dante symbolizes in the tree 'che prima avea le ramora sì sole';[3] beneath the one stands the grifon and a heavenly pageant; beneath the other Cupid, and near by a pageant of the earth, earthy.

With Cupid we return to Boccaccio, and to the *Roman* and to Alain of Lille. We have been on the borders of a Christian Elysium where

> sweet birds sing consorts, garlands grow,
> Cold winds do whisper, springs do flow,

---

[1] *Purg.* xxviii. 142–4.   [2] ll. 207–9.
[3] *Purg.* xxxii. 60.

where the music is fit for the ear of God. But the sense of ambivalence and indeterminacy that has preponderated in the poem hitherto tinges even these six joyous stanzas. These trees, for instance, that at first glance seemed to show Chaucer as a nurseryman, and at a second glance to be variations on a theme of Statius, at a third view are seen to belong to and be reminders of the world of actuality, the world of peace and war, in which ash trees furnish arrows, palms the victors' wreath; in which there is grief and death, elms become coffins, holm-oaks whip-handles, and cypresses symbols of mourning. So in the midst of the forest, when our sense of its paradisal air is keenest, we do not entirely lose awareness of the human world; and if the sweet odours seem to come from Eden, in poetry Eden has no monopoly of eternal spring: it also belongs to the gold-hedged Garden of Venus as Claudian had described it:

> . . . aeterni patet indulgentia veris.
>
> .   .   .   .
>
> intus rura micant, manibus quae subdita nullis
> perpetuum florent, Zephyro contenta colono,
> umbrosumque nemus. . . .[1]

It gives us, then, no shock to come upon 'Cupid our lord'. We remember now the prime theme of the poem, and the kind of vision that the invocation to Cytherea had led us to expect. If at the same time we remember Mr. Lewis's dismissal of the Boccaccian stanzas to come as unChaucerian, and mere Renaissance pageantry, we should also recall that Boccaccio learnt to contrive such pageantry from de Lorris; Chaucer adopted these figures from the *Teseida*

[1] *Epithalamium Honorii*, 55, 60–62: 'There reigns eternal spring . . . enamelled meadows gleam with flowers untouched save by the Zephyr's breath; the boskage is shady'; the boughs live for Venus and only birds approved by her are admitted.

because he had met them long before in the *Roman*; and
in the *Parlement*, as in the *Roman*, they have their part in
a planned movement; a passage from a scene of natural
beauty and delight to one dominated by Amors; whence
in due course we shall come to a place where Nature,
whilst not ousting Amors, reigns supreme.

Certain it is that with Cupid we return to the human
world, to human artefacts (a well, a bow and arrows, a
temple of brass), and to very human attributes and passions.
These personified qualities—part of all courtly poetry from
the *Roman* to the *Thrissil and the Rois* and still later verse—
distinguish this next scene from that described by Statius
and those who followed him in associating the *locus amoenus*
with the abode of Venus;[1] an association that persisted until
Baudelaire announced:

> Dans ton île, ô Vénus! je n'ai trouvé debout
> Qu'un gibet symbolique où pendait mon image . . .

Guillaume de Lorris's allegorical figures are not merely
modiste's models; by changing their stance or costume another poet could effectively convey fresh meaning. In his
Notes to Book VII of the *Teseida* Boccaccio attaches to the
figures that Chaucer now appropriates his own significa-
tions; and Chaucer, who in these thirteen stanzas follows
Boccaccio more closely and continuously than he elsewhere follows any other poet (outside the *Tales*), may have
known and studied these Notes. Yet that he follows the
Italian closely does not mean that he follows it mechanic-
ally: his treatment of the *Teseida* passage in fact shows the
same kind of creative adaptation that we would expect to
find after comparing the *Troilus* with *Il Filostrato*.

To some of the figures with which Boccaccio adorns

---

[1] *v.* Statius, *Silvae*, I. ii. 144 ff. Mr. J. N. Smith drew my attention to this
passage.

PLATE 2

a. Venus and Cupid

b. Venus and her devotees: Achilles, Tristan, Lancelot, Samson, Paris, Troilus

Mount Cithaeron and surrounds the temple of Venus we can easily enough find Renaissance counterparts, such as the brilliant fifteenth-century miniature in a Bodleian manuscript of *Il Filocolo*; where a plump boy of a Cupid stands astride a well against a formal landscape, listening to a more or less naked Venus who appears to him on a cloud, 'but in none'.[1] Yet it is not the presence of pagan deities that gives such paintings an unmedieval quality; an illustration to the *Compleynt of Mars* in an earlier, English manuscript that includes the *Parlement* itself shows us a wholly naked Venus, and more figures of classical myth; and it might equally well serve to illustrate the *Hous of Fame*'s opening dream:

> I saw anoonright hir figure
> Naked fletinge in a see.
> And also on hir heed, pardee,
> Hir rose garlond whyt and reed
> And hir comb to kembe hir heed,
> Hir dowves, and daun Cupido
> Hir blinde sone, and Vulcano
> That in his face was ful broun—[2]

yet neither the *Hous of Fame* nor the *Compleynt* owes anything to Boccaccio or to any other 'precursor of the Renaissance'. All that distinguishes the Italian painting from the English one is a pseudo-classical fullness of form, an embonpoint—and signs of decoration for decoration's sake.

But these are the additions and interpretations of a later artist; and even if we feel them to be concordant with the

[1] Can. Ital. MS. 85, f. 25; repr. in Pl. 2; *v.* also p. 86, n. 1.
[2] ll. 132–9. The miniature (from Fairfax 16) is reproduced in F. Saxl, *Catalogue of Astrological and Mythological Illuminated Manuscripts*, iii. 11 (1953), Tafel vi. The presence of Vulcan often seems to connote an 'honest' Venus: *v.* below.

Boccaccian spirit we are hardly justified in concluding that because Boccaccio's symbolic figures lent themselves to decorative treatment, the function of similar figures in Chaucer is purely decorative. Mr. Lewis himself has warned us in another place that there is nothing of 'Renaissance frivolity' in Chaucer (and we may add that there is less of it in Boccaccio, taken as a whole, than magistrates and readers of 'art' editions of the *Decameron* might think); whilst Chaucer's silent alteration of the order of appearance of these figures should be enough to suggest that he is making his own arrangement of them, his own nexus of the qualities and conditions they signify. These derived stanzas occupy nearly a sixth of his narrative; he is unlikely to have spent them on mere 'ornament'. And soon we glimpse beyond the superficial prettiness forms of doubtful, even of sinister, import; indeed it is this ulterior view that would justify, if any could, talk of Renaissance anticipations; but it is Botticelli rather than Boccaccio who comes to mind: the Botticelli who was influenced by the Florentine platonists; the Botticelli of the *Primavera*, where behind the spring foliage and the poised Graces—both the foliage and the Graces having counterparts in our poem— lurks a disturbing presence, a profound meaning. However we interpret the picture, it is hard to escape the impression that Botticelli is setting forth some of the same aspects of Venus that are Chaucer's concern here. Both artists are doing more than depict Delight and Beauty and Desire: they are relating them to a larger pattern. It is Renaissance pleasure in symbolism, rather than Renaissance voluptuousness, that the *Parlement* prefigures.

The most obvious of Chaucer's changes in sequence is the postponement, till the end of the passage, of the list of those lovers whose stories are painted on the walls of

Venus' Temple, and of whom Boccaccio disposes *before* he describes Venus herself. But this is merely one of the altera-tions—sometimes making for simplicity, sometimes for the opposite—that begin to appear in the very first stanza. In Boccaccio the personified prayer that wings its way from Palamon's lips to Venus' dwelling sees Cupid forging arrows among *bushes* (in which myrtle, proper to Venus, predominates) beside a *fountain* ('Tra gli albuscelli ad una fonte allato').[1] His daughter Voluttà is selecting and tem-pering the arrows in the water of the fountain; and seated beside her are Ozio and Memoria, steeling the darts. Now whatever of Renaissance prettiness we may find in Boccac-cio's scene—and it is certainly not a far cry from it to Oberon's image of 'young Cupid's fiery shaft, Quenched in the chaste beams of the watery moon'—such prettiness is not so easy to find in Chaucer. To him Cupid is 'oure lorde'—the powerful lord and sire named at the beginning of the poem, the imperious *Amors* of the *Roman*, Dante's 'Lord of terrible aspect'. Medieval allegory—and for no frivolous reasons—had made of the winged boy a prince of magnificent array; and there is always something magistral if not godlike in his appearance as Chaucer pictures him. Thus in the *Legend of Good Women* his power is symbolized by his angelic wings and a countenance so bright that

---

[1] *Teseida*, vii. 54. For myrtle *v. Gen. Deor. Gent.* III. xxii. 37c. For the asso-ciation of Cupid with a tree *v.* E. Panofsky, *Studies in Iconology* (1939), p. 101. And with the scene in general cf. Vasari's account of the painting by Bron-zino (*c.* 1546) now in the National Gallery, sometimes described as 'Luxury': 'Fece un quadro di singulare bellezza, che fu mandato in Francia al rè Francesco: dentro il quale era una Venere ignuda con Cupido che la bac-ciava, ed il Piacere da un lato e il Giuoco con altri Amori: e dall' altro la Fraude, la Gelosia ed altre passioni d'Amore' (cit. Panofsky, p. 87). 'Venere' is depicted much as in the *Parlement*, except that she is sitting, not reclining. Her doves may be seen at the bottom left of the picture, and her myrtle near Cupid.

Wel unnethes mighte I him beholde;

And al be that men seyn that blind is he,

. . . sternely on me he gan biholde;[1]

and this presentation owes little to de Lorris or de Meun:
though the *Roman* affirms that this God can 'cherles
daunten' (so Chaucer renders 'cil qui *les amans* justise',
using his favourite verb *daunten* as he uses it of Cytherea in
l. 114 of the *Parlement*), it concentrates on the beauty of
the God of Love's apparel, and gives him a bachelor,
'Swete loking' (Douz regarz), to carry his arrows.[2] Still,
there is nothing to suggest that Chaucer here gave a
signification to Cupid fundamentally different from the
traditional *l'amour du cœur*—the civilized, courtly emotion,
as distinct from the universal appetite, represented by Venus.[3]

Some manuscripts (not necessarily authoritative) make
Chaucer agree with Boccaccio in giving Cupid's daughter
a name: reading *Wil(le)* for *Wel* in l. 214. The contiguity
of *wel* and *welle* certainly rouses our suspicions; and it has
been suggested that *Wille* is the authentic word, deriving
from Chaucer's misreading of the variant *Voluttade* as
Voluntade; but there is some evidence that the text which
Chaucer read had *Voluttà*; and we may assume that he
knew the tradition recorded in Boccaccio's *Genealogia Deorum
Gentilium* from Apuleius that Voluptas was the daughter

---

[1] Prol. G, 233, 237–9. Thus this Cupid is apparently to be distinguished
from the blindfold boy who symbolizes purely sensual love: cf. Panofsky, op.
cit., p. 127, and Lydgate's *Reson and Sensuallyte*, 5379 ff.

[2] The 'Scots Chaucerians' preserve Cupid's majesty: Dunbar (*The Goldyn
Targe*), Henryson (*Testament of Crisseid*), Kennedy (*Passion of Christ*), Scott
('Favour is Fair') all make him a king.

[3] Cf. Boccaccio's interpretation: 'mentis quaedam passio ab exterioribus
illata et per sensus corporeos introducta et intrinsecarum virtutum approbata':
op. cit. IX. iv. 95a. This signification evidently existed alongside that found
in, for example, *RR*, where Cupid often represents sexual passion in men,
Venus such passion in women.

of Cupid and Psyche. These considerations make it the more probable that with deliberate intent he replaced the figure of Pleasure (*Voluttà*) by that of 'Wil'—Will in the sense of 'impulse' or 'desire', a sense exemplified in the frequent medieval antithesis of Will to the rational faculty of Wit.[1] To the formal equivalent of Voluttà he accords a place in the next stanza, where, as 'Pleasaunce', it keeps proper company with 'Lust' (i.e. 'Delight', the Deduit of de Lorris), Array, and Courtesy. On the other hand, Chaucer completely eliminates Ozio and Memoria, who in the *Teseida* put iron heads on the arrows; they were stock figures of courtly love allegory, but even Boccaccio's Notes say little to justify their presence here. That Chaucer knew Ozio's proper function as set forth in the *Roman* is clear from his naming Idleness as porter in his briefer précis of this part of the *Teseida* in the Knight's Tale.[2] Precedent for making Cupid's daughter 'couche with her wyle', or (to follow the easier manuscript reading) 'touche with her file' Cupid's arrowheads, is hard to find. Boccaccio simply says that she tempered the steel, explaining in his Notes that 'she tempers them in the fountains of our false

---

[1] *v.* B. Dickins's edn. of *The Conflict of Wit and Will* (Leeds, 1938), p. 9, and Kemp Malone, *Modern Language Review*, xlv (1950), p. 63, for criticisms of Robinson's note on this passage. Both scholars ignore the description of Voluttà in Boccaccio's Notes: 'la quale s'intende per uno diletto singulare che l'anima sente dentro a se, sperando d'ottenere la cosa amata' (*Teseida*, ed. Roncaglia, p. 420). His explanation in *Gen. Deor. Gent.* IX. v is slightly different: 'cum enim contingit nos aliquid optare, et optato potimur, procul dubio obtinuisse delectamur; hanc delectationem prisci voluptatem vocavere.'

By the sixteenth century Voluptas has become a demonic figure, in contrast to the angelic Virtus: cf. the famous title-page of the *Trionfo di Fortuna* (Venice, 1527). For Renaissance elaboration of the conflict of Wit and Will *v.* J. Seznec's description of Bandinelli's Combat of Ratio and Libido, *The Survival of the Pagan Gods* (New York, 1953), pp. 110–13.

[2] C.T.A. 1940. But Diseuse is feminine in *RR* (525 ff.).

estimation, when because of this delight, born of love and hope, we judge that the things which please us should be preferred to anything else, human or divine'.[1] The arrows themselves are at least as ancient as Ovid, whom Boccac‑ cio duly cites, s.v. 'Cupid' in his *Genealogia*; but in Ovid, as in Apuleius (and Spenser) the distinction is between those of 'sad' lead and those of bright gold.[2] In the *Teseida* Boccaccio does not particularize them; nor does Guillaume de Lorris, beyond saying that some pierce the heart and that the one called 'Fair Semblaunt', though ground 'to cutte and kerve', is anointed with a soothing ointment; but arrows that slay, and arrows that merely wound or pierce garments, are shown in more than one later representation of the Triumph of Love.[3] Thus this line might plausibly be described as illustrating Renaissance refinement; but it is one added by Chaucer, not transferred from Boccaccio; and we now remember that the portal promised cure for

---

[1] *Teseida*, ed. cit. ibid. Cupid is not usually represented in the act of forging his arrows; the Italian illustration from the Canonici MS. (Pl. 2) represents a scene in Boccaccio's *Il Filocolo*, ii, in which Venus 'discese sopra alto monte Citereo, là dove ella il suo caro figliuolo trovò temperante nuove saette nelle sante acque'. Conceivably Chaucer was adapting the scene regularly asso‑ ciated with Venus, of Vulcan working near by at his forge, as in the Fairfax miniature: 'al the while' (l. 214) recalls Alain's *indefessa continuatione* (*v.* p. 95).

[2] Cf. *Gen. Deor. Gent.* IX. iv. The passage in Ovid is *Met.* i. 468 ff.:

> Eque sagittifera prompsit duo tela pharetra
> Diversorum operum. Fugat hoc, facit illud amorem.
> Quod facit, auratum est, et cuspide fulget acutâ;
> Quod fuga, obtusum est, et habet sub arundine plumbum.

Cf. *The Faerie Queene*, III. xi. 46 ff. In *The Kingis Quair*, st. 94–95, Cupid has three arrows 'forgit fair and bright': with the golden he 'smytis soft, and that has esy cure'; that of silver is 'harder aventure', that of steel is 'schot without recure'. In *Paradise Lost*, iv. 763–4, the golden shafts, like Cupid's purple wings, have become symbols of wedded love. (Cf. also *De Venus, La Deesse D'Amor*, 248–50.)

[3] e.g. the Sienese painting reproduced in Burckhardt, *The Civilisation of the Renaissance in Italy*, no. 281.

'dedly woundes', though not for the mortal strokes of Dis/
dain and Danger's spear.

A well or fountain had figured in such scenes since
Claudian wrote:

> Labuntur gemini fontes, hic dulcis, amarus
> alter, et infusis corrumpunt mella venenis,
> unde Cupidineas armavit fama sagittas.[1]

De Lorris had named it 'La Fontaine d'Amors' where
Cupid (he becomes Lord Cupid in the Chaucerian ver/
sion) 'Sema d'Amors la graine',[2] and entrapped youths and
maidens; and that the *Teseida* has reminded Chaucer of
Boccaccio's source here is suggested by his 'Under a tree,
besyde a welle . . .' (l. 211)—which is identical in phrasing
with the Chaucerian rendering of 'je trovai Une fontaine
soz un pin' (ll. 1434–5) as 'Besyde a welle, under a tree...'
(l. 1456). But in the new context of the *Parlement* Cupid in
this position indicates the very moment of our transit from
the world of trees and Nature to the world of art and arrows.[3]
The passage just cited from Claudian has the further in/
terest that it precedes a list of deities that are the ultimate
originals of many of the figures in Chaucer's next stanzas:

> hic habitat nullo constricta Licentia nodo,
> et flecti faciles Irae, vinoque madentes
> Excubiae, Lacrimaeque rudes, et gratus amantum
> Pallor, et in primis titubans Audacia furtis,

[1] Op. cit. 69–71:

> 'Twin fountains flow, one bitter and one sweet;
> This with sweet honey, that with poison blent.
> Cupid in both, 'tis said, his arrows dips.'

[2] *RR*, l. 1589. The image is used by Henryson in one of the most striking
lines in the *Testament of Crisseid*: 'The sede of love was sowen in my face.'

[3] So Alain shows Cupid as having some connexion with Nature, though
she finds him in many ways reprehensible: 'Non enim originalem Cupidinis
naturam in honestate redarguo, si circumscribatur frenis modestiae, si habenis
temperantiae castigetur' (*De Planctu Naturae*, ed. cit., p. 474).

iucundique Metus, et non secura Voluptas,
et lasciva volant levibus Periuria ventis.
quos inter petulans alta cervice Iuventas
excludit Senium luco.[1]

But in their immediate lineage most of the figures in the first of the said stanzas are 'by Boccaccio, out of de Lorris'. Chaucer, whilst in general following Boccaccio's order, omits two of his characters—'Leggiadria' (Grace) and 'Affabilitate'[2]—adds Lust (we must beware of giving the word its modern colour), and turns 'l'Arti' into Craft, expanding Boccaccio's description into: 'the Crafte that kan and hath the myght To doon by force a wyght to do folye'.[3] He removes the qualifying *Van* from Boccaccio's Van Diletto, and places Delight and Gentilesse (Genti-lezza) under an oak. Why he should specify an oak tree here is not apparent; for Boccaccio (though he mentions no tree here) it was a symbol of Diana, Chaucer's 'chaste goddesse of the wodes grene';[4] Boccaccio's 'Bellezza sanza ornamento

---

[1] Op. cit. 78–85:

> Here dwells the Lady License, unrestrained,
> Anger, too quickly moved, Watch wet with wine,
> The artless tear, Pallor, the lovers' friend,
> Audacity at her first thefts ashamed,
> And jocund Fear, and Pleasure insecure,
> And wanton Oaths, the sport of every breeze;
> But innermost is proud and ardent Youth,
> Excluding age from that delicious grove.

[2] 'Affabilitate' has some ethical tincture: cf. Dante's *Convivio*, iv. 17.

[3] ll. 220–1. In the following line Craft is described as 'disfigurat'—a nonce-word, derived from Boccaccio's *sfigurate*; the etymological note in *O.E.D.*, s.v., requires revision.

[4] C.T.A. 2297. MacDonald (*v.* Bibliographical Note) sees the oak as re-presenting the natural, joyous aspects of love, but offers no evidence. We should read 'hemself'(or 'selve') at l. 223. Skeat's punctuation of the Italian (*Chaucer*, i. 69) forces him to take 'Bella imagine nostra' with 'Van Diletto', instead of with the preceding line.

alcun, sè riguardando' (reminiscent of Claudian's picture of Venus gazing at herself in a mirror)[1] is simplified to 'Beaute, withouten any atyr'. Piacevolezza (Charm, Attractiveness) disappears, and instead of Ruffiania (Pimpery, or, possibly, the Bawderie who appears in the same scene in the Knight's Tale) appear Desire, Messagerye, and Mede (only the first of whom is named in the Tale).[2] Ruffiania is the sole character in Boccaccio, or in the original passage in the *Roman*, that one might wish to omit for decency's sake; so that Chaucer's reference to 'other thre—Her names shul noght here be tolde for me', is perhaps meant to cover Leggiadria, Piacevolezza, and Affabilitate; they would have been apt enough names for the three naked Graces who in Apuleius' *Golden Ass* are attendants of Venus and who about this time begin to reappear in depictions of her.[3]

Boccaccio now proceeds to describe the temple proper:

> E'n mezzo il luogo in su alte colonne
> Di rame un tempio vide . . .

For which Chaucer has

[1] Op. cit. 106–8:

> speculi nec vultus egebat
> iudicio; similis tecto monstratur in omni
> et capitur quocumque videt.

(Nor did the mirror's face withhold the truth;
The brightness of the image lights the hall,
Where e'r she looks she's caught by her own charms.)

[2] C.T.A. 1926 ff.

[3] F. N. Robinson's comment on the passage in Boccaccio ('No other figures are mentioned') is misleading: he has not looked further than st. 55.

In the thirteenth-century *De Venus, La Deesse D'Amor* Venus appears accompanied by three maidens (l. 121); cf. also *Altercatio Phyllidis et Floridae*, st. 73. The three Graces are associated with her in (e.g.) the frescoes by Francesco Cossa in the Palazzo Schifanoia, Ferrara; *v.* Burckhardt, op. cit., no. 288. Cf. *Gen. Deor. Gent.* III. xxii. 37a; and p. 147 below.

And upon pilars grete of jasper longe
I saw a temple of bras ifounded stronge.

His changes here can be explained, at least partly, by Boccaccio's commentary, which notes that both copper and brass are metals of Venus, identical in kind, though different in aspect.[1] Chaucer is evidently emphasizing the massy strength of the Temple of Love. Around it, in Boccaccio, dance youths and damsels 'discinte, scalze, in capelli e in gonne' (with gowns flowing free, barefooted, bareheaded), and through it fly 'passere molte', whilst it echoes with the *roucoulement* of doves. Chaucer, who is to introduce the sparrow ('Venus' son') in a different context (l. 351), here mentions merely the doves and the dancers; the dancers are properly dancing near this temple since, in Martianus Capella's phrase, *Terpsichore Venereo sociatur auro*; whilst doves—metamorphosed from Claudian's *volucrum comitatus Amorum*[2]—are the classic symbols of amorous desire, symbols that add a poignancy to Dante's simile of Paolo and Francesca in that fifth canto of the *Inferno* to which we have turned once and shall turn again:

> Quali colombe, dal disio chiamate,
>   con l'ali alzate e ferme, al dolce nido
>   vengon per l'aer dal voler portate . . .[3]

---

[1] Hence in the *House of Fame*, 'Venus clerk, Ovyde' can stand on a pillar of copper (l. 1486). In that poem the story of Dido and Aeneas is written on a table of brass in Venus' temple (l. 142). But the temple itself is made of glass (l. 120)—perhaps to suggest the delusive nature of love such as Dido's—and the dreamer emerges from it into a boundless desert of sand, where (in contrast to the situation in the *Parlement*) there is 'no maner creature/That is yformed by Nature'. The temple threshold in Claudian is of jasper (op. cit., l. 90).

Pratt (*Studies in Philology* (1945), p. 74) quotes Vincent of Beauvais, *Speculum Naturale*, xvi. 45: 'Venus est frigida, humida et temperata, habens de metallis latonem.' Cf. Neckam, *De Nat. Rer.* I. vii.   [2] Op. cit., l. 153.

[3] *Inf.* v. 82–84. For the symbolism v. *Gen. Deor. Gent.* III. xxii. 37b (*aves sunt coitus plurimi* . . .). Cf. Fulgentius, ed. Muncker, p. 71.

'Peace' is present in Boccaccio as in Chaucer, yet seems hardly necessary to the scene until we perceive that she is simply the tranquillity that love requires for its enjoyment: *Venus otia amat.*[1]

Dame Patience Chaucer has a little retouched, giving her instead of 'vista assai tapina' (a somewhat wretched visage) a pale face—and seating her on a hill of sand. She is older—if the Paterism is permissible—than the hill on which she sits. Tertullian had depicted her with brow un- wrinkled by grief or anger, and laughing at the devil; and Shakespeare was to seat her 'on a monument, Smiling at grief' (there is something casual in his image, as if it were familiar). Here in the *Parlement*, her pallor and the shifting sands beneath her presage disappointment and sterility rather than glad submission or eventual fruition. 'Behest and Art' represent 'Promesse e Arte'; there is no need to take the Italian phrase, and still less its English equivalent, for an hendiadys, as Robinson would have it. Jealousy, in the next stanza (which is most elaborately glossed in Boc- caccio's Notes), is altered from 'une donna cruda e ria' (a woman harsh and cruel) to a 'bitter goddess'—an apo- theosis that seems to be Chaucer's own contriving.[2]

All these changes, minor as they are, have their effect on the atmosphere of the scene before us; it grows, in Chaucer's poem, more sultry, more sinister, and at the same time more voluptuous, as we pass from the domain of Cupid to

---

[1] *Remedia Amoris*, 143. Hence in the Fairfax miniature Mars stands before her barefoot and without one of his greaves. Hence also Dryden gives to Venus, in his *Carmen Seculare*, the verse concluding 'Mars destroys, but I repair'—using Alain's image, but doubtless remembering the opening lines of Lucretius.

[2] In the corresponding passage in C.T.A. 1929–30, Jealousy 'wered of yelwe gooldes a gerland And a cokkow sittinge on her hand'; yellow being the colour of jealousy, though neither the marigold as such nor the cuckoo are usually associated with that vice.(With l. 243 cf. Lydgate's version of Deguilleville, 10156.)

that of Venus. The first sensation of innocent pleasure and delight fades into an awareness of the presence of more equivocal emotions and the more sombre aspects of pas-sion. Soon we seem far away from the pure fragrance and temperate freshness of the forest. The curtains at the temple door are stirred by none of the forest's gentle breezes, whilst within the temple the sighs of desperate lovers make sough-ings 'hot as fyr'. It is lit only by the flames kindled on its altars; and the supreme object of devotion is none other than Priapus; and not Priapus as 'god of gardins', his role in the Merchant's Tale and Douglas's Twelfth Prologue—if that were his part here, he would stand in the park, not the temple—but in his most notorious guise ('abito'): naked and lustful. This is 'the monstrous god' much as Cowley was to depict him, as a statue

> With an useless scythe of wood
> And something else not worth a name,
> (Both vast for shew, yet neither fit
> Or to defend, or to beget) . . .[1]

There is little here to connect the image of Priapus with the rationalization that Gunn finds in Jean de Meun's Priapus whose 'viz', endowed by God with 'force de generation', is but another symbol of plenitude; Gunn contends that this phallicism was 'the conclusion drawn by inevitable logical stages from abstract metaphysical doctrines Platonic, Aris-totelian, and Christian in origin and association . . . there is certainly no evidence in the text that Jean de Meun was influenced by any cult of Priapus'.[2] True enough; but

---

[1] 'To the Royal Society', st. 3.

[2] *RR*, ll. 6943 ff. Cf. Gunn, op. cit., p. 215 and note.

Boccaccio (who possessed a copy of the *Fasti*) takes the story of Priapus that Chaucer refers to as a classic example of lasciviousness (*Gen. Deor. Gent.* xiv. vi). Cf. Saxl, op. cit. (1) 11.

Chaucer's description has no metaphysical origins, and there were certainly sufficient allusions in accessible classical literature (including Ovid's *Fasti*) to make his reference to the story of Priapus and the ass intelligible. As if to empha- size the grotesqueness (though hardly, *pace* a recent critic, the humorousness) of Priapic lust, Chaucer decks him with the garlands that in the *Teseida* adorn the temple walls as symbols of success in love. This temple is not different in essence from Boccaccio's; but it *looks* different, set as it is against the fair fresh groves in which Chaucer dwells for so much longer than Boccaccio does; whilst its atmosphere is, if anything, still more wanton, more erotic than Boccac- cio implies.

By postponing the roll-call of hapless lovers that now follows in the *Teseida*, Chaucer here juxtaposes Priapus and Venus. In the *Teseida* Venus dwells in a secret part of the temple, with its own door, guarded by Richezza 'la qual le parve assai da reverire' ('who seemed to deserve much reverence'); and Venus' couch is simply 'assai bello vedere'. Chaucer makes it golden (the goddess is *aurea Venus*, and her temple *radians auro* in Ovid[1]) and hints that she rests only until sunset, night being the time for love; Venus, say the astrologers, is *flegmatica atque nocturna*. For the rest, Chaucer is more reticent than Boccaccio, who dwells on Venus' naked arms and 'pomi rilevati' (high breasts), and says that the purple cloth cover- ing the rest of her person was 'tanto sottil' (so fine-spun) that it concealed almost nothing.[2] Here indeed Boccaccio,

---

[1] *Met.* x. 277; *Ars. Am.* iii. 451. Cf. *Gen. Deor. Gent.* III. xxii. 36d.

[2] *Tes.* vii. 65 (Skeat's text and translation should be corrected). Ruskin associated Venus' purple, symbol of sensual delight (cf. Fulgentius, ed. cit., p. 72), with her shell, 'since from such shells along the Syrian coast was crushed out, sea-purple and scarlet, the juice of the Tyrian dye' (*St. Mark's Rest*, sec. 231).

however much he may moralize in his Notes (and it is a token of Chaucer's artistic superiority that he nowhere finds it necessary to add such moral glosses) shows a Renaissance delight, as well as a Renaissance skill, in the niceties of allurement. In his *Fiammetta*, too, Venus appears in transparent dress; and his references to her in *Il Filocolo* offered opportunity for the frankly voluptuous illustrations such as that found in the Bodleian manuscript (*v*. Pl. 2 and p. 86, n. 1). If we compare his goddess with such later paintings as Jacopo del Sellaio's *Venus* or Botticelli's *Venus and Mars*, it is Boccaccio's picture that is the more enticing. This is the Venus that Faustus remembers when he compares Helen's airy brows to 'the white breasts of the Queen of Love'; she whose degradation begins with Quarles's sneer at 'froth-born Venus and her brat', continues at the kitchen fire of Heine's Tannhaüser, and concludes with her appearance in a pink wrapper in Mr. Auden's *Age of Anxiety*.

Neither here nor anywhere else does Chaucer attempt, *ex ore ipsius*, sensual or prurient suggestion. Not to show Venus' attraction would be to evade one of the very issues that he is concerned with in this poem; yet he can indicate the allure of the half-naked without the hint of a snigger. Even if his manuscript did not here read

> e essa seco per le man tenea
> Lascivia e' l pomo . . .

but, like the text printed by Skeat,

> ed essa il pomo per le man tenea,
> se dilettando . . .,

the context, and the Notes, would make it clear enough that this figure is meant to be the Venus of lascivious enticement, not the deity of *onesto e licito desiderio*; even 'sanza treccia alcuna' ('untressed', l. 268) has an implication of wantonness. The 'good' and 'lawful' Venus is the goddess whose proper function, according to Alain, was to be subvicar of Nature:

Venerem in fabrili scientia peritam meaeque operationis sub-vicariam, in mundiali suburbio collocavi, ut ipsa sub meae praeceptionis arbitrio, Hymenæi conjugis, filiique Cupidinis industria suffragante, in terrestrium animalium varia effigia-tione desudans, fabriles malleos suis regulariter adaptans incudibus, humani generis seriem indefessa continuatione contexeret . . .[1]

But Alain's Nature goes on to say that Venus has aban-doned her proper function; and in many a medieval author her name stands for little else but lasciviousness. We can best judge of the aspect of the goddess that Chaucer has in mind here by comparing his picture with the Venus who replaces Boccaccio's at this point in the Knight's version of the *Teseida*. There Chaucer depicts her with unrestrained delight; not as a sultry, recumbent, Cleopatra-like figure, making the very air love-sick, but 'benigne', 'honourable', and 'digne'; there is no mention or suggestion of Priapus; and the prayer that Palamon offers at this shrine is to be ultimately answered by the gift of a lawful bride:

> The statue of Venus, *glorious for to see,*
> was naked fleting in the large see,
> And from the navel down al covered was
> With wawes grene, and bright as any glas.

[1] 'I stationed Venus, who is skilled in the science of making, in the outer world as the sub-deputy in my undertaking, so that, following the guidance of my judgement, and with the active help of her husband Hymen and her son Cupid, and whilst toiling at the multiple formation of the living things of earth, and regularly striking productive hammers on her anvils, she might link together the human series in tireless continuity': *De Planctu Naturae*, ed. cit. ii. 470. She resembles the chaste *Venus verticordia*, or Ἀποστροφία, who was kin to, but distinct from, *Venus urania*.

A citole in hir right hand hadde she,
And on hir heed, *ful semely to see*,
A rose gerland, fressh, and wel smellinge;[1]

Whatever the precise qualities which Chaucer meant us to associate with that Venus there is certainly nothing of an *Esquire* Petty girl about her. Her 'hour' is the hour of the lark's first morning song; it is hardly dawn when Palamon makes his prayer to her; and Chaucer's lines have the freshness of a dawn wind rippling an azure sea, as it does in Botticelli's more famous portrayal; this is Venus 'with

[1] C.T.A. 1955–61. The citole is an undoubtedly genuine accompaniment of Venus: Professor Gombrich kindly refers me to Saxl, *Der Islam*, iii (1912), pp. 154 ff.; yet I find no references to, or illustrations of, it as such in the fourteenth century, the illustration nearest in date being perhaps that reproduced by Grete Ring, *Painting in France, 1400–1500*, pl. 30 (? *c.* 1420). In Chaucer's *Compleynt of Mars*, Venus is the source 'of sowne of instruments of al swetnesse' (l. 179). The picture of Venus in *The Kingis Quair* is, as might be expected, a composite of those in the Knight's Tale and the *Parlement*: she lies on a bed, but with 'a mantill cast over hir schuldris quite' (st. 96); she wears a chaplet 'of rede rosis full swete' (97); is addressed as 'sterr of benevolence, planet merciable, appesar of malice' (99); and sometimes weeps (116: cf. C.T.A. 2665–6, and Vincent of Beauvais's *humida* (*v.* p. 90 n. 1). James interprets the sighs of l. 248 favourably: 'such as dooth lufaris to be glad' (96). On the other hand, the naked Venus of Charles of Orleans advises 'Ye may as wel chese yow a lady newe' (*English Poems*, ed. R. Steele, E.E.T.S. (o.s.) 215, ll. 4760–875).

James does not place Venus in a temple nor do many medieval writers outside Boccaccio in the *Teseida* (in *Gen. Deor. Gent.* the only reference is from Tacitus, *Hist.* ii. 3), where it perhaps derives in part from Claudian, in part from the medieval version of the rape of Helen according to which Paris met her in Venus' temple on Cythera: cf. Lydgate, *Troy Book*, ii. 3436. Cf. the painting of the scene by Gozzoli, which shows a naked statue of Venus standing on a pillar (National Gallery, no. 288) and the German miniature reproduced by Saxl, *Tafel* xxvii. Lydgate's reference to her statue that 'gives answer and ful solution' (as in the Knight's Tale) derives from Guido (ed. Griffin, p. 69). Boccaccio may well have seen an actual or supposed Temple of Venus (e.g. at Baiæ). Jean de Meun's reference (*RR*, ll. 21073 ff.) is based on Ovid, *Met.* x. 270 ff. In one of the *Carmina Burana* (edn. 1847, p. 138) the *Templum Veneris* is the house of a courtesan.

For statues to *Venus verticordia v.* Valerius Maximus, 8. 15, and Pausanias, 9. 16.

wind blowing upon hir tresse', as she appears to Aeneas in the *Hous of Fame*; both poet and painter have for the moment forgotten their Fulgentius, who says: 'Hanc etiam in mari natantem pingunt, quod omnis libido rerum patiatur naufragia'; they give no hint that these sparkling waves should typify, as Lydgate knows they do, 'the trowble and adversite that is in love'.[1] There is nothing in the Knight's Tale of the seductive Swinburnian languor of hot Mediterranean afternoon that Chaucer has conveyed by a few words in the *Parlement* (and nothing in Boccaccio of Venus' reclining 'Til that the hoote sonne gan to reste'). The one Venus we could think of without incongruity as a deputy of Nature; for the other, 'vulgarly called the god of love', to use the distinction in Boccaccio's Notes, sexual gratification could well be an all-sufficient end; she exhibits herself in just such a way as, according to Macrobius, is distasteful to Nature.[2]

---

[1] Fulgentius, ed. cit., p. 72; Lydgate, *Troy Book*, ii. 2544-5: cf. 5717 ff., on which *v*. Bergen's edn., vol. iv, p. 140.

[2] Cf. p. 50, n. 1. Boccaccio distinguished between two Venuses in *Gen. Deor. Gent.* III. xxiii, but only inasmuch as different accounts of her birth are given. A distinction is clear in Apuleius (*Apology*, xii) on which he perhaps drew for his Notes to the *Teseida*; Apuleius borrows from the *Symposium* 'the lofty and divine Platonic doctrine' that 'the one [Pandemos] is the goddess of the common herd, who is fired by base and vulgar passion and ... fetters servile bodies in the embraces of lust. The other [Urania] is a celestial power endued with lofty and generous passion; she cares for none save men and of them but few; she neither stings nor lures her followers to foul deeds. Her love is neither wanton nor voluptuous, but serious and unadorned, and wins her lovers to the pursuit of virtue ...' (H. E. Butler's translation). As a *celestial* power, Urania could easily be associated with a planet. The Venus of the *Teseida* and the *Parlement* resembles the goddess as described in Apuleius' *Golden Ass*, Book x: '... with the colour of Ambrosia, when she was a maiden, and to the end she would shew her perfect beauty, shee appeared all naked, saving that her fine and dainty skin was covered with a thin smocke, which the wind blew hither and thither to testifye the youth and flowre of the age of the dame ... her body was white as descended from heaven, and her smocke was blewish, as arrived

Yet the two Venuses have something in common besides
the name, or rather, they share the same name because they
share some of the same attributes: beauty, nakedness, com-
pelling attraction; both can bring misery as well as joy.
The duality, not to say confusion, that constantly meets us
in medieval references to Venus corresponds to a real uncertainty in medieval thought about love—unless we should
rather say that if she represents the physical act of love she
must at any period figure as sometimes good, sometimes
bad, sometimes neither. In classical and early Christian
literature Venus often enough represents no more than passion, sensual desire. But the platonic distinction between
a heavenly and a pandemic Venus, though sometimes mis-
understood, was never wholly forgotten; and once the
planet of the name had been characterized as *benevolus* and
benignissimus and procreation had been given its place in the
philosophy of plenitude, 'Venus' inevitably came to denote
marital love as well as illicit.[1] The ambivalence of the
concept is part of the very theme of our poem; and it is
a feature that would doubtless be apprehended easily by an
audience familiar with such allegorical ambiguities as Langland's Lady Meed, who is likewise beautiful, powerful,
and attractive, and likewise good-and-evil. Renaissance
humanists were still able to interpret Venus as either Vice
or Virtue: Filarete puts her in a temple of Vice with
Bacchus and Priapus (cf. the *Parlement*); Ficino makes her
the symbol of *humanity* and all its virtues.[2]

from the sea' (W. Adlington's translation, which hardly brings out the
voluptuousness of the original).

   [1] The distinction between a Venus favouring 'honest' love and a *libidinum dea*
lies behind the assertion of the goddess when she appears in Lydgate's *Temple of
Glas*, that she inspires only 'clene affectioun' (l. 686; cf. ll. 869 ff.). St. Augustine
alludes to three Venuses, including 'conjugatarum' (*De Civ. Dei*, IV. x).

   [2] *v.* E. H. Gombrich, 'Botticelli's Mythologies', *Journal of the Warburg and*

The portress of Venus' part of the Temple is Richesse.
Boccaccio borrows her from de Lorris, and Chaucer goes
back to the *Roman* in characterizing her as 'noble', and
'hauteyn of porte':

> Delez Biauté se tint Richece,
> Une dame de grant hautece,

which Chaucer had rendered as

> Biside Beaute yede Richesse,
> An high lady of gret noblesse,[1]

and near the goddess sit Bacchus and Ceres, as in Boccaccio: in the words of the Terentian tag cited by Fulgentius, 'Sine Baccho et Cerere friget Venus'.

These are the deities whom Troilus curses—along with
Nature and 'Cypride'—when Criseide has to leave Troy
for the Grecian tents: whereas Boccaccio's *Il Filostrato* has
simply 'gli dei e le dee e la Natura'. Chaucer is in accord
with the Notes rather than the *Teseida* itself in identifying
them as the deities of corn and wine, though he does
not go as far as to indicate that they signify 'la gulosità la
quale sommamente seguono i voluttuosi'—an expression
that would be sufficient in itself to show the *significacio* of
Boccaccio's Venus.[2] In the *Teseida* Venus holds the Idaean
apple in her hand—as in some, though not all, medieval
pictures of her; and Boccaccio tells the story of the judge-

Courtauld Institutes, viii (1945), pp. 6 ff. A surprising intrusion of learned
symbolism into popular literature is found in Wittenwiler's *Ring* (trans. G. F.
Jones, Chapel Hill, 1956, p. 30).

[1] *Romaunt of the Rose*, ll. 1033–4. *RR*, ll. 1018–19.

[2] Skeat read st. 66 of the *Teseida* as 'Olíva il collo ben di mille odori . . .',
and he translated accordingly; but it is the place ('luogo') not the neck ('collo')
that is fragrant; Chaucer renders the line correctly, adding 'swote' (l. 274).
Boccaccio gives a realistic explanation of these odours in his Notes. In *Gen.
Deor. Gent.* III. xxii, Venus is said to signify 'usum preciosorum unguentorum,
aromatum fragrantium'.

ment of Paris at length in the Notes; at such length, in fact, as to suggest that it was unfamiliar to his readers; Chaucer may have omitted the apple for a similar reason. On the other hand the story of Atalanta alluded to in the next stanza was sufficiently well known for Robert Holcot to use it in describing a theological course.[1]

The two 'yonge folkes' on their knees before the goddess will not be found in Boccaccio—at least, not here. Yet we surely owe their presence to the two rival lovers who are the heroes of the *Teseida*; Palamon is actually shown kneeling to Venus as he prays the prayer that is to rise to this very temple, and that begins:

> Fairest of faire, o lady myn Venus,
> Doughter to Jove, and spouse of Vulcanus,
> Thou gladere of the mount of Cithaeron,
> For thilke love thou haddest to Adoon,
> Have pite of my bittre teres smarte,
> And tak myn humble preyere at thyn herte.[2]

But of course the petitioners also represent all 'yonge fresshe folkes, he *or* she, In which that love upgroweth with (her) age'; and the mention of them leads very naturally to the trophies of Venus' war with chastity. The allusion to Diana has a very obvious point in the *Teseida*, since it is Emilia, huntress, and devotee of Diana, whom Palemone desires to win; but it is not merely decorative in the *Parlement*: for the heroine of the *Parlement* is likewise to be unwilling to abandon Diana for Venus.

Boccaccio does not actually say that the stories of Callisto

---

[1] *v. Medieval Studies* (Toronto), xi (1949), p. 219 (cited W. A. Pantin, *The English Church in the Fourteenth Century* (1954), p. 145.

[2] C.T.A. 2221–6. Lydgate, in the *Temple of Glas*—a work that is everywhere indebted to the *Parlement*—gives specimen petitions for other lovers in his usual deliberate manner.

and Atalanta (he mentions both maidens of that name) are
painted on the temple walls; he speaks merely of their arms
and apples hung up as trophies; whereas Chaucer refers to
the stories not only here but in the Knight's Tale, where
they are painted on the walls of Diana's temple, left blank
by Boccaccio. As virgins who had tried to resist love but
had learnt, in the Knight's words, that

> Beaute ne sleighte, strengthe, hardinesse,
> Ne may with Venus holde champartye,[1]

they stand here in intentional contrast to the ardent lovers of
the next stanza, who had died from Cupid's fatal strokes.
The only examples of these last that Boccaccio gives are
Semiramis, Piramus and Thisbe, Hercules, and Biblis.
Chaucer trebles the number.

Now muster-rolls of lovers were no new thing. Alain of
Lille has one that includes Biblis, Paris, and Medea,[2] and
Thomas of Hales begins his thirteenth-century *Ubi Sunt* with

> Where is Paris and Heleyne
> That were so faire and fresshe of bleo,
> Amadas and Dideyne,
> Tristram and Iseut and alle þo?

—the first pair and the last being among those cited by
Chaucer. Clearly we are in the presence of yet another
topos. But in tracing it we must not ignore the answer to
Thomas's question, for it is the answer that he would have
us attend to: with Hector and Caesar, he says, they have
vanished like the sheaves of summer. They signify, in

---

[1] C.T.A. 1948–9. The stories are in Boccaccio's *Chiose*.

[2] *De Planctu Naturae*, ed. cit., p. 473. Chaucer introduces Medea when he
adapts Boccaccio's Temple of Venus for the Knight's Tale (C.T.A. 1944).
The puzzling Croesus of Chaucer's list there may be the Crassus, Chresus, of
Alain's. Alain later puts Paris on the robe of Genius also: *Illic Paris incestuosae
Cupidinis* [v. l. *turpitudinis*] *mollitie frangebatur*: op. cit., p. 518.

effect, the transience of earthly happiness, the imperman-
ence of love.

The trail of this literary commonplace becomes clear in
the *Confessio Amantis*, where the poet, as in a swoon, sees
'Cupid with his bowe bent' and an assembly 'like unto a
Parlement . . . of lovers'; amongst those present being, besides
almost all those named in Chaucer's stanzas, Lancelot,
Guinevere, and Galehalt.[1] Gower may here be attempting
to improve on Chaucer, as Chaucer had improved on
Boccaccio. Chaucer himself holds other such roll-calls
in the Balade embedded in the *Legend of Good Women*, in
the *Hous of Fame*, and in the *Book of the Duchesse*; and in the
Balade *Against Women Unconstant*, which may be his, his
Criseyde is included along with Dalyda and Candace.[2]
But the list in the *Parlement* has the special interest that, like
so much else in the poem, it takes us back to Dante. The
lost lovers are almost the first sinners we meet among the
damned after passing through the gate that we have found
Chaucer adapting to his own use in this poem. The very
first among them is Semiramis,

> di cui si legge
> che succedette a Nino e fu sua sposa.[3]

She is first likewise in Boccaccio ('sposa di Nin', he calls
her, perhaps echoing Dante); and this circumstance, not
unlike one noted elsewhere,[4] would be enough to send

---

[1] *Confessio Amantis*, viii. 2450 ff. For similar later references *v.* Schick's note
to l. 50 of the *Temple of Glas* (E.E.T.S. (o.s.), 60, 1891).

[2] For Candace *v.* ibid., l. 137 n. The story goes back to the Pseudo-Callis-
thenes. Giotto actually painted Hercules, Dido, Paris, Helen, and some others
on the walls of the Castelnuovo at Naples (now lost). Boccaccio includes
Achilles and Cleopatra in *Gen. Deor. Gent.* ix. iii, and takes Dido to represent
the enticements of lust in Book xiv. xiii.   [3] *Inf.* v. 58.

[4] *Medium Ævum*, xxii (1953), p. 114; cf. J. L. Lowes, *Modern Philology*, xiv
(1917), p. 131.

Chaucer back to that fifth canto of the *Inferno*, where he would find not only Helen, Cleopatra, Paris, Tristram, but 'più di mille ombre', all named by Virgil to Dante but not by Dante to us. There he would also find, as we have seen already, the adulterous Francesca and Paolo: but they were as yet lovers of purely local notoriety—they perhaps owe their modern fame almost as much to Romanticism, and Stephen Phillips, as to Dante; and Chaucer replaces them by his own Troilus, as if *his* fame as a lover could already be taken for granted.[1]

The substitution produces the same effect as most of Chaucer's changes of Boccaccio's stanzas: it increases the pervading sense of ambivalence, of indeterminacy. Of almost all the other lovers it can be said that their love was in some sense adulterous or lustful. Cleopatra and Semiramis are damned, the one because in Dante's words she had been 'lussuriosa', the other because 'libito fe' licito in sua legge'. Dido, Pyramus, and Thisbe belong to those 'ch'amor di nostra vita dipartille'—they had committed the sin of self-murder. These five, at least, represent the very breakers of the law, and the lecherous folk, that in the *Somnium* as Chaucer had paraphrased it were doomed to 'alwey whirle aboute th'erthe in peyne'. 'Trew Troilus' carries no such obvious stigma; yet his love was inordinate (in the sense that he would not recognize human limitations), and inasmuch as it disregarded marriage and procreation might be said to be unlawful. Courtly lover though he is, he belongs also to classical story, and it is as if something of the perilous

---

[1] For Chaucer's Scots followers Troilus became the ill-fated lover *par excellence*: cf. Kennedy's *Passion of Christ*, l. 39, and Douglas's *Palice of Honor*, where 'trew Troilus' occurs with 'false Enee' and with Chaucer's Palamon and Arcite. The source of the medieval conception of Achilles, Curtius notes, is the *Ilias Latina*. With Troilus, Tristan, Lancelot, and Paris he figures as a suppliant on the Louvre Troy: *v*. Pl. 2.

frenzy of love in the form that it afflicts the men and women of classical story had touched him too. It brought him, like these others, to a bitter end. Too late he

> damned al our werk that folweth so
> The blinde lust, the which that may nat laste;[1]

and that Chaucer means us to think of his despair and piti-ful death, as well as of Dido's, Tristram's, and the rest, the last line of the stanza makes clear: 'And al hir love, *and in what plyte they dyde*'. Nor must we assume that the last stanzas of *Troilus* show his soul secure in a Christian heaven, or in anything like it. His final station is not specified as the 'eighthe spere' but 'theras Mercurye sorted him to dwelle'; and in referring to Arcite's final destiny in the same context, Chaucer, or his Knight, is careful not to commit himself:

> His spirit chaunged hous, and wente ther
> as I cam nevere, I can nat tellen wher.
> Therfor I stinte, I nam no divinistre.[2]

This is not agnosticism in the modern manner; but it does diminish the effect that Boccaccio aims at when he describes Arcita's ascent through the spheres—that of linking him with such heroes as Lucan's Pompey and Aeneas as pre-sented by Mapheus Vegius in the book he added to the *Aeneid*; heroes who, according to Isidore's definition, 'by their wisdom and courage are worthy of heaven'.[3]

If the dream had ended here Chaucer could not but have awakened with the same 'busi hevinesse', the same puzzle-ment about the 'dredful joy' of love that he had felt as he closed Macrobius. In the *Somnium* he had found an account of heavenly felicity rounded off with a warning on the fate

---

[1] *Troilus and Criseyde*, v. 1823–4.
[2] C.T.A. 2809–11.
[3] *Etym. Lib.* I. xxxix. 9 (ed. cit.).

of lecherous and unlawful lovers. In the dream he has passed from a vision of earthly felicity to pictures of the wretched end of those who spend themselves in passion; pictures that show, in the words he used of the ill-fated Troilus, 'swich peyne and wo as Loves folk endure.' This renewed sense of the woe that Venus-worship may bring comes upon us gradually, almost imperceptibly. At first we notice only what represents all that is pleasurable and inno-cent in love—Youth, Array, Gentilesse, Beauty, and Delight. Only slowly do the darker shades appear—Craft, Fool-hardiness, Flattery, Jealousy, phallicism, death. Within the temple of Delight, to use Keats's image, is the shrine of Melancholy (in Keats, too, it is hung with 'cloudy trophies'); Joy's hand—Keats continues to supply a gloss—is ever at his lips, bidding adieu. The effect of 'aching Pleasure nigh turning to poison' perhaps owes as much to Boccaccio's commentary on the *Teseida* stanzas as to the stanzas them-selves. But the effect of sharp contrast that Chaucer is now to achieve owes nothing to Boccaccio at all. Boccaccio leaves us, and Palemone's prayer, in the temple. Chaucer, for whom the temple in the last resort signifies sultriness and sorrow, suddenly takes us outside again to the temperate air, green grass, pellucid streams, where he and we can be 'solaced' by the singing birds. From the fever and the fret, and that unrest which men miscall delight—if Shelley's phrases, like Keats's, fall almost too pat it is because we are near the birthplace of that Romanticism which was to issue in *The Sorrows of Werther*, *Adolphe*, and *Dominique*—we escape to breathe again the freshness of the open park; and its pure beauty is now figured as a medieval poet always figured pure beauty, in terms of light:

Tho was I war wher that ther sat a quene
That, as of light the somer sonne shene

Passeth the sterre, right so over mesure
She fayrer was than any creature.[1]

Whether Chaucer as he reached these lines thought for the last time of the *Somnium*, with its eloquent description of the sun as 'dux et princeps et moderator luminum', is incapable of proof—and inessential to our argument. It is the force of the simile, the sudden change in speed and direction, that we must attend to. The brightness of Venus pales with the coming of the sun;[2] and by specifying the *summer* sun the comparison points at once to this queen's supreme power and beneficence. And just as at the end of the Proem the invocation to Cytherea startled us into alertness, so here the sudden rise and roll in the verse corresponds to a change of tone from doubt and questioning and gloom to radiant affirmation. We can always trust to the beat of Chaucer's lines, to the pace of his rhythms. Now they assure us that we have come to the core and climax of the poem.

[1] ll. 298–301.
[2] '... dux et princeps et moderator luminum reliquorum, mens mundi et temperatio, tanta magnitudine, ut cuncta sua luce lustret et conpleat' (loc. cit. iv. 2); in the next sentence Venus is described, with Mercury, as simply a companion (*comes*) of this great sun (cf. Pl. 1).

CHAPTER III

Nature and Venus

Then forth issewed (great goddesse) great Dame Nature,
With goodly port and gracious Maiesty
Being far greater and more tall of stature
Then any of the gods or Powers on high;

. . . .

So hard it is for any living wight
All her array and vestiments to tell,
That old *Dan Geffrey* (in whose gentle spright
The pure well head of Poesie did dwell)
In his *Foules Parley* durst not with it mel.
The Faerie Queene, VII. vii. 5, 9

lo vinco d'amor che fa Natura.
Inferno, xi. 56

Quantas rerum flectat habenas
Natura potens, quibus immensum
Legibus orbem provida servet,
Stringatque ligans inresoluto
Singula nexu, placet arguto
Fidibus lentis promere cantu.
De Consolatione Philosophiae, iii, m. 2

IN Chaucer's transport as he begins to speak of Dame
Nature, and in the exalted position to which he here
assigns her—twice within twenty lines she is called 'noble',
and this poet does not use such epithets lightly—we may
discern the last effects of the impact made by philosophy on
poetry in the time of Alain of Lille and again in the time of
Jean de Meun. Differing as these eclectic poets do, they yet
agree that Nature is the vicegerent of God, and that only
God can tell her ineffable beauty:

Car Deus, li beaus outre mesure,
Quant il beauté mist en Nature,
Il en i fist une fontaine
Toujourz courant e toujourz pleine,
De cui toute beauté desrive;
Mais nus n'en set ne fonz ne rive.[1]

As for Jean she is 'oficiaus qui toutes choses a fait naistre', 'conestable', and 'vicaire', and for Alain 'Dei proles genetrixque rerum, vinculum mundi ... Dei gratia, mundanae civitatis prima vicaria procuratrix',[2] so for Chaucer she is 'vicaire of th'almighty Lord'. And as Bernardus Silvestris (who first gives Nature life in medieval allegory) has described her by a phrase echoing the Salutation to the Virgin: *Natura uteri mei beata fecunditas*:[3] so Chaucer applies to her a phrase from the same Salutation: 'full of grace' (*gratiae plena*).[4] She puts all created things in true perspective. Her throne is no shifting mound of sand, but a flowerdecked hill. The flowers are no more merely 'ornament' than are the figures outside Venus' Temple; they are the symbol of Fecundity; and it is as such symbols that they will appear— if we accept Professor Wind's view—on a gown in Botticelli's *Primavera* and on that held out to his Venus as she comes from the foam. Nature needs no temple of jasper or of brass, with painted walls and smoking altars. At *her* forge, to use the image adopted by de Meun, she is for ever renewing the links of 'la bele chaiene doree'. She governs

[1] *RR*, ll. 16233–8.
[2] *De Planctu Naturae*, ed. cit., pp. 458, 511.
Conversely, Deguilleville, in his *ABC*, uses 'vicaire' of the Virgin: 'He hath the maked vicaire and maistresse Of all the world', as Chaucer puts it in his rendering of that poem.
[3] *De Mundi Universitate*, ed. Barach and Wrobel (1876), ii. 5; *v*. also Appendix.
[4] Cf. *gracia Nature*, in Alain's *Anticlaudianus*, i. 52, iv. 88.

PLATE 3

a. Nature and a poet

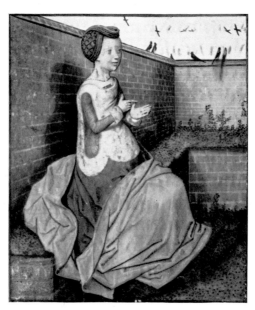

b. Nature as portrayed in *Le Roman de la Rose*

all things that propagate after their kind—in this poem symbolized by the birds now assembled submissively before her. To accept her is to reject dualism.

This hardly sorts with the view of Nature held by the earlier medieval exegetes and later hermetic philosophers, who both conceived of Nature as a vast array of Emblems; but it is at least equally different from the 'scientific' view of Nature that we ascribe to Francis Bacon and the Royal Society. It was the outcome of the thirteenth-century's discovery of the *Physics* of Aristotle, inciting men to examine afresh the nature of the visible world: a discovery as revolutionary in its effects as the opening up of the new world of observation that Bacon's title-page would have us associate with his *Novum Organon*. The philosophers of the School of Chartres had invested *Natura* with the function of a platonic world-soul. But the new knowledge of Aristotle encouraged poets to endow her with new attributes. That Chaucer went beyond Jean de Meun to the fountain-heads of neo-Aristotelian teaching—viz. to the works of St. Thomas and the schoolmen of Paris—it is neither necessary nor possible to prove. Nor need we here consider—though the inquiry would be worth making, and not irrelevant—the impact of this new learning on the older Boethian philosophy, in which Chaucer, no less than de Meun and his contemporaries, was firmly grounded. The results and adjustments following this impact belong to a history of philosophy. But they were evidently not confined to lectures in the Schools: the *Roman de la Rose*, we have seen, often appears to be coloured by the bolder speculations of young students sitting over their wine in the taverns of the Quartier Latin; and Chaucer may likewise have been stirred by the talk of his 'philosophical' Oxford friends like Gaddesden and Strode, members of the college

of Buckingham, Bradwardine, and Bredon.[1] It was perhaps not only the books of 'auctoritees' but intercourse with
such men as these that stirred him to set forth the new vision
of Nature in bright new images.

Thus the crowded scene of the *parlement* that he now finds
in session not only gives us the sense of his being hemmed
in as by farm-yard fowl thronging round their feeder—

> erthe and eyr and tree and every lake
> So ful was that unnethe was ther space
> For me to stonde, so ful was al the place—[2]

it also figures the philosophers' *Naturae plenitudo*, the doctrine
that lies at the heart of the *Roman* and that we have already
glimpsed in this poem. And when he specifies 'every foul
that comth of engendrure' he is not so much excluding the
phoenix 'that no second knows, nor third' (James I found
room even for that fabled bird in a scene imitated from this
in his *Quair*) as he is expressing the neo-Aristotelian emphasis on generation and corruption, found likewise in the
Roman:

> Toujourz choses engendrables
> Engendreront choses semblables . . .[3]

Such was the attraction of this theme that Chaucer was to

---

[1] *v.* F. M. Powicke, *The Medieval Books of Merton College* (Oxford, 1929),
pp. 23 ff.

[2] ll. 313–15. 'erthe and see' is the reading of all manuscripts except Gg and
Ff, which have 'erthe and eyr'.

Chaucer's dreamt-of 'house of tidings' is similarly characterized: being 'fild
ful' not only of tidings but of folk:

> That certes in this world nis left
> So many formed *by Nature*,
> Ne deed so many a creature,
> That wel unethe in that place
> Hadde I oon footbrede of space. (*Hous of Fame*, ll. 2038–42.)

[3] *RR*, 17515 ff.

return to it—blending it, characteristically, with Boethian doctrine—in that peroration of Theseus which seems to be infused with the poet's own feeling:

> That same prince and that moevere, quod he,
> Hath stablissed in this wrecched world adoun
> Certeyne dayes and duracioun
> To al that is *engendred* in this place
>
> . . . .
>
> And therfore, of his wise purveyaunce,
> He hath so wel biset his ordinance
> That speces of thinges and progressiouns
> Shullen enduren by successiouns
> And nat eterne be, withoute lie.[1]

Even so had Natura, in Alain's *Planctus*, emphasized that *meum opus est mutabile*.

The Lady Nature, beautiful and beneficent, who presides over this process of continuous creation, Chaucer juxtaposes with the enclosed, passive Venus Pandemos— equally, in Pater's phrase, 'the depositary of a great power over the lives of men', yet, whether in Boccaccio, Botticelli, or Chaucer, 'never without some shadow of death'. But the juxtaposition is not new. It had been made, after a fashion, 200 years earlier, in Jean de Hanville's *Archithrenius*.[2] Jean, having briefly shown us *Veneris domus aurea*, and in much greater detail the goddess's attendants, brings us three thousand lines later to a woman of ageless beauty, surrounded by flowers. She is the lady *Natura*, who discourses on the divine creation of the world and the universe and on the desirability of marriage; few poems had greater popularity in the thirteenth and fourteenth centuries; several commentaries were written on it; it must have been known to Jean de Meun, and to the author of *Les Échecs*

---

[1] C.T.A. 2994-7, 3011-15.   [2] *v.* Appendix.

amoureux.[1] Chaucer may not have read it; but in making
the appearance of Nature the climax of his poem, in displaying her superiority over Venus in beauty and power,
he follows the pattern that Jean de Hanville adumbrated.

If Chaucer's readers today fail to note this juxtaposition
of Venus and Nature, his greatest disciple did not. The
catalogue of trees in the First Book of *The Faerie Queene*,
with its 'builder oake', 'sailing pine', 'vineprop elme', suggests that the *Parlement* was in Spenser's mind as he began
to write that epic; it certainly was when he ceased. The
unfinished Mutability Cantos owe their very being to 'the
Foules Parley'—which Spenser names in his poem, just as
Chaucer names Alain's *Pleynt of Kynde* in his. Like the
Parlement, the Mutability cantos give us a debate before the
great goddess, Nature; the birds—and with them all other
creatures, and the gods—are arranged by Nature's sergeant,
Order, even as in Chaucer each is in 'his owne place'.
Spenser's Nature, like Chaucer's, pronounces her 'doom';
and Chaucer's simile for her surpassing beauty gives Spenser a hint for *his* description of her splendour; 'it the Sunne
a thousand times did pass'.[2] His Lady Nature sits upon a
hill, in a pavilion not wrought by craftsman's 'idle skill',
but made of dainty trees, with flowers of sweet odours at
her feet; Chaucer's sits on a hill of flowers in a sweet green
glade, and 'of braunches were hir halles and hir boures'.
For her 'array' Spenser, like Chaucer, refers us to Alain.
Mutability, moreover, speaks in terms that (like Theseus'

---

[1] *v.* ibid. and Pl. 3 (a). A similar miniature in the *remaniement* of this poem is
reproduced by Seznec, *The Survival of the Antique Gods*, p. 108.

I find no pictures of Nature seated on a hill of flowers. Mr. Charles Mitchell
has pointed out to me that early Renaissance representations of Thalia (who
shares some of Nature's attributes: cf. *Gen. Deor. Gent.* XI. ii. 113a) show her in
a similar posture.

[2] *The Faerie Queene*, VII. vii. 6.

peroration) are reminiscent of Cicero's doctrine as Chaucer has paraphrased it in the *Parlement*:

> all things stedfastnes doe hate
> And changed be; yet being rightly wayd
> They are not changed from their first estate;
> But by their change their being doe dilate:
> And turning to themselves at length againe,
> Doe worke their owne perfection so by fate:[1]

whilst the two extant verses of the following canto, with their loathing of 'this state of life so fickle', their yearning for the time when

> all shall rest eternally
> With Him that is the God of Sabbaoth hight:
> O that great Sabbaoth God, graunt me that Sabbaoths sight—

these are in the very tone of Chaucer's African, and show the same blend of Christian and platonic language as his concluding lines:

> Than shul they come into this blisful place,
> To which to comen, God the sende his grace.

The cantos describing the Garden of Adonis and the Bower of Bliss, read in the light of Spenser's Chaucerianism, display features adapted from the Park of Dame Nature and the Temple of Venus respectively. The abode of Venus was, to be sure, a theme favoured by Renaissance poets: as William Julius Mickle puts it when comparing the scene in the *Parlement* with the luxuriant isle of Venus in the *Lusiad*, 'the subject is common, and the same poetical feelings in Chaucer and Camoens pointed out to each what were the beauties of landscape and of bowers devoted to pleasure'.[2] Tasso's island of Armida is another varia‑

---

[1] Ibid. 58. St. 57 is evidently based on Alain's *Anticlaudianus*, i. 210 ff.

[2] *Lusiad*, 3rd edn. (1798), p. 339. The passage in Camoens is interesting as

tion on the theme, and certainly Spenser had read Tasso.
Yet a modern critic will find more than 'poetical feelings'
in Acrasia's bower: in fact Spenser has allegorized *his*
Italian original much as Chaucer gave new allegorical
significance to *his*. And some details of the bower—details of
which Mr. Lewis has vividly shown the significance—he
would find suggested nowhere save in Chaucer. Thus this
bower, corresponding as it does to Chaucer's temple, is
guarded by a dishevelled porter holding 'for more formality'
a staff that is perhaps the priapic sceptre disguised or mis-
understood, and a mighty mazer, signifying Bacchus, whilst
in a porch sits Excess,

Clad in faire weedes, but fowle disordered,
And garments loose, that seem'd unmeet for womanhed—[1]

even as the women about Chaucer's temple were 'in kirtels,
al dishevele'. The fountain, like the temple, is artificial
(even in its ivy), and paved with the jasper that the temple
pillars are made of. The ducking damsels whom Mr.
Lewis has aptly if unkindly christened Flossie and Cissie
seem like 'the *Cyprian* goddesse'; like her they are blonde,
and half-naked, showing their limbs as through a veil;
whilst the wanton lady of a later stanza lies (like a Cleopatra) on a bed of roses, faint from heat, and arrayed 'or
rather disarrayed', in a veil

That hid no whit her alablaster skin

. . . .

Her snowy brest was bare to readie spoyle—[2]

showing familiarity with such *topoi*, which tended, as Curtius shows, to survive
longer in the Iberian peninsula than elsewhere.

[1] *The Faerie Queene*, II. xii. 55. Ruskin (who, incidentally, sees the influence of
Boccaccio's account of the Cyprian Venus in the *Genealogia* on the programme
of Carpaccio's St. George at Venice) has noted the likeness between the depic-
tion of brutish paralysis in the following stanzas and Botticelli's *Mars and Venus*
in the National Gallery (*St. Mark's Rest*, sec. 227).　　　[2] Ibid. 77–78.

a picture corresponding to Chaucer's picture of Venus resting on a bed of gold

> Til that the hoote sonne gan to weste.
>
> . . . .
>
> And naked fro the breste unto the hede.

To show, on the other hand, the likenesses between the open park of the *Parlement*, where Nature presides, and the Garden of Adonis in the sixth canto of Spenser's Third Book would mean citing some twenty stanzas. It may be enough for the present purpose to note that Spenser's garden—strongly walled with gold and iron, but with double gates wide open—has

> all the goodly flowres
> Wherewith dame Nature doth her beautifie.[1]

Here 'all plenty and all pleasure flows'; there is no room for fell rancour or the fond jealousy that is the cause of the sorrow in Chaucer's temple. 'Franckly ech paramour his leman knowes' and (as in the finale of the *Parlement*) 'ech bird his mate'. In this 'joyous paradise', as in Chaucer's, there is continual spring; and the pleasant arbour is 'not by art, But by the trees own inclination made.' Cupid has laid aside his 'sad' darts—those that bring grief with love. All is in accord with the command of the Almighty: increase and multiply. The medieval doctrine of plenitude, as transmitted by Chaucer, thus finds in Spenser its last great poetic utterance.

Yet between Chaucer's park and his temple precincts there is, as we have noticed, no clear division. Nature's glade is not precisely located, Cupid's well seems to be under one of the sempiternal trees, there are doves roosting on the temple as well as on the forest branches; contrariwise, some of the birds to whom we shall soon be listening

[1] III. vi. 30.

use language of 'yonge folkes' in love, and the formel
heroine knows of Cupid and Venus, though she refuses
to serve them 'as yet'. Is it fanciful to see in this shading of
one scene into another the suggestion that the realms of
Nature and of Love march together, that however different
their climates may be, no sharp impenetrable boundary
divides them? In like manner, Spenser gives to his bower
some 'parklike' features that we might expect rather to
characterize Adonis' garden. On the plain where the bower
stands the jovial heavens suffer nor storm nor frost to fall,

> Nor scorching heat, nor cold intemperate
> T'afflict the creatures, which therein did dwell,
> But the milde aire with season moderate
> Gently attempred, and disposd so well
> That still it breathed forth sweet spirit and wholesome smell.[1]

Deceptive as it is, the garden even has paradisal music like
that in Chaucer's park:

> For all that pleasing is to living eare
> Was there consorted in one harmonee
>
> . . . .
>
> The joyous birds shrouded in chearefull shade,
> Their notes unto the voyce attempred sweet;[2]

It is, of course, precisely this *semblance* of an Earthly Paradise that gives the bower its allure. Spenser is determined
not to underrate its attraction, its escapist charm. Here men
find

> what ever in this worldly state
> Is sweet, and pleasing unto living sense,
> Or that may dayntiest fantasie aggrate;[3]

But the very words *worldly*, *fantasye*, and the repeated re-

---

[1] II. xii. 51.
[2] Stt. 70–71. I cannot find the mechanical birds that Mrs. J. W. Bennett
(*Sir John Mandeville*, 1955, p. 46) thinks Spenser borrowed from Mandeville.
[3] St. 42.

ference to the senses, should put us on our guard. Soon we find that besides some natural beauty there is here an attempt of Fancy to 'out-work' Nature. The gate of Ivory (with its Homeric suggestion of the false, of wishful dreaming) set in the thin fence that surrounds the garden, bears its own warning; it pictures the story of Jason and Medea: one of those stories that are found on the walls of Venus' oratory as Chaucer describes it in the Knight's Tale; and that tale provides sufficient exegesis:

> . . . Lo, alle thise folke so caught wer in hir las,
> Til they for wo ful ofte seyde 'Alas'.[1]

The *significacio* of Spenser's garden and bower Mr. Lewis has convincingly set forth. 'The one is artifice, sterility, death; the other, nature, fecundity, life.'[2] ' 'Tis all enforced, the fountain and the grot'; so Marvell's Mower would condemn the Bower; but the path thither lies through green fields, just as the path to Chaucer's temple (as to the Garden of Delight in the *Roman*) lies through green glades and fragrant gardens. In both poems it is always Nature at her fairest that conduces to love. But both poems are concerned less with the beginnings than with the ends of love. In the temple as in the bower, love, pleasurable and innocent enough in its inception, becomes an end in itself. All of the lovers whose stories are painted on the temple wall are paid with the wages of death. None (save 'the moder of Romu-lus', exceptional in other ways) bear children. Prosaic, even impertinent as this last comment may seem to the romantic, it would not have seemed so to the speculative

---

[1] C.T.A. 1951-2.
[2] *The Allegory of Love* (Oxford, 1937), p. 326. His interpretation has been challenged by N. S. Brooke, *The Cambridge Journal* (April 1949); but none of Mr. Brooke's arguments, even if accepted, affect the present exegesis of the *Parlement*.

and supposedly cynical de Meun any more than to the devout and orthodox Langland. Once love does become all-sufficient, these poets no less than Chaucer, Alain, and Spenser seem to imply, it joins hands with wantonness and unnatural vice, and the ways thereof are the ways of death. Nowhere does Spenser show himself more 'medieval' than in his adherence to this doctrine. The difference from Chaucer is chiefly one of scale. Chaucer, with his usual passion for compactness, has treated the two aspects of love in a single sequence: the open park, Cupid at the edge of the temple precincts (where he can prick with his arrows birds and beasts as well as men and maidens?); the initial delights and later perils of love; the murky temple; the worshippers and accompaniments of Venus and their latter end; then the return to the fresh, green glades, and the spectacle of Nature presiding over the mating birds, whom we have already glimpsed in the park, as they 'besyed hem hir briddes forth to bringe'. The outskirts of the temple merge on the one side with the park and on the other with Nature's 'launde': as if to show that courtoisie is meet and commendable if regarded not as an end in itself but as part of the preparation of Youth for adult life and marriage. Spenser, on the other hand, working in his large Renaissance tapestries, has space to picture separately the dual sequences of the love that leads to harmony and procreation and the love that ends in sterility and death; and he can give to each sequence a setting of 'so faire a place as Nature can devize'.[1] Whether he would have employed the imagery of Chaucer's park in describing the approaches to the Bower if he had felt that Chaucer had first in mind an Earthly Paradise in the strict Dantean sense is a question unnecessary and unanswerable. As Chaucer had reshaped

---

[1] *The Faerie Queene*, III. vi. 29.

parts of Dante to his own purposes, so Spenser might remould Chaucer. And we have not yet done with his remouldings. For in the tenth canto of Book IV we come to
yet another pleasaunce 'walled by Nature', another pair of
gates, another array of trees, another picture of innocent
love, and another Temple of Venus, though guarded not
by Richesse but by Concord—'a sober dame'. This temple
(like the one in the Knight's Tale) is fuming with incense,[1]
and (like Venus' in the *Teseida*) decked with garlands. Its
statue of Venus 'covered in a veil' has about the shoulders
a flock of little loves—*putti* as old as Claudian,[2] who likewise describes them as brothers of Cupid—'Daun', Spenser
titles him, following Chaucer: his law he compels all
creatures to obey. Round the altar are

> Great sorts of lovers piteously complayning,
> Some of their losse, some of their loves delay,
> Some of their pride, some paragons disdayning,
> Some fearing fraud, some fraudulently fayning—[3]

and for a moment we seem to be back with Chaucer's
Flattery, Behest, and Art. But then comes the memorable
prayer to Venus as Queen of Beauty *and of grace*, no indolent
voluptuary, but the tireless vicegerent of creation: her grace
being that which Chaucer had seen in Nature:

> The ioy of Gods and men, that under skie
> Doest fayrest shine, and most adorne thy place,
> That with thy smyling looke doest pacifie
> The raging seas, and makst the stormes to flie;
> Thee goddesse, thee the winds, the clouds doe feare;

. . . .

[1] IV. x. 37. Cf. C.T.A. 2281, and n. in my ed. of the Knight's Tale.
[2] *Epithalamium Honorii*, 72–73:
> mille pharetrati ludunt in margine fratres
> ore pares, aevo similes, gens mollis amorum.
[3] St. 43.

So all the world by thee at first was made,
And dayly yet thou doest the same repayre:
Ne ought on earth that merry is and glad,
Ne ought on earth that lovely is and fayre,
But thou the same for pleasure didst prepayre.[1]

No reader of Chaucer coming upon this paean but will recall Boccaccio's lovely hymn to a Venus who, like Spenser's, cannot be labelled simply Urania or Pande׳mos; a hymn into which Chaucer injects his own masculine force and serious feeling:

Pleasaunce of love, O goodly debonaire,
In gentil hertes ay redy to repaire.
O verray cause of hele and of gladnesse,
Yheried be thy might and thy goodnesse!

In hevene and helle, in erthe and salte see
Is felt thy might, if that I wel descerne;
As man, brid, best, fish, herbe and grene tree
Thee fele in tymes with vapour eterne.
God loveth, and to love wol nought werne;
And in this world no lyves creature,
Withouten love, is worth, or may endure.[2]

If we are to give Spenser's Venus any label, it will be 'verticordia' or 'conjugatarum'.[3] Her purposes are one with Nature's: so that the birds who, 'privily pricked with thy lustfull powres', chirp to this Venus out of their leavy cages, may very properly remind us of those who were 'prest in [Nature's] presence' in the *Parlement*, and

---

[1] Stt. 44, 47. Spenser is here translating Lucretius, *De Nat. Rer.* i. 1 ff.—a passage that Chaucer does not seem to have used, though it would be accessible to him in Priscian.

[2] *Troilus and Criseyde*, iii. 3–14. l. 12 is markedly different from Boccaccio's '[ti senton] gli homini e gli dei' (*Il Filostrato*, iii. 75)—'men and gods [as well as birds, &c.] feel thee'.

[3] Cf. pp. 95, n. 1, 98, n. 1.

of the 'smale fowles' of April at the beginning of the Tales
of Caunterbury. Nearby stands Amoret herself, attended
by Womanhood, Shamefastness, Cheerfulness, Modesty,
and—sole survivor of Boccaccio's lay-figures—Comely
Courtesy, the true, the acceptable descendant of Courtoisie.

Thus in this last scene of Spenser's all the elements that
he accounts as innocent and good in park and temple,
garden and bower, lie compacted. Art finds its proper
place: no tree or flower of any worth 'But there was planted
or grew naturall'.[1] The gardener—Shakespeare was to take
up the analogy in a pregnant passage in *The Winter's Tale*—
is the true artist whose work complements Nature's by
bringing order into wildness, yet neither imitates nor defaces
hers. The 'gardens' of Adonis could not be Spenser's last
word; no Platonist could dissociate them from gardens of
the same name in the *Republic*, where they are the very
symbol of unreality. It is rather to this pleasaunce in Book
IV that Spenser would direct us; and in it, as in Chaucer
and Alain, along with Venus there is Nature, and Nature
is the goddess of orderly creation. For plenitude does not
imply chaos; creation does not mean confusion. If there is
a place for the Artist, the Maker, in this pleasaunce or in
the world, it is because Nature herself is supreme artist
(interestingly enough, the analogy was first suggested, however dimly, by Macrobius, who in his *Saturnalia* compares
Virgil, *Natura parens*, and the creator of the universe). And
if there is a place for Amoret, it is because with her, so Mr.
Lewis teaches us, the age-old debate between Venus and
Diana—the debate that is to occupy the rest of our poem—
comes to an end; an end that Chaucer, who always
assumes that marriage is the proper consummation of love,
would hardly have found surprising. For Chaucer, we

[1] St. 22.

have seen, as for Jean de Meun, Nature represents 'the age-less fecundity, the endless and multiform going on' of life. Jean's Dame Nature, says Mr. Lewis, 'sweeps aside traditional love-lore, *and* traditional condemnation of it . . . and passes easily and inevitably into the expression of Jean's delight in natural beauty'. Now traditional love-lore is certainly still present in the *Parlement*: we found it in the stanzas based on Boccaccio, and we are soon to have still more of it, in the pleas of rival suitors that Chaucer himself devises; whilst traditional condemnation of it is not very different from the sentiments expressed by African or those soon to be voiced more stridently by duck and goose. Yet in the perspective of the whole, Chaucer's goose and duck count—and he meant them to count—for little by comparison with that natural beauty which he finds in the paradisal park: not a still-life beauty, but one of which the creatures who fill earth and air are an animated part. We have not here to do with what Mr. Lewis dismisses as 'the usual medieval recipe of May morning and singing birds'; indeed, the time is not May, but mid-February. As the trees that Chaucer saw first in this vision were 'clad with leves that ay shall laste, *Eche in his kinde*', so these birds are 'of every kinde that men thenke may'. They thus assemble '*alwey fro yere to yere*'—displaying, like the trees, Nature's age-less fecundity. What Jean expresses in long monologue, elaborate *descriptio*, and scholastic phrase, Chaucer images forth by a variegated show of birds that would be familiar in character and colour to every reader since they were part of everyday medieval life. They abound in medieval manuscript borders because they abounded in field and forest, farm-yard and fen. Few of them, it might be said, would be mating in an English February; but the Valentine tradition was stronger than requirements of realism. More-

over, it is not the hatching throstle's shining eye or the
livelier iris twinkling on the burnished dove that prompts
Chaucer to write about the birds of spring; it is their busy-
ness, their infinite variety of function, expressive of tireless
divine bounty.

Chaucer's Nature, when compared with de Meun's,
may appear to have something homely and matter-of-fact
in her address. Yet in many a 'miracle' related by Gautier
de Coincy the Queen of Heaven herself scolds just as
downrightly ('moult aireement'); and the downrightness
in no way detracts from the divinity and grace that the poet
ascribes to Nature in words strikingly like her own in the
Physician's Tale:

> He that is the formere principall
> Hath maked me his vicaire-general
> To form and peynten erthely creatures
> Right as me list; and eche thing in my cure is
> Under the mone, that may wayne and waxe.[1]

This Nature has nothing in common with the conventional
Nature of the panegyrists except personification. As *vicaria
Dei auctoris*—so she described herself in Alain's *Planctus*—
she makes *all* creatures 'to the worship of my lord'. She
paints the rose and lily, and gives colour and 'figure' to the
birds no less than to this Virginia, who, like Desdemona,
is in very truth 'the cunningst pattern of excelling Nature'
(both, that is, show Nature surpassing herself)—and not
least, we shall see, because 'she floured . . . with alle
attemperaunce'—an attribute that Spenser would not fail to
note. This Nature, as already hinted, is the same that appeared in wonderful beauty to Alain, to hold a dialogue—
it is a reminder that the new poetic-philosophic pattern

---

[1] C.T.C. 19–23. Deguilleville also has Nature's realm end at the moon.

developed out of the old—not unlike Philosophia's with Boethius; and in the Sapphics that Alain addresses to her:

> Quae tuis mundum moderans habenis
> cuncta concordis stabilita nodo
> *nectis*, et pacis glutino *maritas*
> caelica terris . . .[1]

there is (besides the notion of Nature as a moderating, tempering force) a phrase that Chaucer now remembers as he defines Nature as the vicar of god who

> hoot, cold, hevy, light, moyste and drye
> Hath *knit* by even noumbre of accorde.[2]

Whether Chaucer meant us here to think of Nature or of God himself as making this nexus is immaterial; in the *Roman* (ll. 16792–7) it is God who *creates* and Nature who *guards*; but Alain was drawing on a passage from Macrobius that Chaucer had read just before he wrote this poem:

Quas ab hoc numero [quaternario] deus mundanae molis artifex conditorque mutuatus insolubili inter se vinculo elementa devinxit, sicut in Timaeo Platonis adsertum est, non aliter tam controversa sibi ac repugnantia et naturae communionem abnuentia permisceri, terram dico et ignem potuisse et per tam iugabilem conpetentiam foederari, nisi duobus mediis aeris et aquae nexibus vincirentur. Ita enim elementa inter se diversissima opifex tamen deus ordinis opportunitate conexuit, ut facile iungerentur.[3]

---

[1] *De Planctu Naturae*, ed. cit., p. 458:
> Thy reins the universe's course are guiding,
> Thou all things with firm knot of concord joinest,
> And with the bond of peace dost firmly marry
> Earthly and heavenly.

[2] Lines 380–1: *v.* Note at end of this chapter.

[3] 'Borrowing the means from the number [four], the Creator of the Universe bound together the elements in an unbreakable chain, as was affirmed in Plato's *Timaeus*; in no other way could the elements of earth and fire, so

Jean de Meun, taking a cue from Macrobius, or Virgil (who had found a golden chain in the *Iliad*, VIII. 19), made these links into

> La bele chaeine doree
> Qui les quatre elemenz enlace
> Trestouz enclins devant ma face; [i.e. the face of God].[1]

But only Chaucer, fusing in his characteristic fashion Alain, Boethius, and de Meun (and perhaps not forgetting Dante's 'Amor che muove il sole e l'altre stelle'), was to name this chain the Chain of *love*—thus identifying love with the operations of Nature: it is his Troilus, not Boc-caccio's, who hymns the God who 'with his bonde, Love, of his vertue liste to cerclen hertes alle' as 'auctour of Kynde':[2] and it is his Theseus, not Boccaccio's, who, alluding to the four elements by their compounds, speaks of the chain that binds them as made by the First Mover who

> Whan he first made the faire cheine of love,
> Greet was th'effect, and heigh was his entente;
> Wel wiste he why, and what thereof he mente;
> For with that faire cheine of love he bond
> The fir, the eir, the water, and the lond
> In certein boundes, that they may nat flee:[3]

What makes this speech doubly relevant to our purpose is that it is a proem to a marriage, and that a marriage between

opposed and repugnant to each other, and spurning any communion of their natures, be mingled together by the two means of air and water. For thus, in spite of the utter diversity of these elements, the creator harmonised them so skilfully that they could be readily united.' (*Commentarium*, I. vi. 24.)

[1] *RR*, ll. 16786–8.

[2] iii. 1765–7: based on Boethius, II, m. viii, where this love is said to knit 'sacrement of mariages of chaste loves'. But neither Boethius nor Boccaccio (who adapts the passage in *Filostrato*, iii. 74 ff.) has any reference to the author of Nature. Chaucer, again, has Troilus, odd as it may seem, invoke Hymen (ib. 1258; glossed in H4 as 'deus vinculorum'). [3] C.T.A. 2988–93.

a 'gentle' knight who has served 'with wille, herte and mighte', and a maid 'that fairer was to sene Than is the lilie on the stalke grene': such a marriage, in fact, as is proposed in the *Parlement*. The God who ordained bonds between the elements, who 'al this wide world hath wroght', or-dained also the bond of matrimony that finally united Emily and Palamon:

> Bitwixen hem was maad anon the bond
> That highte matrimoigne or mariage.

And here it is that Chaucer's philosophy of love is seen to wear a different aspect from de Meun's. Of wedlock, Christian or pagan, de Meun takes little or no account. To him Nature is the procreative force that overrides all human forms and ceremonies. Wherever he found sug-gestion of or support for this doctrine, it was certainly not in Alain. True, Alain has no discussion of marriage as such, beyond the pictures that he paints on Hymen's robe:

Ibi tamen sacramentalem matrimonii fidem, connubii paci-ficam unitatem, nuptiarum indisparabile [*v.l.* inseparabile] iugum, nubentium indissolubile vinculum, lingua picturae fatebatur intextum. In picturae etenim libro umbratiliter legebatur quae nuptiarum initiis exultationis applaudat sole-mnitas, quae in nuptiis melodiae solemnizet suavitas, quae connubiis conviviorum arridebat generalitas specialis . . .[1]

But the presence of Hymen in his allegory is in itself note-worthy; and still more significant is his use of marriage as the symbol of concord; he conceives of Nature's own operations in terms of it: 'Omnia sibi [sc. Deo] invicem legitimis pro-

---

[1] 'Yet pictorial language showed that there was woven the sacramental pledge of matrimony, the peaceful unity of connubial bliss, the firm yoke of marriage, the knot of wedded folk, that shall not slide. For in that writing one could darkly read what ceremonious delight cheers the beginning of marriage, what sweetness of melody attends it, what special widening of the festive circle happily accompanied weddings' (*De Planctu Naturae*, ed. cit., p. 503).

portionum connubiis maritavit.'[1] To turn from the Temple of Venus to the 'launde' of Nature is to turn from the *Roman* to the *Planctus* and to a new range of images that enable Chaucer to express his sense of marriage as a concord and the supreme achievement of love. To him the marriage feast is a symbol of 'alle blisse and melodye';[2] such melody and such bliss are the characteristic features of the park, not of the temple.

The *Pleynt of Kynde*, as we have already noted, is not the only work by Alain that Chaucer knew. The *Hous of Fame*, in its general ordering, no less than in a specific reference, shows that he was equally familiar with the *Anticlaudianus*, which he may even have read at school.[3] In this dream-poem Nature, desiring to make a perfect man, holds council with her sisters the Virtues in her paradisal wooded garden of everlasting flowers and fragrance. The trees are full of singing birds:

> Syrenes nemorum, cithariste veris, in illum
> Convenere locum mellitaque carmina sparsim
> Commentantur aves, dum guturis organa pulsant.

---

[1] 'He wedded all things to himself in the lawful wedlock of proportion' (ibid.). Further, for Alain's Natura man's 'complexions' resemble the *concors discordia* of the elements, and—the passage is relevant to a discussion of a poem with a Prologue such as the *Parlement*'s: 'sicut contra ratam firmamenti volutionem motu contradictorio exercitus militat planetarum, sic in homine sensualitatis rationisque continua reperitur hostilitas. Rationis enim motus, ab ortu coelestium oriens, per occasum pertransiens terrenorum, coelestia considerando regyratur in coelum. E contrario vero sensualitatis motus planetici erratici contra rationis firmamentum, in terrestrium occidentem, obliquando labuntur' (p. 451). ('As the army of the planets opposes the fixed rolling of the firmament in contrary motion, so there is in man an unceasing warfare between sensuality and reason: the motion of reason, arising from a celestial source, passing through the level of earthly things, being centred on heaven, returns thereto. The erratic planetary movements of sensuality, on the other hand, operating against reason, fall into earthly decline.')

[2] C.T.A. 3097.

[3] Cf. Bolgar, op. cit., p. 261.

Pingunt ore liram, dum cantus imbibit istos
Auditus, dulces offert sonus auribus escas.[1]

Within the wood and on a mountain top stands a columned
hall decorated with paintings not of dead lovers but of dead
heroes and dead philosophers—though two of the heroes
are shown as in conflict with Venus:

> Ypolitique pudor Veneris subductus habenis
> Gaudet et excepto luget Cytherea pudore.
>
> .   .   .   .
>
> Fractus amore Paris, Veneris decoctus in igne,
> Militat in Venerem;[2]

whilst Nature is seen binding the elements—for Alain as
for Chaucer it is her primary activity:

> . . . fidei nexu civilia bella refrenans
> Et fratrum rixas, elementis oscula pacis
> Indidit et numeri nodo meliore ligavit.[3]

Prudentia (who represents Plato's *sophia* rather than our
modern 'Prudence', and who speaks of *hoc commune bonum*),
being urged by Racio and Concordia,[4] ascends to heaven

---

[1] i. 92–96.
> There the spring's lutanists, syrens of the grove,
> Poured forth their honeyed song, or parleyed loud
> Whilst some made deeper music. Listening ears
> Drink in their songs, which counterfeit the lyre.

[2] i. 150–1, 179–80:
> Hypolitus, once sham'd and subdued
> By Venus' reins, rejoices, whilst she mourns
> That the disgrace is now obliterate
>
> .   .   .   .
>
> Once scorched by love, broken by Venus' power,
> Paris now fights against her.

[3] i. 194–6:
> She curbed by bond of faith the civil wars
> And strife fraternal, setting kiss of peace
> Upon the elements, which tight she bound
> In number's better knot.

[4] ii. 305.

in a chariot built by the Seven Liberal Arts, learning in
her flight, like Chaucer in the *Hous of Fame*, the causes of
'snowes, hailes, reynes, windes':

> Inquirit que materies, que nubis origo,
> Quomodo terra madens proprio sudore resudat
> In nubes celoque suos componit amictus.
>
> . . . .
>
> Unde trahunt ortum venti, que semina rerum
> Inspirent motum ventis causasque movendi; . . .[1]

—but learning it at much greater length than Chaucer
allows to the lesson. As Racio has promised, she beholds
the planets and sees

> Quas Venus illecebras, que tristia gaudia, tristes
> Leticias, mala dulcia, pocula fellea terris
> Offert et felle mellito cumpluit orbem.[2]

Like Cicero's Scipio, she passes beyond the spheres into
the empyrean, where she meets Theologia (*poli regina*), and
recovering from her swoon in the presence of the Virgin—
for whom, as we might expect in the twelfth century, the
most ecstatic and sustained poetry is reserved—comes at
length into the presence of God himself. He grants her request for a perfect soul for a perfect body, and himself

---

[1] iv. 248–50, 258–9:
> How comes a cloud, what its material;
> How earth, once soaked in its own sweat, exudes.
> Clouds that envelope it and join with heaven—
> All this she learnt; and whence the winds arise
> And what the seminal force behind the winds
> That sets them moving . . .

The *vagantes aerios cives* of ll. 273 ff. are, as W. P. Ker noted, the 'eyrish
bestes' ('many a citezein') of *Hous of Fame*, ll. 930–2.

[2] ii. 122–4:
> What Venus' blandishments and what her joys
> With sorrows blent, what her sad happiness
> And bitter sweet, and proffered chalice sour,
> What honeyed gall she rains upon the earth.

creates Anima, on a model supplied by Noys. Prudentia
returns to earth, and, the Vices having been vanquished,
a new Golden Age begins. Love and Harmony reign
once more; whether sexual love obtains we are not told;
but nothing in Alain's philosophy or theology would be
against it.

The Summary appended to the work, which Chaucer
almost certainly knew, concludes:

> Per huius autem libri scientiam comparatur illius super-
> celestis propositionis iudicium; Noti sesytos, [= γνῶθι
> σεαυτόν] id est, cognosce te ipsum. . . .

It is the text from which St. Bernard and St. Bonaventura
were ever preaching, and reminds us, like the eminence
accorded to Theologia, that Alain himself was a Cistercian
and a theologian before he was a poet: the author of
*Parabolae, seu de regulis sanctae theologiae, Contra hereticos,
Distinctiones.* In one sense Chaucer's whole work represents
a fresh awareness and understanding of this text, a fresh,
empirical study of mankind and of the human heart; and
his work, too, could be summarized like Alain's: *humanae
naturae cognitio*:

> Per hunc enim librum cognoscit homo quid ex Deo habeat,
> quid a Natura ministrante recipiat, quid a Fortuna suscipiat,
> quid a Vicio contrahat.

But in the *Parlement* he is chiefly concerned with *Natura
ministrans*; Alain's concept of Nature—the poetic sublima-
tion of Chartrain philosophy—came in still more aptly
for him than for de Meun, and Alain's ornate mannerisms
(some worthy of Amanda Ros herself) do not prevent
Chaucer from perceiving its power.

In the *Parlement* Nature is not only the dominating and
controlling figure of the birds' assembly; she stands in

counterpoise to the austere other-worldliness that characterizes African's preaching in the Proem. Not that there was a fundamental irreconcilability between the *Somnium* itself and the doctrine of Nature as Chaucer understood it; the case was, rather, that certain dualistic implications in this political and ethical tract by a Roman adherent to a traditional Greek philosophy had been so heavily underlined by Macrobius that it was impossible for any medieval reader to ignore them. The greatest achievement of the twelfth and thirteenth centuries was to make better-balanced and catholic pronouncements on the relation of man to society as well as to the physical world; and Alain's allegory, however defective, is the first poetical expression of this achievement. We do not have to read Alain in order to understand, to 'enjoy' Chaucer; but we shall be in less danger of underrating the serious part of Chaucer's purpose if we note that for both poets Nature speaks in the same tone —the tone of authority. And Chaucer's Nature is no less authoritative for being, for the most part, benign. She speaks in 'esy voys' (l. 382), 'with facound voys' (l. 521); and even her manner of giving judgement is mild; 'Foules, tak hede of my sentence, *I prey*' (l. 383). She presides (as God's regent) over the parliament because it is the occasion of the general mating, and it is by mating of like with like that she replenishes the earth. Suitors may speak of 'sovereyn ladies', 'mistresses', 'servants'; to her they are all simply 'feres' (l. 410) or 'makes'—the latter being a word she uses no less than thrice (ll. 389, 631, 657). But nothing in such usage implies libertinism or free love, and all Rousseauian connotations of 'nature' we must banish from our minds. Nature—or Kind, to use the native English word, as Chaucer himself does—is often synonymous in medieval usage with law; but the law of kind is not that ruthless 'natural law' by which a later century was to account for the survival of the fittest. It is ineluctable, to be sure—'no man', says Chaucer in *Troilus*, 'may fordon the lawe of kynde'; but, like the divine moral laws, to be properly obeyed it must be loved. Hence it is that in the *Book of the Duchesse* Chaucer speaks of the happy age in which poets

> [fables] put in ryme
> To rede, and for to ben in mynde
> Whyl men loved the lawe of kynde.[1]

Hence, again, Nature is constantly associated not with blind passion or instinct but with Reason. Thus in the *Anticlaudianus* Racio holds the most respected place in Nature's Council; whilst in Langland (who will scarcely be suspected of indulging in fantasy or heterodox speculation) part of Kind's lesson to the dreamer is that birds and beasts follow Reason in the times of their engendering and in succouring their young; it is only fallen man who is blind to the laws of Nature and of Reason.[2]

We need not, therefore, look for anything heretical or fanciful in Chaucer's delineation of Nature. Rather, her presence alone should be sufficient to suggest that nothing in the fowls' confabulations which we are about to hear will be allowed to mar the dignity of Reason.

[1] ll. 54–56.
[2] *Piers Plowman*, B. xi. 326–61. Cf. Appendix.

Note *on* 'Even noumbre of accorde'

The only fourteenth-century example of the phrase 'even number' given in O.E.D. is *Piers Plowman*, B. xx. 268: 'Hevene hath evene noumbre, and helle is without noumbre', which is placed under the heading 'exact, precise'. Skeat, whilst glossing *even* in Langland's line as 'the opposite of odd', in his Notes thereto explains the first half of the line by reference to Rev. vii. 4–8: 'and there were seated an hundred and forty and four thousand'—which is both an exact and an even number; the second half he refers to Job x. 22, where the land of darkness is described as having *nullus ordo* (the verse on which the Parson comments: 'alle thinges ben ordred and numbred, but they that ben dampned ben nothing in ordre, ne holde none ordre'). Behind Chaucer's line, as behind Langland's, there certainly lies the Augustinian view of number as the principle of order and form, of beauty and perfection, of proportion and law; everything in which there is order and measure is to be ascribed to God (cf. F. Copleston, *History of Philosophy*, ii (1950), pp. 77, 85). Unambiguous examples of the phrase 'even number' itself are not found before the fifteenth century; but the sense 'exact, precise' easily shades into 'equal' which is found as early as Laȝamon, and the adj. 'even' = opposed to odd is found in Trevisa's *Bartholomaeus* (1398; cf. also *O.E.D.*, s.v. 'odd', 2). If we bear in mind the medieval suspicion of odd numbers—illustrated in the view that Lucifer upset the harmony of the angelic hosts in reducing their ten orders to nine by his defection (cf. Towneley play of Noah, l. 10)—it seems clear that l. 381 refers to the *quatuor elementorum concors discordia* of Alain (cf. Skeat's note and the citation from Chaucer's rendering of Boethius, iii, m. 9 at p. 160 below).

So much is necessary by way of preliminary before we can consider the force of 'of accorde'. The passage in Boethius suggests that it should be taken as a separate adverbial phrase meaning 'harmoniously', the notion of harmony following naturally upon, but not being identical with, that of evenness. Cf. the French 'Par l'acort (de trestouz nos omes)' which occurs in *RR*, l. 10688, where it is rendered 'by evene accord' in the *Romaunt*, l. 5818; there the meaning is clearly 'unanimous agreement'. The same phrase occurs in l. 668 of the *Parlement*; but there the context suggests a rendering 'male matching with female of his own kind, harmoniously'. Miss Cecily Clark (*Essays in Criticism* (1955), p. 407) renders it 'by *mutual* agreement'; but though such agreement is implied it can scarcely be said that the phrase, in itself, yields such a meaning.

CHAPTER IV

Love's Meinie

'Si le Paradis est un jardin, il y pousse des arbres; et s'il y pousse des arbres, comment voulez-vous qu'il n'y vienne pas des oiseaux?'
HENRI BOSCO, *L'Âne Culotte*

Many of the winged tribes have various sounds and voices adapted to express their various passions, wants and feelings—such as anger, fear, love, hatred, hunger and the like. All species are not equally elegant; some are copious and fluent . . . the language of birds is very ancient, and, like other ancient modes of speech, very elliptical.
GILBERT WHITE, *Selborne*

THE St. Valentine's Day assembly that gives the poem one of its titles occupies little more than half of it. Partly because it displays much lively humour, partly because it is thought to contain clues to the date of the poem, it has received far more attention from critics than the three hundred lines or so that have occupied us thus far. But it is only when we have learnt from these earlier passages what Chaucer's method in this poem is—and in particular what use he makes of 'matere' found in other poets—that we can appreciate his manner of proceeding now.

It is easy to find in Gower, Machaut, Deschamps, Oton de Graunson—all poets known to Chaucer—analogues for bird-convocations, while before them Jean de Condé had written his *Messe des Oisiaus* and Jordanus of Osnabrück his *Pavo*.[1] It is also easy to find *demandes d'amour*—

[1] For the former *v.* Scheler's edn., cited in Appendix; for the latter *Romanische Forschungen*, vi. 46, and P .W. Damon, *Modern Language Notes*,

PLATE 4

English birds

debates as to the claims of rival lovers or the propriety or gentilesse of their actions. Manly has pointed to the ex/ ample of Boccaccio's story (*Il Filocolo*, iv) in which an un/ married lady has to choose among three suitors distinguished the first by bravery, the second by courtesy and liberality, the third by wisdom. It is not so easy to find such a *demande d'amour* debated by birds, or, before Chaucer's time, to find English poems for St. Valentine's Day; here the nearest analogue that Manly could discover is in the *Fablel dou Dieu d'Amors*, in which the claims of *vilaine gent* are main/ tained by *malvis* and *gais* against the *espreviers*, in an assembly presided over by a *loussignos*; the *Complaynt d'Amours* (some/ times attributed to Chaucer himself), though it celebrates St. Valentine's Day, 'Whan every fowel chesen shal his make', offers no such *tençon*, and probably belongs to the fifteenth century.[1]

There is a closer similarity with Oton de Graunson's *Songe Sainct Valentin*.[2] When a man falls asleep from

lxvii (1952), pp. 520 ff. It is doubtful whether Chaucer knew either poem. For other bird/assemblies *v.* Seelman, *Jahrbuch für nd. Sprachforschung*, xiv. 101– 47. The only relevant part of *La Messe* (early fourteenth century) is the Intro/ duction, describing a May/night Mass in honour of Venus chanted in due form by the birds, with the nightingale officiating and the popinjay preaching a sermon. After the birds have asked for absolution for their sins in love, a high seat is prepared for Venus, in a delightful pleasaunce, 'si riches et d'œvre si fine/Que bien sembloit œvre devine'. If Chaucer knew the poem it may have given him a hint for the bird/assembly presided over by a goddess—for him not Venus, but Nature. Whether the allegorical 'Speech of the Birds' of the great Sufi poet Attar (*fl.* 1230) had any influence on these poets is a question outside our province. English writers who had introduced bird/assemblies were Odo of Cheriton (*Narrationes*, 55) and Banastre (v. *Blancheflour et Florence*, *Rom.* xxxvii. 221–34, ll. 345 ff.; *v.* also ll. 73 ff.).

[1] For comments on the attribution v. *Medium Ævum*, xviii (1949), pp. 36 ff.

[2] All quotations are from the edition by A. Piaget, *Oton de Grandson, sa vie et ses poésies* (Lausanne, 1941); the 'Songe' (449 ll.) is printed on pp. 309–23. Whether or not this Savoyard poet was the first to write a St. Valentine's Day poem, his are the first known examples of the genre.

weariness, begins Graunson—in a manner not unlike
Chaucer's—he will dream of some marvel 'bonne pour lui
ou dangereuse', as he, Oton, did one St. Valentine's Day.
He dreamt that as he wandered in search of a precious
stone he came upon an assembly of birds of every kind.
Each chose its mate (*per*)—though only for a year—according to its 'degree';

> Et font ensemble le demour,
> Pareille de cuer et d'amour;

and

> bec et bec, masles et femelles,
> Ilz se embrassoient dez elles.

They are presided over by an eagle who

> faisoit a chascun raison,
> Selon le jour et la saison,

and who demands of a peregrine falcon why he is not
mated. He replies that as he cannot have the tame falcon
whom he desires and has waited for faithfully, he will have
no one. This falcon, who rules the skies, and never wearies
in well-doing, is

> en la garde d'un gentilhomme —
> Nul besoing est que je le nomme,

and he dare not ask for her as his *per*. The noise of the birds'
departure wakes the poet, and sets him thinking of those
birds who 'd'amour ont douleur et joye'. He has learnt that
one should not blame 'les gens se ils veulent amer', and
that as birds choose mates at their own will, so should men:

> Amour est chouse naturelle,
> Mais elle ne sera ja telle,
> Si loial ne si bien servie,
> Ne tant a son droit assouvye
> Entre lez oyseaulx et les bestez,
> Qui n'ont point de sens en leurz testez . . .

This summary of Graunson's fable and its monologues includes all points that offer any correspondence with the *Parlement*. The question of the female bird's consent is not once raised.

Now Chaucer owed to Graunson the substance of the *Compleynt of Venus*, where he hails him as 'flour of hem that make in Fraunce'; and it is possible, as Braddy has argued, that Chaucer had read the *Songe*. But it is too much to claim, as Braddy goes on to claim, that the *Songe* is the model for the *Parlement*, or that it has a number of 'focal elements' which 'cast a new light' on the leading situation. Graunson's voluble peregrine falcon, who holds the centre of the stage throughout, hardly compares with any of Chaucer's suitors. To 'birds of lower kind' Graunson gives never a note. There is no hint in his dream of intervention by them and other birds in such an affair; and while Chaucer's birds delight to recover their mates, Graunson insists that most birds are inconstant, 'newfangle'. Finally, it is not Nature but an eagle that presides over the French session; the closest we come to any mention of Nature there being the sentiment 'Amour est chose naturelle'. Graunson makes as much of the differences as of the likenesses between the loves of birds and of men and women. In tone the two poems are wholly different: the French is formal, if not flat; the English 'a gay and vigorous dissertation'. Perhaps the most that Chaucer owed to the former—as distinct from other works in this genre—was a suggestion or two for his fable. The notion of introducing other birds besides eagle and falcon as lively characters with speaking parts seems to be his own, and so (except for a partial precedent in Alain, soon to be noted) is the assignment to Nature of the role of presiding judge. Once more the real lesson to be drawn from study of a supposed 'source' is that

Chaucer's shaping spirit of imagination remoulds such sources to his own desire, with effects almost Coleridgean.

Gower's two St. Valentine's Day balades, which have a 'gentilesse' and formal charm of their own, illustrate a convention rather than supply a source.[1] In one the lover addresses the lady as 'mon belle oisel', and wishes that he and she could be like the Ceyx and Alcyone whose meta-morphosis Gower lovingly commemorated elsewhere:

> Com dieus muoit en oisel lour figure,
> Ma volenté serroit tout tielement
> Qe sanz envie et danger de la gent
> Nous porroions ensemble par loisir
> Voler toute francs en nostre esbatement:

In the other she is 'com la fenix souleine':

> Chascun Tarcel gentil ad sa falcoun,
> Mais j'ai faili de ceo q'avoir voldroie:

In both there is talk of election: each bird

> semblable a sa mesure
> Une compaigne honeste a son talent
> Eslist tout d'un acord et d'un assent;

Nature is 'pleine de favour A ceos oiseals q'ont lour elec-cion'. But the genre evidently requires that St. Valentine should be given the commanding place in these poems:

> Saint Valentin l'amour et la nature
> De toutz oiseals ad en governement;

---

[1] *Works*, ed. Macaulay, i. 365. Other examples in English are: Chaucer's *Compleynt of Mars*; Charles of Orleans's first poem (*English Poems*, ed. cit., ll. 53; cf. 2455–80); Lydgate's *Flour of Courtesy* (which is much indebted to the *Parlement*); and Rolland's *Court of Venus* (S.T.S., 1884). For Manly's suggestion that 'cours amoureuses' were held on St. Valentine's Day there is no evidence beyond what he himself produced of such a court in Paris in 1400.

and the likeness in phrasing between them and the *Parle-ment* is not of a kind that enables us to say that one friend was borrowing his conceits from the other. What the com-parison chiefly brings out is the differences between the two poets even when they are following a similar pattern.

The link between the 'noble emperesse Nature' and Chaucer's bird-assembly is provided by Alain's *Pleynte of Kynde*, which he now refers to by name (l. 316). Editors since Skeat have duly noted that whereas in the *Planctus Naturae* the birds figure as innumerable ornaments on the robe of Nature, Chaucer has given them life, speech, and motion. They have *not* noted that Alain has some living birds who do honour to Nature at her approach in spring, much as Chaucer's do honour to her as they leave: 'Aves vero, quâdam naturae inspiratione, alarum ludo plausibili joculantes, virgini venerationis faciem exhibebant'[1]—though Alain says nothing of their mating. Descriptions of a robe like this of Nature are so common (there are others in the *Planctus*, and in the *Anticlaudianus* Concordia wears one adorned with pictures of *castus amor*) as to suggest that it formed an accepted *topos*, popularized, perhaps, by teachers of rhetoric. In *Les Échecs amoureux* the mantle represents all creation; and Cupid's garment in the *Roman de la Rose* is cut to the same rhetorical pattern.[2] But Chaucer not only departs from the convention of the robe; he swerves at once

---

[1] Ed. cit., p. 446. Cf. also p. 461: 'Aves vero variis sigillatae naturis meae directionis regimine, sub alarum remigio fluxus aeris transfretantes, praecordiali-ter meis inhiant disciplinis.'

[2] *v.* p. 151, n. 2. Alain cannot specify what figures were embroidered on her under garments: 'sed tamen ut quaedam fragilis probabilitatis remedia docuerunt, opinor in herbarum arborumque naturis ibi picturae risisse lasciviam' (p. 443, cf. *Parlement*, ll. 302–4). Of the animals on the tunic he says: 'histrionalis formae representatio, quasi jocunditatis convivia, oculis donabat viventium'; he aimed at the vividness that Chaucer achieved.

away from the poetic to the parliamentary. The birds that crowd into Nature's presence behave for all the world like the lords, burgesses, knights of the shire that thronged West/ minster Hall during the session of a fourteenth-century parliament—a parliament that was still as much a court of law, a royal council, as a law-enacting body. Primarily it was a place of consultation and debate; and 'debate' or 'consultation' is what this word connotes in, e.g., the *Parlement of the Thre Ages*, or the *Roman*, when Amors summons a *parlement* of barons at ll. 10784 ff.: a passage im/ portant for us as indicating that Chaucer, on a hint from Alain, has substituted Nature for Amors as president. In parliament the king gave his dooms, and in his own person listened to the Commons' pleas.[1] There Chaucer himself sat in 1386 as knight of the shire for Kent; and there he would learn how the Commons chose a Speaker (the title indicates the original function) 'to diffyne Al her sentence, and as hym lyst, termyne' (ll. 529–30), and 'presented' him to the king; a custom to which this poem provides the first allusion.[2]

The royal Nature who presides over our assembly is no arbitrary monarch: she governs 'by statute' and 'rightful

[1] Cf. the use of *parlement* in *Piers Plowman*, B. iv. 47 ('bille' = petition); *v.* also Willi Pieper, 'Das Parliament in der m. e. literatur', *Herrig's Archiv*, 146, pp. 187 f. The French sense of a 'court' is dominant in Charles of Orleans: cf. ed. cit., l. 2887; *v.* also p. 168 and C.T. 2112 ff. (not in Boccaccio).

[2] l. 531. O.E.D. does not record this parliamentary sense; but cf. *Rot. Parl.* iii, 17 Ric. II (1393–4), 310:

'Joefdy ensuant, les Comunes *presenterent* au Roi en plein Parlement Monsr. Johan Bussy pour lour comune Parlour, & ledit Monsr. Johan Bussy fist protestatioun en manere accoustume; & a cause que la dite protestatioun sembla honeste & resonable, *le Roi accepta*.' (Cf. l. 532: 'she accepteth hym . . .').

The dismissal of the birds (ll. 655–75) corresponds to the dismissal of a parliament: cf. op. cit. 29 (1 Ric. II, 1377): 'le Roi, en plein parlement . . . lour donnast congie a departir'.

ordenaunce'.[1] She is not only the goddess of fecundity:
she stands for harmony and decent order, which means
hierarchy: not a rigid and mechanical hierarchy, but one
as richly various as that scale of creatures of which these
birds form a part. 'It is necessary', says St. Thomas, in
setting forth this principle of the *scala Naturae*, 'that God's
goodness, which in itself is one and simple, should be
manifested in many ways in his creation: because creatures
in themselves cannot attain the simplicity of God. Thus it
is that for the completion of the universe there are required
divers grades of being, of which some hold a high and
some a low place in the universe. That this multiplicity of
grades may be preserved in things, God allows some evils,
lest many good things should be hindered.'[2] Thus each of
the birds has its 'owne place' (l. 320), with 'foules of ravine'
highest, and waterfowl lowest—the regular and recognized
order.[3] Yet the lowest are not despicable: they share the
general joy of living, and the particular joy of mating.
Nature 'onques ne fis chose vilaine': we shall, it is true,
find some evil-intentioned birds in this array: the lapwing is
false, the cuckoo murderous. But—'God allows some evil
things lest many good things should be hindered.' Again,
what one bird lacks another has—to each its special pro-

---

[1] For the distinction between ordinance and statute *v.* Stubbs, *Const. Hist.*
II. xvii, sec. 292. Ordinance in the senses 'direction how to proceed, established
rule', is used in English first of the Deity; the sense 'royal decree' not being recorded before Chaucer's time; that of 'decision' is found first in Dunbar. The
distinction between *ordinance* and *statute* became rigid almost at the time that
Chaucer was writing; *v.* E. A. Jolliffe, *Constitutional History of Medieval
England* (1937), p. 378 and n. 1.

[2] *Summa Contra Gentiles*, ii. 45. Cf. *Inf.* xxxi. 52 ff., on Nature's just and
prudent creation of beasts like elephants and whales.

[3] So St. Ambrose, in the *Hexaemeron* (v. 13), speaks first of waterfowl 'as
it is hard to raise one's thoughts suddenly to birds of the air' (cited by W. O.
Hassall, *The Holkham Bible Picture Book*, p. 60); *v.* Skeat's note on l. 323.

perty and propriety. And it is noteworthy that Langland, Chaucer's greatest contemporary, like him turns to birds to illustrate this divine purpose in Nature's variety:

Kynde knoweth the cause hym selve—and no creature elles.
He is the pyes patroun—and putteth it in hire ere
That there the thorne is thikkest to buylden and brede;
And Kynde kenned the pecock to cauken in swich a kynde...[1]

The 'ordenaunce' governing the birds has harmony as its aim and, like the ideal order of society, is freely ac- cepted, not enforced. Nature allows, even insists, that the formel, the maiden, is to have free choice among those who love her. Without mutual affection there can be no 'accord'; it is the very word used of the happily wedded (and high- born) lady of the Franklin's Tale—in which so much that is implicit in the *Parlement* is expanded in human terms:

Prively she fil of his accord
To take him for hir housbonde and hir lord,
Of such lordshipe as men han over hir wyves;
And for to lede the more in blisse her lyves
Of his free wil, he swoor hir *as a knight*
That never in al his lyfe he, day ne night,
Ne sholde upon him take no maistrye
Agayn hir wil, ne kythe hir jalousye.[2]

—there being no room in this relationship for the Gelosia that brought bitterness into Venus' Temple. And once again Chaucer's sentiments chime with Langland's:

For no londes, but for love, loke ȝe be wedded,
And thanne get ȝe the grace of god and good ynogh to live with,

---

[1] *Piers Plowman*, B. xii. 226 ff. (cf. the whole passage with xi. 336 ff.). Line 226 recalls St. Bonaventura's answer to the question why God did not, if he could, make a better world: *quia voluit, et rationem ipse novit* (I *Sent.* 44. 1. 1 ad 4).
[2] C.T.F. 741–8.

it is those who wed for money and regardless of 'curtesye' who suffer:

> In gelesie ioyeless and ianglynge a bedde
> They live here lif unlovely til deth them departe.[1]

Only since the nineteenth century has 'love-match' come to connote disparities of the duke–chorus-girl kind beloved of newspapers. In Chaucer's century any liking for this kind of romanticism was satisfied by such stories as *Aucassin and Nicolette*—or the Franklin's, or the Knight's. In the Knight's Tale, Palamon is 'a kinges brother sone, pardee'; and if Theseus can urge that even though he were 'a poure bacheler' (in degree of knighthood) his service would still make him worthy of Emily's hand, this represents the limit beyond which 'gentil mercy' could not pass; whilst in the other tale the suitor who durst hardly avow his love because his lady came 'of so heigh kindrede' is himself of no lower rank than a knight. The Nicolette who is loved as a slave-girl turns out to be a long-lost daughter of a king, just as the banished man of the *Nutbrown Maid* is really an earl's son, the Ophelia who is to regard Hamlet as a prince 'out of her star' is yet a courtier's daughter. In the *Parlement* Nature will not insist that the formel's suitors should be her exact equals in rank. She would wish the formel, her 'gentileste' creature, to wed the royal bird because he is likewise 'gentileste' and 'most worthy' (l. 635); but her harmony and hierarchy would not be shattered were she to choose one of the other suitors. They (like Griselda) can make up in worthiness what they lack in rank; and merely to seek 'worship' is to recognize the virtue of order, of degree. All that Nature insists on is this recognition—and the voluntary principle. She will have no forced marriages,

---

[1] *Piers Plowman*, B. ix. 175–6; C. xi. 270–1.

no coupling, in Langland's phrase, of a young wench
with an 'old feble', leading as it does to the adultery and
'derne love' of the Merchant's Tale, and so to discord, the
hindering of generation, and the restricting of Nature's
fecundity.

In all this there is nothing discordant with the Christian
doctrine of sacramental marriage as the parson teaches it:

God maked it . . . *in paradys*, and wolde himself to be born in
mariage. . . . This is verray mariage, that was established by
God er that sinne bigan, whan *naturel lawe* was in his right
poynt in paradys; and it was ordeyned that o man sholde haue
but o womman, and o womman but o man [otherwise] ther
ne sholde neuere be pees ne reste amonges hem . . . A man sholde
bere him wyth his wyf in suffraunce and reverence.[1]

'Womman sholde be felawe ("fere") unto man.' The purpose of marriage, continues the parson, is engendrure of
children, to replenish Holy Church, the Christian commonwealth, 'by *good linage*'. Originally, and ideally, then,
marriage is paradise on earth. In *Cleanness*, an unim-
peachably orthodox poem by a contemporary of Chaucer,
God says:

> I compast hem a kynde crafte & kende hit hem derne,
> & amed hit in myn ordenaunce oddely dere,
> & dyȝt drwry þerinne, doole alþer swettest,
> & þe play of paramoreȝ I portrayed my seluen;
> & made þerto a manere myriest of oþer,
> When two true togeder had tyȝed hem seluen,

---

[1] C.T.I. 77; cf. E. 1330–6. A full exposition of the parson's teaching on
marriage (which includes a condemnation of 'amorous love') would not be to
the present purpose, which is simply to indicate at what points it touches
Nature's; but amongst these might be included his view of folk who 'peynen
more to doon than to hir appetyt suffiseth'; such excess is equally condemned by
Nature, with her emphasis on the Mean (*v*. p. 191 below).

Bytwene a male and his make suche merþe schulde come
Wel nyȝe pure paradys moȝt preve no better
Elles þay moȝt honestly ayþer oþer welde.[1]

We see now why Chaucer could take hints for the setting of this poem from Dante's cantos on the 'paradiso terrestre'. We can see too how much romantic love learnt from Christianity. The Parson had claimed that marriage 'maketh the hertes al oon of hem that been ywedded, as well as the bodies', long before Malory's lady of the lake told her lover's slayer that 'two bodyes thou hast slain in one herte, and two hertes in one body',[2] or Donne affirmed that

> We were mutuall Elements to us,
> And made of one another.

St. Thomas himself had laid the ethical basis for the parson's views. For him marriage involved 'amor', 'dilectio', 'intensa amicitia'—and 'amicitia in quadam aequalitate consistit'; without monogamy there would not be 'liberalis amicitia', but servility. And it happens that in defending the marriage-bond he argues, as Chaucer might, from the behaviour of certain birds: by divinely implanted instinct the male bird remains with the female 'ad educationem foetus'; so also ought the man to remain with the woman. Since generation was instituted 'ad bonum naturae' and for the conservation of the species, it should be governed by laws for the common good.[3]

Chaucer, then—to sum up this part of our comment—

---

[1] *Cleanness*, 697–705: 'Elles' = provided that.
[2] *Works of Sir Thomas Malory* (Oxford, 1954), p. 52. Alain had used a similar expression for David and Jonathan: 'Cum sint diversi, non sunt duo mente sed unus' (*Anticlaudianus*, ii. 186). Cf. 1 Samuel xviii. 3.
[3] *Contra Gentiles*, III. cxxii. 6; cxxiii. 6 ff.

would recognize no antithesis between 'nature' and 'order'. Christian religion as well as Christian philosophy would make him feel—to adapt some words of Chesterton—not only that there are certain proper things to say, but also that there are certain proper things to do; 'Man was a ritualist before he could speak'. *Amour courtois*, with all its so-called conventions, would never have arisen but for this deep-rooted feeling. Ritual, far from being inimical to Nature or to Love, is fostered by them. It is the cycle of the seasons that first produces ceremonies. It is the lover who duly seeks 'worship and honour', and like the Franklin's knight does 'penaunce', in hope 'to stonden in his lady grace', that is most like to win her love. Moreover, observances of Nature—such as the ritual devotion to May 'with alle thy floures and thy grene' which every creature 'of gentil herte' performs, whether a Squire or a Theseus, an Arcite or an Emily—accord and blend with the observances of love: pagan in origin, doubtless, but refined from the pagan indecency of Venus' Temple—just as St. Valentine's day observances themselves represent a refinement of pagan practice; and when Chaucer's birds assemble on another occasion, to praise St. Valentine, the distinction between Love and Nature almost disappears: in the Prologue to the 'Legend of Cupid's Saints' (mistitled the *Legend of Good Women*) they 'diden observaunces'

> That longeth unto love, and to Nature—
> *Construeth that as you list, I do no cure.*[1]

So in *Troilus* Love is not to be withstood, since it is 'a thing so vertuous *in kinde*'. It is not surprising, then, that the same rapture which informs Chaucer's praise of Nature in our poem rings through his adaptation of Boc-

[1] Prol. G, 150-2.

caccio's hymn in *Il Filostrato* to the love that is 'veray cause of heele and of gladnesse'. Gladness and health are the pleasures promised us by the verse of gold on the gates of the park; and Chaucer, like Boccaccio, identifies the love that is their cause with the planetary Venus. As we have seen already, the distinction between planet and goddess was not absolute: the beneficent power that the planet symbolized was inevitably identified with 'honest', health ful love; and since sexual love comes within the province of Nature, the force that promotes it can be regarded as an agency with purposes accordant, though subservient, to Nature's own. Thus it is that Douglas's birds

> Louys thar lege with tonys curyus
> Baith to Dame Nature *and* the fresch Venus[1]

—'fresch' is noteworthy—and Dunbar's cry 'Haill princes Natur, haill Venus luvis quene';[2] and in the *Parlement* itself the name will occur (l. 652) in a context that associates Venus with the Nature of the park rather than with the enclosed goddess of the temple. If her name is used with such different associations it is because no one can say where Love that is part of the whole procreative process of Nature becomes that passive self absorbed divinity who brings not joy but pain. There is mystery here that neither

---

[1] So the planet is sometimes represented by the foam born goddess accom panied by Cupid and the Graces, e.g. in the drawing mentioned at p. 96, n. 1, and in the calendar in the fifteenth century book of hours, B.M. MS. Add. 11866 (f. 4*v*.—juxtaposed to 'charitas'); cf. descriptions in fourteenth century manuscripts of Michael Scot's *Liber Introductorius* (e.g. MS. Bodley 266), one of which is printed in *Der Islam*, iii (1912), p. 175.

[2] *Eneydos*, Prol. xii. 247 ('louys thar lege'—praise their Lord'); *The Thrissil and the Rois*, l. 63. 'Fresch'—which Chaucer uses more than once of the goddess —translates Virgil's 'candida' in *Eneydos*, viii (*Aen.*, l. 608). Dunbar applies it to the planet in his *Ballad of Lord Barnard Stewart*, l. 77.

Chaucer nor any other poet can plumb. Yet of one thing we may be certain: that when he invoked Cytherea it was not because he had dreamt of the Temple of Venus. To be sure, the promise of health and gladness was addressed to Love's servants, and we have found some of these in that temple. But we are soon to meet others, obedient to Nature's laws above all, and we are to sense the 'bliss and joy' of the birds who have found their loves. If they give praise there/ for not to Venus but to Nature it is because the law that Venus, in the words of the *Troilus* hymn, 'han set in universe' ,must be read and followed in the light of Nature's overruling 'statutes'; whilst if the inscription had pertained only to the servants of Venus in the temple, the poem must have concluded four hundred lines earlier than it does.

Obedient to Nature as the goddess of Order, each bird on this festal day takes its proper place. It was the all/ inclusive pattern, the sense of glorious richness in diversity produced by the juxtaposing of each genus and species, that fascinated Chaucer (and many a medieval philoso/ pher) more than the 'inscape', the anatomy, of the separate animal, tree, or flower. Thus, for all Chaucer's delight in the daisy, we could hardly tell from his references alone what sort of flower it was; it is the contrasting white and red that he loves; just as he is content to say that the flowers Emily gathers are 'party white and red', or that a meadow is 'with floures swote enbrouded al'. Often as the lily and the rose are named, it is chiefly in simile (so the formel and Criseyde blush like the fresh red rose); we must wait till Henry Hawkins's *Partheneia Sacra* for an exact word/ picture of the lily. Chaucer has told us nothing of the shape or colour of the trees in the park, but only of their uses; and now when we come to the list of birds, which in its deliberate formality balances the tree/list, only one of these birds—the goshawk 'with his fethres dunne and grey'—is given any attribute of colour. The rest are characterized by their qualities, and in the language of the Bestiaries; and it is the Bestiaries' insistence on *significacio*, and indifference to zoological categories or probability that we must bear in mind as we scan Chaucer's assembly, or those of his successors: such as the author of *The Kingis Quair* (who includes elephants, dromedaries, and unicorns in his paradisal zoo); or Henryson, who convenes, *inter alia*, 'the tame cat, wildcat, and the wild woodswyne' in his 'Parlement of four futtit Beistis' for the *Trial of the Fox*; or Skelton, who summons 'all maner of byrdes in their kind' (including the 'estridge', 'tassell gentle', and 'byrde of Araby') to Philip Sparrow's funeral.

But the Bestiaries did not sum up all medieval bird-lore. Besides them there was 'al this new science that men lere'; and Chaucer, as always, blends old and new, imposing on a seemingly miscellaneous array what is almost Aristotle's order—birds of prey, birds that live on worms, seedfowl, and waterfowl. He makes use, too, of traditional associations that owed nothing to the bestiaries. Thus, though the bestiaries told him that the eagle 'with his sharpe look perceth the sonne' when it renews its youth:

> —up he teð
> til that he the heuene seð
> ðurgh skies sexe & seuene.
> til he cumeð to heuene.
> So right so he cunne,
> he houeð in the sunne—[1]

it was not from them he learnt that it was a 'royal' bird—

---

[1] Middle English Bestiary (ed. in J. Hall, *Selections from Early Middle English*, i (1920), p. 177).

'imperial', as the Book of St. Albans has it.[1] Again, if he follows Alain in calling the next bird, the goshawk, a 'tyrant', it is probably because 'tyrant' already had that special association with birds of prey which we find in *The Phoenix and the Turtle*:

> From this session interdict
> Every bird of tyrant wing
> Save the Eagle, feathered king.

'The gentil faucon' (l. 337) is a regular synonym for the peregrine: hence Skelton's Merry Margaret is

> Gentle sa falcon
> or hawk of the tower—

where 'gentle' means *noble*: hawking, as Chaucer indicates when he adds that the falcon 'with his feet distreyneth the kinges honde', being pre-eminently the sport of kings.[2] The jealousy of the swan is, says Burton, a fact 'confirmable by observation and ocular inquiry';[3] though that it sings against its death, as Chaucer states, is simply a fiction that survived Pliny's scepticism, to yield another line in *The Phoenix and the Turtle*, and the opening of Weelkes' loveliest madrigal. Chaucer's Anelida compares herself to this bird

---

[1] In *The Thrissil and the Rois*, Dame Nature gives the 'King of Fowles' judicial powers over the other birds (ll. 120 ff.).

[2] As 'royal' birds, falcons, and hawks were regularly given to the king: cf. *De Scaccario*, ed. Johnson, p. 121. For the 'hardiness' of the sparrowhawk cf. Neckam, I. xxxii ['tower'=O.F. *tour*, soaring flight: cf. p. 151 n. 1].

[3] 'R.T. in his blason of Jealousie telleth a story of a Swan about Windsore, that finding a strange Cock with his mate, did swim I know not how many miles after to kill him, and when he had done, came back and killed his hen.... For my part, I do believe it may be true; for Swans have ever been branded with that Epithete of Jealousie' [Burton then cites l. 342 of the *Parlement*]: *Anatomy of Melancholy*, pt. 3, sec. 3. memb. 1, subsec. 1. Cf. Browne, *Pseudodoxia Epidemica*, III. xxvii. To Skeat's references add Neckam, I. xlix (where Ovid is quoted). Alain does not mention jealousy.

which 'ayens his deth shal singe in his penaunce': she is, in fact, in the plight of Dido—the very plight pictured on our temple walls. Here is one of the many cross-associations between park and temple suggesting that the bird-world has its analogies with the human; associations that to an audience familiar with beast-allegory would immediately suggest themselves.

We are moving down step by step from royal eagle, noble goshawk, and falcon, to sparrowhawk, and merlin. With the dove, swan, and owl we come to seedfowl, water-fowl, and inferior fowls of ravin. But for Chaucer, as for Shakespeare, the owl (cf. l. 343) is pre-eminently 'the shrieking harbinger, foul precurrer of the fiend', Lady Macbeth's 'fatal bellman, Which gives the stern'st good-night.'[1] By now it is evident that the poet is not depicting a conventional concourse of the kind of songsters that make tuneful a spring morning, or limiting himself to the gay birds of medieval ornament, such as the popinjay and chalaundre, finch, woodwale, and 'archangel', that bedeck Cupid in the *Roman*.[2] The nightingale, to be sure, is here,

---

[1] It is the hierarchic order of birds that gives point to the later comment on the murder that the owl presages:

> 'Tis unnatural,
> Even like the deed that's done. On Tuesday last
> A falcon, towering in her pride of place,
> Was by a mousing owl, hawked at, and killed (*Macbeth*, II. iv. 11–13);

the 'unnaturalness' of a king being murdered (supposedly by his grooms) being parallel with the killing of a beautiful and noble falcon by a bird despised by its own kind (in the Squire's Tale the owl is one of the *false* birds painted on the mew that Canace makes for the deserted falcon). For other instances of Shakespeare's use of traditional bird-associations cf., e.g., the adulterous wren of *Lear*, IV. vi. 115, and the detested kite, ibid., I. iv. 286.

[2] *RR*, ll. 865 ff.; *Romaunt*, ll. 890 ff. (cf. *Sir Gawain and the Green Knight*, ll. 610–12). For a discussion of variants in the original, and of 'archangel', v. *English and Germanic Studies*, iii (1949–50), p. 34, and *Notes and Queries*, vol. 175, 1938, p. 332.

as she is in the *Roman* (where likewise she is found among
'the fresshe leves newe'), but beside her is the tame and
household bird, the ruddock, or redbreast. And with each
stanza enter birds distinguished not by their beauty or their
song, but by their hostility to other living things: the goshawk 'doth pyne To briddes for his outrageous ravyne',[1]
the sparrowhawk preys on the quail, the merlin on the lark,
the heron on eels, the swallow (not here the Procne who
with sorrowful lay wakens Pandarus, or the purifier of the
air from pestilence) murders the innocent honey-sipping
insects, the drake destroys its own kind, the magpie 'jangles'
(*garrulae repraesentatrix jactantiae*, says Neckam); whilst dead-
lier human vices now appear in feathered form: treachery
(the lapwing is still the symbol of this evil for Shakespeare's
Lucio), cowardice, lechery (the popinjay is 'ful of deli-
casye'), and disobedience to natural law (the cuckoo is
'evere unkinde'). Birds themselves, says Lydgate, echoing
popular belief, hold in despite 'Jayis, Pyis, Lapwyngis &
these Oulys'.[2] Chaucer in short, blinks none of the ugliness
and violence to be found under the leaves of life. He needed
no Tennyson to tell him that animal nature was red in
tooth and claw; this painter of ideal gardens, ideal maidens,
ideal knights, is as 'realistic' now as when he wrote the
Reeve's Tale or described how Arcite lay, 'as blak as any
cole or crowe, His brest tobrosten with his sadel-bowe'.

Interlaced as are these realistic traits with other human
attributes, they make us aware that this *parlement* is in some
sort at least an image of the everyday world, and prepare us
for the contentions and rivalries that are soon to come.
Whether or not Chaucer had read such works as Robert

---

[1] ll. 335-6. Cf. *The Thrissil and the Rois*, where Dame Nature bids the eagle
'lat no fowll of ravyne . . . devoir birdys bot his awin pray' (ll. 125-6).

[2] *Temple of Glas*, st. 25c.

Holcot's *Super Libros Sapientiae*, in which the nobility are allegorized as fowls of rapine, he certainly could not assume that his readers had done so;[1] and in any case he must, like any poet worth the name, suggest his own correspondences, such as might be sufficiently discernible without the aid of footnotes. When the cock appears as 'orloge of thorpes lyte', the ever-mating sparrow (*libidinosa*, says Neckam) as 'Venus son', and the turtle-dove as 'wedded'; the distinctions between the world of bird and man begin to blur; so that by the time we reach the formel eagle she can be described, without our feeling any incongruity, in almost completely human terms as

> The most benygne and the goodlieste;
> In hir was every virtue at his reste,
> So ferforthe, that Nature hir selfe had blisse
> To loke on hir, and ofte hir beke to kisse—[2]

this last couplet recalling the scene in the *Planctus* where Nature kisses the lovely maiden Castitas '. . . osculi praeludio complexus connubio, mentalem foris depinxit affectum'.[3] Later (l. 448) Nature addresses her affectionately as 'daughter'—a term that did not necessarily indicate filial relation. She can blush out of modesty and be compared, like any courtly heroine, to 'the fresshe rede rose newe'. The use

---

[1] For this suggestion *v.* E. Rickert, *Modern Philology*, xviii (1920). 1 ff. Miss Rickert also suggested that the waterfowl represent the merchants—'because their wealth was founded on the import and export trade'. Skeat notes Alain's 'tanquam vulgaris astrologus, suae vocis horologio loquebatur discrimina', comparing *Troilus and Criseyde*, iii. 1415. Conversely, in the Prologue the Host becomes 'oure aller cok' (C.T.A. 822). A variant occurs in the Nun's Priest's Tale, C.T.B. 4043-4. Cf. Henryson's *Cok and the Fox*, l. 498.

[2] ll. 375-8.

[3] *De Planctu Naturae*, ed. cit., p. 505. Castitas is described as a maiden 'In cujus pulchritudine tanti artificii resultabat solemnitas, ut in nullo claudicaret Naturae digitus polientis . . . rosam cum lilio disputantem in facie . . .' (ibid.); cf. ll. 442 ff., and C.T.A. 1038.

of the bird-parable relieves Chaucer of any obligation to describe with the usual rhetorical fullness all the details of feminine beauty, whilst allowing him to emphasize the maidenly virtues. For this blending of the human and the animal his descriptions of other heroines should have pre-pared us. The Criseyde on whom he lavishes his greatest art is 'as fresshe as faucon comen out of mewe';[1] the lively Alison of the Miller's Tale is 'As any wesel [that favourite medieval pet] . . . gent and smal'; whilst in the Squire's Tale the two worlds inter-penetrate so completely that a falcon can speak of a tercel ('that semed welle of alle gentilesse') falling on his knees, of Paris and Jason being unworthy 'unbokelen his galoche', and of the newfangle-ness of birds as a human narrator would:

> Men loven of propre kinde newfanglenesse
> *As briddes doon* that men in cages fede . . .[2]

In the *Parlement* the nearest we come to this kind of identity is the duck's oath, the second tercelet's 'hang me by the neck'; and these touches making for the poem's liveliness and humorous charm would hardly appear incongruous to a medieval audience, familiar as it was with fables and pic-tures in which beasts treated each other according to human forms and ceremonies, and fond as it was of talking crows, jays, or magpies like that in the *Seven Sages* which 'couthe telle tales alle apertlich, in Freinch langage'.[3] How closely

---

[1] *Troilus and Criseyde*, iii. 1784. The simile is not in Boccaccio. Falcons were shut up in mews during the summer so that they might moult their feathers and recover their youthful beauty.

[2] C.T.F. 610–11.

[3] Cf. e.g., the Rat Fable in *Piers Plowman*, B, Prologue, and in Bishop Brinton's contemporary sermon, printed in Camden Society, 3rd ser., lxxxv–vi. 316. The sculptures and illustrations showing beasts revenging themselves on other beasts (e.g. the cat carried to burial carved on a capital at Tarragona; the fox hanged by geese in MS. Royal 10 E. iv (mid-fourteenth century; repr. M.

the medieval mind paralleled the behaviour of birds and men (a proclivity that helps to explain the great medieval popularity of the *Metamorphoses*) we can also infer from a phrase that Andreas Capellanus gives to a lover addressing his mistress: 'You should not call me by the dishonourable name of kite but by the honourable one of tercel.'[1]

So it was natural enough for Chaucer—whether or not he knew of such St. Valentine's Day poems as Graunson's—to put a lovedebate into the mouths of birds, and in especial of birds like falcons and eagles whose traditional or actual associations with courtly folk or occupations made them proper types of courtly lovers. The formel, like an ideal heroine of romance, is a paragon of beauty and of gentilesse—though the emphasis on her virtues and benignity puts her above an Emily or a Dorigen; and the suitors contesting for her will behave like courtly suitors, using the language of an Arcite or a Palamon. Some of the other birds remind us of different aspects of human passion as portrayed in or around Venus' Temple. Thus the swan recalls to us the 'Jalousye' depicted there as 'the bitter goddesse'; the sparrow, Venus' own son, is here as elsewhere the symbol of her sensuality, the peacock 'with his aungels

---

Rickert, *Painting in Medieval England* (1954), pl. 132*a*; cf. misericords at Malvern and Sherborne); Neckam's story of a goshawk that a British king ordered to be hanged as guilty of treason for killing a royal eagle, though in selfdefence; the killing of cats that were thought to be witches' familiars—all illustrate the treatment of beasts as if they were responsible creatures.

[1] *De Arte Honeste Amandi*, second dialogue (which has the further interest that it includes a statement by the woman to the effect that Love leaves it to the choice of each woman to love or not—as Nature leaves it to the formel in the *Parlement*).

For examples of Shakespeare's use of bird correspondences v. *Troilus and Cressida*, III. ii. 54 (Pandarus commenting on the lovers: '. . . the falcon as the tercel, for all the ducks in the river'), and *Romeo and Juliet*, II. ii. 159 (Romeo is a 'tassel gentle').

fethres brighte', of the 'Aray' who stood outside the temple;[1]
whilst the meek-eyed doves, the same that flutter round
Venus' statue in the Knight's Tale and in the Fairfax
miniature, we have seen already sitting on her temple walls.
Finally, as if to emphasize these correspondences, Nature
herself soon speaks in just such terms of sympathy for
lovers as Chaucer uses in the *Troilus* when he prays for
love's servants

> That god hem graunte ay good perseveraunce
> And sende hem mighte hir ladies so to plese . . .

even as Nature prays:

> But which of yow that love most entryketh
> God sende him hir that sorest for him syketh.[2]

Yet no less striking than the resemblances between the
bird-world of the park and the passionate world of the
temple are the differences; the prime difference being that in
the one we meet only lovers, in the other birds (with few
exceptions) whose hearts are set on mating, 'signifying
matrimonie'. Though the formel's suitors illustrate some
aspects of courtoisie, they have no more thought of the
secrecy that conditions the action in, say, *Troilus and Criseyde*
(as in *Anna Karenina*), than they have of the adultery taken
for granted in Andreas's *De Arte Honeste Amandi* (as in *La
Cousine Bette*). The significance of this difference will appear shortly. Meanwhile we may note, first, that true and
happy wedlock is symbolized by the turtle-dove, whilst the
monogamous stork stands for the punishment of adultery;[3]
and next that for many of the birds—the crane, crow,

---

[1] Angels were traditionally represented with peacock feathers; striking early
examples survive in the Museum of Catalan Art, Barcelona.

[2] *Troilus and Criseyde*, I. 44–45; *Parlement*, ll. 403–4.

[3] A belief (says Speght) as old as Aristotle; in the *Gesta Romanorum* (chap. 82)
an unfaithful stork is killed by her mate and by other storks. Speght claims

cuckoo, raven, and thrush—though 'everych of hem did his besy cure' to choose a mate, love is by no means the sole or consuming interest. That it takes all sorts to make a world has now become, in Cowley's phrase, 'a very vulgar saying', the expression of an amused if not a condescending tolerance. To Chaucer it was one of the profounder, albeit piquant, implications of the philosophy of plenitude. And if he is making any specific point in the *Parlement* it is surely this: that for all the preoccupations of the romancers and poets, and for all the values that inhere in love, the world of lovers is not the whole world; love is but a 'function' of Nature. Human society, here symbolized by the birds, has, like the natural world, its infinite gradations. It includes both 'lered' and 'lewed'—and African has told us (l. 46) that both have equal chances of heavenly happiness. Love may be said—and in a Christian view may well be said—to bind it together. To mate and to marry is to carry out the divine injunction to increase and multiply. But mating and marriage are not the sole purposes of society—that organic unity in which each person, each class has a proper function and a proper place. Within

that it 'forsaketh the chimney tops of houses if the man or wife of the place commit adultery'.

The description of the pheasant, 'scorner of the cok by night' (l. 357), may refer to the characteristic mentioned by Neckam (1. xlii): 'Masculi certo tempore pares eligunt et illo dumtaxat tempore quo commiscentur simul habitant masculi cum suis comparibus. Alio enim tempore per totum annum seorsum habitant gallinae seorsum galli.' 'O (adds Neckam), si usum phasianorum in hac parte imitarentur mulieres nostri temporis!' Skeat offers other explanations. As for the 'raven wys', Neckam (lxi) notes that 'prae sui multa calliditate . . . doctorem . . . in sancta ecclesia repraesentat'.

Anyone who has watched a thrush will be tempted to emend 'olde' (l. 364) to 'bolde', but it is reputedly long-lived. For the crow's 'voice of care' cf. Isidore, *Etym. Lib.* xii. vii. 44: 'quam aiunt augures hominum curas significationibus agere . . .'; and Dunbar's *The Fenyeit Freir of Tungland*, l. 115.

society should be order, but not isolation. The parliament itself both shows and symbolizes creatures dwelling to⁄gether, if not in the perfect unity which is the divine ideal, and Nature's, at least in some approach to concord. In listening to a love⁄debate at all this mixed assembly shows its recognition of love's binding force. Yet love is not the sole concern of it members.

For Nature the root of concord is order. 'By order shul ye chese', she now says, 'after your kynde' (ll. 400–1). How⁄ever uncertain we may be as to exactly where each bird would come in the scale of creatures, or what class or func⁄tion in fourteenth⁄century society it would represent, we are left in no doubt of the gap between the 'gentles'—falcon, formel, tercel—and the churls—ducks and geese who be⁄have like the 'goosish peple' of whom Criseyde bade Pandarus beware, and who, when moved by mob⁄feeling, so easily become, in Chaucer's eyes no less than Shake⁄speare's, the 'stormy peple, unsad and ever untrewe'.[1] It is by scorn of the intangibles of life—to which the virtues of gentilesse belong—that *l'homme moyen sensuel*, the Miller or the Reeve, is likely to betray himself, even whilst claim⁄ing to 'know a gentleman when he sees one', and so forth. But of these virtues Chaucer, even in his most sceptical or other⁄worldly moods, never loses sight. And so, though his Nature would have all birds choose their 'feres', he hints at a distinction between the noble birds, who take their 'for⁄mels', and the rest, who take their 'makes'; a distinction implied also by the last tercel when he speaks of each bird crying out to be gone 'forth with hys make *or* with hys lady dere' (l. 466).

It is to the gentles, the aristocracy, that our formel⁄heroine belongs. Nature holds her 'on hir honde'—that is,

[1] C.T.E. 995.

on her wrist, as the elegant lady holds her falcon in the Duc
de Berri's *Tres Riches Heures*; and she is 'of shap the
gentileste'. Just as Jean de Hanville has Natura commend
to the marriage bed a maiden who is not only beautiful but

> morum
> Ingenio felix, virtutis filia, natu
> Nobilis, et thalamos meditanti nubilis anno;
> Pulchra, pudica tamen,[1]

so Chaucer suggests that the formel has more than bodily
beauty. She is not an Alisoun (whose physical attractions
the Miller describes at length, but to the complete exclusion
of other qualities); she is more like Anelida, who was

> of swich fairnesse
> That Nature had a joy hir to bihelde;
> And for to speken of hir stedfastnesse
> She passed both Penelope and Lucresse:[2]

She is still more like Virginia; for Anelida is twenty, and
ripe for love, whilst the maid Virginia

> twelfe yeer was and tweye,
> in which that Nature hadde swich delyt.
> For right as she can paynt a lilie whyt
> And reed a rose, right with swich peynture
> She peynted hath this noble creature
> Er she were born, upon hir limes free.
>
> . . . .
>
> And if that excellent was hir beautee,
> A thousand fold more vertuous was she,
> In hir ne lakked no condicioun
> That is to preyse, as by discrecioun.[3]

[1] Ed. cit., l. 386.

[2] *Anelida and Arcite*, ll. 80–82. Alain, too, describes Nature as admiring her
own handiwork in Largitas, ed. cit., p. 507. Penelope and Lucretia are amongst
the examples of chastity cited by him, p. 505.

[3] C.T.C. 30–35, 39–42. Cf. Isidore, *Etym. Lib.* IX. vii. 29: *in eligenda uxore*

Both the formel and Virginia, in brief, are singled out by their 'vertu' and their 'gentilesse'. Both are 'shamfast in maydens shamfastnesse'. Both are 'floured in virginitee'. Neither has reached the stage of life at which to refuse to wed, like Gower's Rosiphelee, would be to refuse to ac⸗quiesce in Nature's purpose of continuating society. Vir⸗ginia avoids foolish dalliance and wine⸗bibbing:

> Bacus hadde of hir mouth right no maistrye;
> For wyn and youth doon Venus increce—[1]

so the family doctor puts it, using the language of the Temple, in which 'Venus' means amorous desire. Lastly, in both characterizations there is a hint that Nature's concern with these her creatures is but part of a larger concern for the harmony of all things beneath the moon: just as the Doctor conceives of her as saying

> My lord and I ben ful of oon accord;
> I made hir to the worship of my lord.
> So do I alle myne othere creatures—[2]

so in the *Parlement* all her creation is knit by even number of accord. Before Chaucer's Nature utters a syllable he dwells on this power of binding the elements 'by numbres proportionables', so that, as he words it in his version of Boethius, 'the colde thinges mowen accorde with the hote thinges and the drye thinges with the moiste; that the fyre, that is purest, fleye not over⸗hehe. . .'.[3] For Boethius this power is an attribute of God himself; but Claudian, in

quattuor res inpellunt hominem ad amorem: pulchritudo, genus, divitiae, mores. Melius tamen si in ea mores quam pulchritudo quaeritur. So a woman looks in a husband for *virtus, genus, pulchritudo, sapientia: ibid.* 28.

[1] *Ibid.* 58–59.

[2] *Ibid.* 25–27.

[3] *Lib.* iii, m. 9. Chaucer adapts the passage in that last speech of Theseus' with which so much else in the *Parlement* may be linked: cf. pp. 124–5.

his *De Raptu Proserpinae*, a poem that Chaucer cites more than once elsewhere, assigns it to Nature.[1]

Whatever the precise meaning of the phrase 'even noum-bre of accorde', we may be sure that its echoing of the melody 'of strenges in accord' at the beginning of the dream' (l. 197), and the recurrence of 'by evene accord' at the end (l. 668), are not fortuitous. The melody of the paradisal park was Nature's melody, itself an echo of the divine harmony that gives music to the spheres, and that Lorenzo invoked in the happy garden at Belmont. The 'easy voice' with which Nature speaks now and through-out the parliament likewise expresses this assured concord; and she is speaking completely in character when she states her 'sentence'—her *sententia*, her considered opinion—that mates must be chosen in proper sequence (ll. 392, 400). But as the vicar of God she insists, equally, on 'free will'—not, of course, in a strict theological sense (though it is a common factor in the love between man and woman and the love of both for God)—but because wedded harmony is impossible without such freedom: witness the Franklin's 'Love wol nat ben constreyned by maistrye . . .',[2] witness also that other poem of wedded love—*The Kingis Quair*; where again we have a park-setting, with birds making dulcet harmony and thanking love, 'that had their makis wonne'; as the poet listens

> sudaynly my hert become hir thrall,
> For ever, *of free wyll*;[3]

whilst Chaucer's manciple describes this free will (or some-thing very like it) as one of the qualities

---

[1] i. 248–53. The passage closely resembles that in Boethius. For Chaucer's knowledge of Claudian's poem cf. *Hous of Fame,* l. 449, C.T.E. 2232; and p. 54 n. 1 above.

[2] C.T.F. 764.

[3] St. 41.

which that Nature
Hath naturelly set in a creature.[1]

Only mutual affection can produce the perfect bliss that
was promised at the portal of the park. We are never ex-
plicitly told how this bliss compares with the eternal bliss
that African had promised as the reward of those who love
the common profit. But if Nature, vicegerent of God,
gives her blessing to the free unions that yield this happiness
they and it can hardly be in the poet's mind, sinful or suspect. He does not imply that it is the *Summum Bonum*—it
remained for Browning to assert that; he does imply that it
is a desirable good:

And whoso may at this time have his grace
In blisful time he com into this place![2]

That the royal tercel who first speaks pleads as a complete courtly lover engaged in a *débat d'amour* is obvious
enough; and the resemblance to the *locus classicus* for such
avowals (*Roman de la Rose*, ll. 2220 ff.) is striking. These
are the 'techeles termes of noble [luf] talking' such as the
Green Knight's household hopes to learn from Sir Gawain.
At once, and more than once, he disowns Nature's term
'fere', and insists that the formel is not his equal but his
'lady sovereigne'; he has yet not learnt the Franklin's paradox that his mate may be 'his lady, certes, and his wife
also'. He uses, and with evident sincerity, all the terms of
Frauendienst, and makes all its gestures. In terms and substance the speech resembles Troilus' letter to Criseyde, and
first oral confession of his love,[3] any differences in tone

[1] C.T.H. 161–2. [2] ll. 411–12.
[3] v. *Troilus and Criseyde*, ii. 1065 ff.; iii. 98 ff. Both suitors claim that they will
die for love—a claim rarely substantiated, even in the romances.

Gardiner Stillwell has already noticed the resemblance to Graunson's
'Balade de saint Valentin' (ed. cit., p. 226).

arising from the important underlying difference that the one is a public the other a private avowal; the one a plea, if implicitly, for a maiden's consent to marriage, the other a prayer to a wished-for mistress. Just as Troilus (who in Criseyde's dream becomes a noble eagle) 'as hir man wolde ay live and sterve',[1] so this tercel 'ever wol hir serve, Do what hir lyste, to do me lyve or sterve' (ll. 419–20). Like Arcite, he would gladly die, so it be in his lady's presence; Arcite, indeed, would wish his ghost to serve her even after his death; and just as it is hard to find even a hint of satire in the account of his dying moments, so it is hard to believe that Chaucer is here indulging in any sort of parody. Like Arcite, again, this tercel knows that he has no claim on his lady 'by right'; and the last word of his petition proper is 'routhe'—as Arcite's was 'Mercye, Emilye'. His argument that 'oghte she be myn thourgh hir mercy, For other bond can I noon on hir knette' (ll. 437–8) has been ridiculed: the ideal lover, according to Mr. Stillwell, 'never said that the lady ought to submit to being tied with his one bond, whatever it was'. But the bond is nothing more than a faithful lover's due claim on her 'mercy'; and in his behaviour, as in that of the other suitors, there are none of the more ambiguous or sinister concomitants of courtship as we have met them in or near the temple, and as they appear in *Troilus* or the Knight's Tale: there is nothing of Jealousy or Craft or Meed or Flattery; nothing of Arcite's anger or fatalism, nothing of Troilus' despair or fear. Instead of the feverishness of the temple there is restraint, fixity, humility—that paradoxical humility which, like the religious man's, 'aspires to that which is beyond its desert'. There is, for some men at least, a stage in love in which the very futility of the passion enhances it and exalts

[1] i. 427. The line (and the dream: ii. 925 ff.) is added by Chaucer.

the lover. Will Ladislaw, as presented in chapter 47 of *Middlemarch* (with the help, we note, of medieval-sounding allegorical debate) is such a one. The conventions that these suitors employ were verifiable from experience. Nor is the formel a lay figure, a 'cruel fair', taken out of stock. If she blushes, it is with the 'rosy hew' of Criseyde, to which Chaucer had given a new signification:[1] she is behaving— it is perhaps necessary to insist on this in the middle of the twentieth century—as a young girl of gentle birth and breeding would behave.

The tercel 'of lower kinde' (lower, evidently, in degree, cf. l. 453: representing a 'knight bachelor', perhaps, not a royal prince) speaks less formally, with all the vigour of a human rival, basing his claim first on length of service; it is apparently a claim not to be given heavy weight, since Nature does not in the event indicate any preference for this tercel. The arguments at this point offer a variation on those between Palamon and Arcite over their claims to Emily; but whereas Palamon is acutely jealous, and Troilus has to simulate jealousy, here the jangling and the jealousy of the temple are mentioned only to be spurned. 'Fals', 'unkinde', 'jangler', 'jalous'—the tercel uses these epithets almost as though he were carefully distinguishing himself from the lapwing, cuckoo, magpie, swan that have just been so described. And when this tercel swears to act 'hir honour for to save', 'honour' carries more than the sense of 'reputation', which is all that Criseyde sometimes seems to give it: even Boccaccio links it with chastity ('l'onestà

---

[1] The phrase in question (op. cit. ii. 1198), though answering verbally to Boccaccio's 'Ella divenne rossa immantinente', has quite a different implication in Chaucer: in *Il Filostrato* Criseida is blushing with a sense of immodesty; her subsequent letter shows her as fully aware of what she is doing; whilst Criseyde is only 'half-willing, half-reluctant to be led'.

salva, e la castità mia'), and Anelida certainly does when she says 'Myn honour save—meke, kind and fre' and con֊ fesses that she was her knight's 'as fer as it was right'.[1] There is something attractively honest and impulsive about this *cavaliere sirvente*, who swears by St. John, and speaks so bluntly. If he rebel against the code, he is prepared to take the particular punishment that fits a rebel's crime: 'do me hongen by the hals'.

The third suitor is no less pungent, even though—or because—he has the shortest length of service. He seems to feel some disadvantage in speaking last. His hint that Nature, in her eagerness to speed the mating, will not hear him out, is hardly justified; but it is a touch of verisimili֊ tude with its own parliamentary point: we think—and it matters little if we are anachronistic—of a private member trying to speak on the motion for the adjournment before some one notices that there isn't a quorum.

Each suitor shows something of the intensity of the Prince of Arragon or Morocco standing before Portia's caskets. But now, as often, Chaucer swerves away from the intense and the touching to the bustle of the actual and the practicalities of every day. In contrast to his follower Lydgate, who loses no opportunity of 'rehearsing' at length, 'the chere and the speking' of the lovers in the *Temple of Glas*, he never gives us more than is dramatically necessary. In contrast to his friend Gower he never 'holds' the note of pathos. As he breaks off the story of Ceyx and Alcyone ('hit were to longe for to telle'), and leaves the question of Arcite's metempsychosis to 'speken forth of Emilye'; so now he comes suddenly back to the parliament. Like all parliaments, it is impatient of long speeches; like most

---

[1] *Anelida and Arcite*, ll. 267, 224. For other examples of the phrase cf. Schick's note to the *Temple of Glas*, l. 342.

fourteenth-century parliaments, it is full of members eager
to get home—to be 'delivered', in the technical phrase that
Chaucer here aptly introduces.[1] This 'courtly love', the
noisy birds imply, isn't the only thing in the world; people
have more to do than listen to rival suitors all day—the
same period of time, we may note, that Chaucer has spent
pondering African's speeches to Scipio, before this dream.
But—now the unforced perceptive humour of the poem
grows dominant, the stir of everyday life grows louder—it is
those who think least of love and its demands who assume
that they are most competent to pass judgement on the case
and that they have a right to do so: to wit, the goose, the
cuckoo, and the duck, of all birds the most insistent in their
noises—'thorgh myn eres the noyse wente tho', says Chaucer,
reminding us for the last time of his silent presence in this
dream-scene. The humorous intent is clear when the selfish
and self-willed cuckoo, of whom the proverb ran that he
'can synge noon oþer songe but of hymself',[2] takes it upon
him, to speak for the common good, and out of supposed
love for his fellows—the pretence of 'charite' (l. 508) gains
in irony if we remember that in the *Roman* Raison sharply
contrasts 'charité' with selfish passion—whereas it is the
modest turtledove, here reluctant to pronounce of her own
accord on such a delicate point, who is later chosen by the
seedfowl to speak for them all.

Throughout the next hundred lines we keep the sense of
noisy jargoning, the ceaseless going on of life, the chattering
and murmuration that birds do make towards evening
('dounwarde drow the sonne wonder faste'), when rooks

---

[1] Cf., e.g., the *Anonimalle Chronicle* (ed. V. H. Galbraith, 1927), p. 83: 'Ils
vodroient delivrer le dit parlement a pluis tost qils purrount.'

[2] Cited by Phyllis Hodgson, *Review of English Studies*, xxiv (1948), p. 8, from
Ignorancia Sacerdotum, MS. Bodl. Eng. Th. c. 57, f. 47.

and starlings confabulate, and thrushes sing as if for ever. *Parliamentum*, we should now remember, can bear the sense, *inter alia*, of '*noisy* discourse'.[1] The sense of clamour could hardly be conveyed more briskly than by the sharp, clack‑ing gutturals of

> The goos, the cokkow, and the doke also
> So cryede 'kek kek, kokkow, quek quek', hye.[2]

They had given voice before in medieval verse, but never *en masse*. Not so does Alain's Nature summon *her* council to order—'concepta severis Vultibus exponens, dextraque silencia dictans'.[3] Chaucer's Nature is to Alain's as is the eagle in the *Hous of Fame* to that in the *Purgatorio*. His pur‑pose is not to parody, but to restate some of Alain's doctrine as of Dante's, in 'facound voys'. When Nature silences the 'lewednesse' of those who are chattering of matters outside their competence[4] she becomes for a moment, though with‑out perceptible diminution of dignity, almost a henwife, with her 'hold your tongues there!' Yet her homely phrase only proves her affinity with another of Chaucer's goddesses —the Juno who in the *Book of the Duchesse* addresses her messenger to Morpheus as if he were a very schoolboy: 'Go bet . . . now understond wel, and tak keep . . . Go now faste, and hye the blyve.' This touch of the colloquial amidst the formal phrases of debate and such 'sentence' as

---

[1] Cf. 'There is to be no clamour, *parliamenta*, or vain conversation' (*Oculus Sacerdotis*; *v.* Pantin, op. cit., p. 199).

[2] ll. 498–9. The cuckoo's cry is found earlier in 'Sumer is icumen in', the goose's in the tale of the False Fox who
> Toke a goos fast by the nek
> And made her to sey wheccumquek
(*Secular Lyrics of the XIVth and XVth Centuries*, ed. R. H. Robbins, 1952, p. 45).

[3] *Anticlaudianus*, i. 211–12.

[4] l. 519. 'murmour' in this line perhaps has a scholastic undertone: S. Thomas calls his opponents *murmurantes*.

the dove's 'Office uncommitted ofte anoyeth' perhaps has
precedent (outside of Aristophanes' *Birds*) only in the
twelfth-century *altercacio* between the owl and the nightingale. The crowded, noisy scene reminds us more of the
former than of the latter; and it is doubtful whether English
comedy has ever come closer to the Aristophanic vein (the
nightingale episode in the Greek reminds us that the vein
is not incompatible with lyricism); but the colloquialisms
('Come of!' . . . 'not worth a flye' . . . 'by my hat' . . . 'mo
sterres than a paire') are used with the freshness and economy
that characterize Chaucer's art at its highest.

Nature decrees that each 'folke'—each estate of the bird-
realm—shall choose a spokesman to give its 'verdit' (the
word means hardly more than 'opinion')—though until
the goose had announced that 'I wol say my verdit fayre
and swythe For waterfoul' (ll. 503-4) there had been no
hint that the birds were to be allowed any say in the matter.
Indeed the modest dove ('oon the unworthieste . . . and litel
of connying' is how she describes herself) had noted the
impropriety of interfering in things 'of which he neyther
rede can ne synge'. But Nature is doing no more than
humour the birds. Like a fourteenth-century king-in-par-
liament—who could always conclude debate with a nega-
tive 'le roi s'avisera'—she retains the power to deal with the
matter herself. And terms like 'judge', 'verdict', 'doom',
'sentence', 'termine', 'pleading'[1] should not lead us to
think that Chaucer has forgotten the parliamentary setting:
they should rather remind us that parliament was still, in

---

[1] On some of these *v*. Willi Pieper, op. cit. 'Termine' is first recorded in
English in a legal context: cf. A-Fr. 'oyer et terminer', q.v. in *O.E.D.* 'Pleyn
eleccioun' (l. 528) is not found elsewhere; but it is obviously influenced by 'in
pleno parliamento', &c., where 'plenum' implies 'regular, formal' (cf. Miss
Helen Cam, *Trans. Royal Hist. Soc.* 1944, p. 13).

many of its functions, a court of law. There is no evidence that the various classes in a fourteenth-century parliament had separate spokesmen, or proctors, but possibly they did, on certain occasions. In any case, Chaucer is aiming at *vraisemblance* rather than complete exactitude.

The nobility speak first, through their spokesman, the falcon-tercelet, chosen, in courtly French phrase, 'by pleyn eleccioun'; his noble breeding shows not least in his polite-ness when interrupted ('yf that I dorste it say, ye doon me wrong')—in contrast to the goose's strident blustering. The formal presentation of this tercelet resembles, we have seen, the presentation of a Speaker in parliament; but it is equally important to note that Nature listens to him 'with glad entente'; for a noble so chosen has some right and reason to advise the young of his own class or kin—and the tercelet does no more than advise—what 'were sittingest for hir, *if that hir leste*' (l. 350). At first he seems to have in mind just such a solution as the nobility would approve: a tournament in which the rivals contend in single combat. The three rival knights in Jacques de Baisieux's *Trois Chevaliers* are likewise tested in tourney;[1] and the rivals' eagerness for this solution is as much a sign of their nobility as of their sincerity. Chaucer's Knight would have under-stood and approved: 'every lusty knight', says he,

> That loveth paramours and hath his might,
> Were it in Engelond or elleswhere,

would like to engage in such a tournament:

> To fighte for a lady, bencitee,
> It were a lusty sighte for to see![2]

But one of the suitors, the royal bird, is so obviously pre-eminent in rank, family, and prowess (on this last he had

---

[1] *Trouvères Belges*, ed. A. Scheler (1876), p. 162.   [2] C.T.A. 2112 ff.

been properly and modestly silent) that the falcon concludes by submitting that no such trial of arms is necessary. The falcon's speech is the model of 'politesse' ('*Sires*, ne taketh noght agref, I preye'), not least in the final refusal to identify the suitor he prefers:

> Of these thre she wot hirself, I trowe,
> Which that he be, for it is light to knowe.[1]

Nor does he forget Nature's condition: 'if that hir leste' (if she be so inclined): a condition, if we may believe the Knight's Tale, and other romances, not always considered in such debates, and certainly not always regarded in feudal society. The waterfowl, meanwhile, waddle off to a caucus—'her hedes leyde togeder', applies neatly to a crowded duck-pond, just as 'large golee' suggests their noisy quack-ing; these are the birds 'lowest in the dale', the lowest class of society, that loves noise and crowds. The gawky, self-important goose, with her long neck and insistent screech, dominates the meeting and wins a unanimous vote:

> Herkeneth which a reson I shal bringe;
> My wit is sharp, I love no taryinge.[2]

But it is in this very act of praising her own cleverness that she shows her folly, whilst she quite forgets that 'the ques-tion before the House' is not what advice to give to the rivals, but what is the best choice for the formel. As it is, the goose's counsel is worthy of Dinadan, that 'madde talker' who in the Arthurian romances takes just such a rough-and-ready attitude to the questions of love.[3] Any suitor *par amours* would be as shocked by the goose's 'But

---

[1] ll. 552–3.   [2] ll. 564–5.

[3] Or cf. Beaumains' words to the Red Knight: 'thou to love that lovyth nat the is but grete foly' (Malory, ed. Vinaver, p. 515).

she wol love hym, lat hym love another' as Troilus is by the desperate Pandarus' consolation that there are as good fish in the sea as ever came out of it. The sparrowhawk speaks for all folk of gentle birth or feeling when he ridi-cules the goose, who does not even realize that to love, or cease from loving 'lyth not in his wit ne in his wille';[1] it is part of the 'wonderful wirkinge' of love alluded to at the outset of the poem that, as Arcite puts it,

> A man mot nedes love, maugre his heed
> He may nat fleen it, thogh he sholde be deed.[2]

Of the next class—the seedfowl—the turtle-dove is the chosen representative; and she speaks in the frank un-equivocal terms of the worthy burgesses and knights of the shire, the only commoners that a fourteenth-century parlia-ment admitted. In marked contrast to the goose, she has to be pressed to give her opinion. In upholding the ideal of constancy she is simply being true to her own nature. It is the ideal that she traditionally represents, and for which she is canonized in *The Phoenix and the Turtle*; and it is an ideal that is not the nobility's monopoly: *Virtus nobilitat hominem.* This was true in the literal sense inasmuch as worthy citizens and yeomen of this class could rise to knighthood; and it expresses the well-established medieval belief—there is nothing revolutionary about the Wife of Bath's assertion of it—that 'he is gentil that doth gentil dedis'. But the turtle-dove, it has been suggested, asks more of a bereaved lover than *amour courtois* itself required—hers is the touching fidelity found often in the humblest classes—and her affirma-tion, simple and moving as it is, hardly contributes to

---

[1] l. 573; it presumably refers back to ll. 567 ff., *him* and *his* referring to each of the rivals.

[2] C.T.A. 1169–70.

the debate. She is, in fact, sidetracked by the goose's garrulous irrelevances, and as each suitor has already averred or implied constancy we are not very far forward; whilst the duck's retort nearly reduces the discussion to a slanging match, a flyting. To him, whose life, as the tercelet soon reminds us, is bounded by the midden, such unrewarded fidelity is ridiculous; it 'gets you nowhere', and his 'Ther ben mo sterres, god wot, than a payre' not only echoes the goose's sentiments: as a proverb it identifies the duck with the plain blunt men who in Chaucer, and the world at large, rely on proverbial philosophy. 'Daunceth he murye that is mirtheles?' he asks; and the tercelet can only reply: 'What love is thou canot nat see ne gesse.' But the duck's impatient interruption does serve to make plain the demarca- tion between the birds. Those that are gentle by birth or manners—falcon, sparrowhawk, turtle-dove—range them- selves together; and the cuckoo, without even going through the formalities of an election as the representative of his class, reveals at once his vulgar pushfulness. His very diet has made him suspect from the outset—'worme, or thing of which I telle no tale'; especially if we recall that to live in the forest and eat worms is described in the Man- ciple's Tale as the lowest kind of wretchedness. And now he speaks out of unabashed self-interest.

> So I (quod he) may have my make in pees,
> I recche nat how longe that ye strive.[1]

This from the bird that had claimed to speak 'for comune spede'. It was mere pretence—pretence being the essence of the bird that (so John Clare noted) assumes the character of the lordly hawk. We see now that his only notion of love

---

[1] ll. 605–6.

or 'charite' (*v.* l. 508) or peace is to live for himself, undis-
turbed. The duck may display all the limitations of the
plain man who knows what he likes and has no time for
sentiment; but after this naked avowal of the cuckoo's he
appears a positively amiable soul. And the merlin is prompt
to seize on the discrepancy between the cuckoo's professed
zeal for the public weal and his actual disregard for Nature's
order. According to Neckam the cuckoo was the very
exemplar of acquisitiveness—*proclamans et dicens 'Affer, affer'*
—a point that will doubtless appeal to those who see in the
bird the type of fourteenth-century business-men 'characterized by boundless avarice'. Not without reason did the
Old Testament enjoin: 'The cuckoo have in abomination'.
It is 'ever unkinde'—it breaks Nature's laws, even (l. 612)
slaying that smallest, timidest of birds, the dunnock, or
hedge-sparrow. This is the bird that *ought* to live unmated:
'Lyve *thou* soleyn, wormes corrupcioun!' (l. 614). The
taunt is triple-barbed. First, the cuckoo is addressed as
corruption personified, an agent of evil—just as the Parson
describes a wicked priest as the *corrupcioun* of his village.
Secondly, it feeds on the worm, which itself feeds on
decaying matter; worm and bird have their function in
Nature, but the associations evoked here are of foulness and
death. Lastly it is 'soleyn', isolated and unsocial:

> The cuckoo shouts all day at nothing,
> In leafy dells alone.

Thus at the extreme opposite to the 'gentileste' formel stands
this 'ungentle gull'; the phrase is Shakespeare's and applied
to the cuckoo-like usurping Bolingbroke; but the sense of
'ungentle' is Chaucerian, and behind it is a folk-tradition
as old as the Anglo-Saxon Riddles. There is a touch of
rhetoric in the merlin's speech, and a touch of a 'lered'

man's scorn in its close: 'Go, *lewed* be thou, whyl the world may dure!'[1]

As Nature enjoined silence when first she heard the 'murmour of the lewednesse behinde', so now she again calls the assembly to order, with a reminder that 'I com- maunde here'. As Chaucer has been busy all day over Macrobius, with no apparent result, so the 'business' of these debating birds had brought them 'never the nere' (l. 619) by sundown. It is now obvious that such a mixed and motley gathering is incapable of agreement or of ever reaching a sound judgement on what, after all, is a delicate and personal affair. Nor was it part of the *débat* convention —the convention to which in this poem Chaucer gives a parliamentary setting—that a verdict must be delivered: none is given, for example, in the *Owl and the Nightingale*. Yet through the chirping and the chiding we have caught an intimation of the attitude that Nature would have her creatures take. What the tercel has proposed is essentially what Nature will advise. And that this bird was shouted down makes no difference to the outcome. For this is no twentieth-century parliament working by whips and majority rule. The Plantagenet monarch, summoning par- liament as and when he willed, might listen himself to the debates of his subjects, or consider their petitions. But he had the final decision and the power of dismissing the assembly he had summoned of his own accord. Much more then, does Nature, presiding over her own creation.

Her final counsel is not, as might appear at first, merely a repetition, in terms appropriate to the formel's case, of the

---

[1] l. 616. Cf. *The Cuckoo and the Nightingale*, ll. 50, &c. In *La Messe des Oisiaus* the cuckoo tries to annoy the lover-birds by his cry 'tout cuku':
'Il en fist maintenant cuer irasca/De ce k'il lor fist tel laidure' (ll. 310-11).
But Venus bids them not to destroy him—he cannot help his evil nature.

general conditions that she had laid down at the beginning
of the assembly. After indicating that as 'argumentes' the
speeches of the rivals are indecisive—and confirming, in
passing, the falcon-tercelet's view that 'hit may not here discussed be Who loveth hir best'—Nature now declares, not
that the formel must be willing to mate with the one who
chooses her (a condition adequate only until it appears that
she is the choice of more than one) but that the final choice
must rest with her: she

> Shal have right him on whom hir herte is sette
> And he hir that his herte hath on hir knette—[1]

as if to imply that the bird she chooses will be the one that
is 'meant' for her. Nature, who knits all things equally,
knows that this is the royal tercel, and so counsels her to
accept him. For though there be little to choose between the
pleas of the rivals, and though each may have served as
faithfully as in him lay, there is, objectively—and this only
Nature, who 'may nat lye' (l. 629), can know—something
to choose between the rivals themselves as regards worth
and gentilesse. It is the tercelet's emphasis on these attributes (ll. 550 ff.) that Nature now endorses. The royal
bird has passed through all the tests of knighthood, and
emerged as the proven chevalier, *sans peur et sans reproche*.
Nature, we are to infer, so frames her creatures—including
man and woman—that like will draw to like. But according to medieval allegory and medieval belief she does not
act, or prompt to action, contrary to Reason. So in the
Anticlaudianus Racio had the last word at her council.
And so now she is careful to say

> If I(t) were *Resoun*, certes, then wolde I
> Counseyle you the royal tercel take.[2]

---

[1] ll. 627-8.
[2] ll. 632-3. Two manuscripts (Gg and Pp) read 'If I', the rest 'If it'.

Reason would certainly counsel this, if only because it was by such harmonious alliances that peace between nations, in the Middle Ages, was brought about and preserved. Yet Nature, being God's vicegerent, does not compel creatures to mate as she would wish, even though she fore sees which union will be the most harmonious (and the most fruitful).

The noble virgin whom Nature counsels but does not constrain is no Rosiphelee resisting the law of Kind and the dictates of the heart.[1] She asks for delay simply that she may be sure of her choice:

> I axe respit for to avise me
> And after that to have my choys al fre.[2]

(her 'ye gete no more, although ye do me deye', we may imagine to be addressed to the *congregacio* rather than to the Almighty Queen). Like Emily, before the tournament, she is still a servant of Diana, the 'chaste goddesse of the wodes grene'—of the very trees in which the birds were sitting— and would not *yet* transfer her devotion to 'Venus ne Cupyde':[3] she will neither seek a lover herself nor submit to the embraces of a man. This is not the dallying of the kind of girl who

> neither knows how t'enjoy
> Nor yet let her lover go.

Still less is it the medieval equivalent of 'This is so sudden!'

---

[1] Cf. *Confessio Amantis*, iv. 1245 ff.

[2] 'Free choice' is, of course, a rendering of *liberum arbitrium*; but it would be hazardous to read theological implications into the words. Chaucer's use of 'eleccioun' is dutifully copied by Lydgate in describing those 'maried in her tendir age . . . wiþoute fredom of eleccioun, Wher love haþ seld dominacioun' (*Temple of Glas*, ll. 210–12).

[3] l. 652. For women's service to Venus cf. *Romaunt of the Rose*, ll. 3705–10, where the reference to such service is added by Chaucer.

It is instinctive femininity; here at the end of the vision modesty becomes dignity—as if in conscious contrast to the alluring half-naked Venus at the beginning. The point is perhaps less quickly taken in the twentieth century than in the fourteenth, when the interest of the speech would lie, not so much in the request for a respite as in the claim to a 'choys al fre': the realities of feudal life—or for that matter, of aristocratic life in any century before the present, allowed little such freedom; Michel St. Pierre does not even now allow it to his post-war *Aristocrates*. Yet Chaucer is here championing it, or at least admitting the possibility of it, even when the maiden is of such rank that her betrothal is the whole commonwealth's concern. In literature, admittedly, such a situation was not new: it was the very condition that provided the element of suspense in many a *demande d'amour*. But elsewhere—e.g. in Giovanni da Prato's *Il Paradiso degli Alberti*[1]—the choice is allowed by Venus, or Minerva. In Chaucer the significant fact is that it is allowed by a far higher divinity, Nature.

Nature's subsequent last words to the rivals:

> Beth of good herte, and serveth, alle three;
> A yeer is not so longe to endure,
> And eche of yow peyne hym, in his degree,
> For to do wel; for, god wot, quit is she
> Fro yow this yeere . . .[2]

may seem scarcely to sort with the 'sentence' that we have just extracted from her advice to the formel, since they appear to imply that the two birds of lower degree have something to serve for. But there is no real disparity. They introduce a hint of the possibility that happy mating *might*

---

[1] For this work *v.* W. E. Farnham, *P.M.L.A.*, xxxii (1917), p. 492.
[2] ll. 660–4.

take place between men and women of different rank.
Nature is less rigorous than the social codes, for her pur'
poses are vaster; she is also less rigorous than the romances:
in 'The Squyre of Low Degre' the king's daughter imposes
a probation period of seven long years. The main emphasis
here, however, is on the ennobling, the maturing, effect
of service by which the brashness, the callousness of youth'
ful love, is rubbed away; and by which alone the sincerity
of the rivals' claims can be tested. We move beyond the
world of knights and tourneys here: if tourneying were the
solution, the turtle'dove, and Nature, would have accepted
it much earlier. The service implied is primarily, of course,
that of 'courteous word and noble deed'; so Troilus, after
he has confessed his love

> gat him so in grace
> That eche hym loved that loked on his face.

> For he becam the frendlieste wight,
> The gentilest, and eek the moste free,
> The thriftiest, and oon the beste knighte
> That in his tyme was or might be.
> Dede were his japes and his cruelte,
> His heighe porte and his maner estrange,
> And eche of tho gan for a *vertu* change.[1]

Not only does he grow in humility and other 'graces'; he
begins to show sympathy and consideration for others. The
psychological truth of this *A Shropshire Lad* confirms:

> Oh, when I was in love with you
> Then I was true and brave,
> And miles around the wonder grew
> How well I did behave . . .

But Chaucer emphasizes its effect on the lover's attitude to

[1] *Troilus and Criseyde*, i. 1077–85.

other people: *amor* may approach the specifically religious virtue of *charitas*[1]—just as 'Do wel' (to contemporaries of Langland, at least) has religious as well as 'courtois' connotations; and if the rivals are to impress the formel in whom 'was *everi* vertu at his reste' they must display every virtue.

Striking is the resemblance in place and function between Nature's peroration and that of Theseus before *his* 'parlement'. Theseus, who, 'like a god in trone', more than once in that tale acts, like Nature, as a mouthpiece or conscious agent of divine purpose, recognizes, like her, 'the virtue of necessity': a phrase which he himself uses and which, being as yet unvulgarized, would convey far more of its original philosophical content than it does today. His view that it is wisdom to 'take it weel that we may nat eschue' answers to Nature's:

> Now syn it may non other wyse betyde,
> Quod tho Nature, heere is no more to sey.[2]

Like Nature, Theseus (who himself begins by discoursing of Nature and 'speces of thinges and progressiouns'), delights in 'excellence' and 'worthy fame'. And like Nature he is concerned to knit together mates fitted for each other: Emily's role resembles that of the reluctant formel, Palamon, who has served her 'with wille and herte and mighte' is like a faithful tercel—'a kinges brother sone, pardee'. Emily, Theseus urges, should take him 'for housbonde and for lord': marriage with the beloved being here not only compatible with the strictest adherence to the courtly code, but the very reward of practising it. And Theseus' final plea for Palamon—

---

[1] Troilus invokes 'Charite' as well as Love: iii. 1254.
[2] ll. 654–5; cf. C.T.A. 3043.

Syn he hath served yow so many a yeer
And hath for yow so greet adversitee,
It moste been considered, leeveth me,
For gentil mercy oghte to passen right—[1]

corresponds with, and illuminates, Nature's counsel to the
rivals: Theseus, like Nature, believes that such service is a
test of love. So Palamon weds Emily 'with blisse and
melodye', and they live thereafter 'in richesse and in heele'.
It is an enlargement of the scene that is repeated countless
times in the final act of our Fowls' Comedy, when Nature
gives to each bird its mate 'by even accord'. We began with
the harmony of the eternal spheres, in the paradisal park we
heard birds singing in harmony angelical. Now birds
break forth in song again. Not all of these birds are angelic,
our poem clearly shows; but it shows equally clearly, and
not least in its close, that all of them have a place and function in God's multifold scheme of harmonious creation.

[1] C.T.A. 3086–9.

Envoy

'Sirocchie mie uccelli, voi siete molto tenute a Dio vostro Creatore,
e sempre ed in ogni luogo il dovere laudare, imperocchè v'ha dato
libertà di volare in ogni luogo, anche v'ha dato il vestimento
duplicato et triplicato, appresso, perchè riserbò il seme di voi
in nell' arca di Noè, acciocchè la spezie vostra non venisse meno;
ancora gli siete tenute per lo elemento dell' aria che egli ha
diputato a voi; . . . e però guardatevi, sirocchie mie, del peccato
della ingratitudine, e sempre vi studiate di lodare Iddio.' Dicendo
loro san Francesco queste parole, tutti quanti quelli uccelli com-
inciarono ad aprire i becchi, ed istendere colli, e aprire l'ali, e
reverentemente inchinare i capi infino a terra. . . .

I Fioretti di S. Francesco, c. xvi

Haile Bishop Valentine, whose day this is,
    All the Aire is thy Diocis,
    And all the chirping Choristers
And other birds are thy Parishioners,
    Thou marryest every yeare
The Lirique Larke, and the grave whispering Dove,
The Sparrow that neglects his life for love,
The household Bird, with the red stomacher,
    Thou mak'st the black bird speed as soone,
As doth the Goldfinch, or the Halcyon;
The husband cocke lookes out, and straight is sped,
And meets his wife, which brings her feather-bed.

DONNE, *An Epithalamion*

Well dost thou, Love, thy solemn Feast to hold
    In vestal February;

PATMORE, *The Unknown Eros*

SUDDENLY we have arrived at the secret of the joy that
pervaded the delectable wood. The delights of that place
were conveyed in terms of music and birdsong, and now the
birds express their joy in blithe chorus. As he beholds the

mates embracing with connubial tenderness, the poet again communicates his own pleasure by a change in the tempo of his verse:

> A! Lorde, the blisse and joye that they make!
> For eche of hem gan other in winges take
> And with hir nekkes eche gan other wynde,
> Thanking alway the noble goddesse of kynde.[1]

Gower's Ceyx and Alcyone, metamorphosed into sea birds, likewise embraced each other 'as they couthe'; but whereas in Gower this represents pathetic consolation, in Chaucer the embrace is the fulfilment of happiness. The time of singing of birds is come—it comes earlier, doubtless, 'in Fraunce,' where the tune to which they sing was made (l. 677), and where the cult of Saint Valentine arose. There are no nuptials to celebrate. Yet the tone and spirit of these closing stanzas are those of an epithalamium, with the measured 'solemnite' that belongs to the greater epi-thalamiums like Donne's and Spenser's, as well as to the lesser ones like Herrick's or Abercrombie's; formally, in fact, they correspond to the lines describing the marriage that closes the *Archithrenius*, one of the earliest antecedents we have found for the *Parlement*:

> Nec minus et mima nemorum circumsonat ales,
> Et modulos crispat nativi pectinis arte;
> Ruris alauda chelys, lyricen Philomena rubeto,
> Per vada cantor olor, citharaeda per aequora siren,
> Corvus 'Ave' dicens, homo linguae psittacus usu,
> Pica salutatrix, lasciva monedula fando,

---

[1] ll. 669–72.

Turdula prompta loqui, facundo graculus ore,
Et quaecunque stylum valet usurpasse loquendi.[1]

No cloud is over *this* sun, the delight is without alloy of
'drede'; the 'grete worthinesse' of love is subsumed in a
larger sense of praise and gratitude; and this honouring of
Nature is no unique experience but as constant and recurring as the 'wuldortorhtan weder' of spring. Graunson and
others insist on the newfangleness of birds. But Chaucer
now goes out of his way to attribute to them constancy in
love and devotion just as in the *Legend of Good Women* he
goes out of his way to have the 'tidif' ask forgiveness for its
inconstancy and 'unkindness'.[2] Here Art and Nature are
reconciled in a song whereby the birds enlist the one to do
honour to the other, and music and sweet poetry agree:

> . . . yere by yere was alwey hir usance
> To synge a roundel at hir departinge,
> To do Nature honour and pleasaunce.[3]

It is part of the complex balance and interplay of functions
ordained by Nature that this roundel should be sung by
those 'smale foules' (l. 684)—they will include James I's
'lytill swete' nightingale, and the ruddock, who sings even
before winter is over—that have earlier been mentioned as
present at the assembly, though as yet they have taken no
part in it. But each bird, like each colour, stone and flower,
has in the medieval view its special 'virtue', complement-
ing those of its fellows. If the peacock outshines in beauty

[1] Ed. cit., p. 390:
> 'With birds in mimic voice the wood resounds
> As tunefully they strike their trembling lyres
> —Shy nightingale, and lark, and syren swan.
> Ravens croak 'Hail', parrots find human speech,
> Magpies bid welcome, with the sportive dove,
> And eager thrush and jackdaw eloquent. . . .'

[2] Prol. F. 153 ff.　　　　[3] ll. 674-6.

he is 'loth for to here'; it is the littlel ark—'the lasse fowle'—
that, as Langland reminds us, 'is the loveliest of leden'.
Hawk and eagle, for all their majesty, cannot make music:
this is the office reserved for the little birds

> That slepen al the night with open ye
> —So priketh hem Nature in hir corages.

If Chaucer does not here enumerate 'the blackbirds and
thrushes, robins and finches, and such feathered inches as
titmouse and wren', it is perhaps partly because he wishes
to observe proportion and decorum, partly because he has
already arrayed them in his translation of the *Roman de la
Rose*.[1] The usual time for such bird choruses is, in poetry
at least—*vide* the Prologue to the *Legend of Good Women*, and
The Kingis Quair, which imitates it—the month of May; and
in fact our birds are proleptically hymning the summer sun:

> Now welcome, somer, with thy sonne softe,
> That hast this wintres weders overshake.[2]

This is the refrain of their reverdie—which Chaucer rightly
calls a roundel; and no song could close this poem in
praise of concord more fitly than a roundel: for it is the
most harmonious type of song, the most illustrative of concord in its pattern and in its music.

It is a song of assured love as well as of approaching
summer: love and its season being the theme of all Chaucer's
roundels, not excluding Palamon's—of which we are vouch-
safed only the refrain:

> May, with alle thy floures and thy grene,
> Welcum be thou, faire, fresshe May,
> In hope that I some grene gete may.[3]

---

[1] *Romaunt of the Rose*, ll. 655 ff.

[2] ll. 685–6. Cf. Douglas's *Eneydos*, Prol. xii. 252 ff., and Hoccleve's roundel,
'Somer, that rypest mannes sustenance' (*Poems*, ed. Mason, p. 62).

[3] C.T.A. 1510–2.

The chant has its place in the organization and movement of the poem. Everything else may have been dream,
but this is the accompaniment of dawn, the full dawn-
chorus that we hear in spring or summer, the sober certainty
of waking bliss. As Langland is startled out of one of his
Visions by loud jangling between Piers and a priest, Dunbar (in *The Thrissil and the Rois*) by gunfire, the dreamer-
within-the-dream in the *Book of the Duchesse* by 'smale
foules a gret hep', and the poet by a bell 'As it had smitten
houres twelve'; so now Chaucer is wakened by 'the shout-
yng whan hir song was do'. We remember now that he began by poring over old books to learn 'a certain thing', never
fully defined, but clearly pertaining to love, since the night-
dream that follows his day of study is dominated by themes
and images of love. That the dream was not as dispiriting
as the study, and that African's promise to requite him
'sumdel' was not false, appears, if from nothing else, from
the terms in which he addresses Cytherea as he begins the
account of it, and from the delight that vibrates through
the stanzas at the close. The exclamatory 'A! Lorde! the
blysse and joye that they make!' (l. 669) is in the same key of
ineffable wonder as the praise of divine might and noblesse
in the *Hous of Fame*. Wakened with this music in his ears
he can turn back to his books with a renewed and surer
hope that his search is worth the making. Something at
least he has learnt—thus we may safely gloss the final
stanza—some inkling of the place of love in the scheme of
things. With a modesty that is only superficially a literary
convention, and at bottom a token of Chaucer's essential
humility before the wonder and mystery of life, he refrains
from extracting any rule-of-thumb moral from his fable,
or from suggesting that he has discovered final truth about
love:

> I hope, ywis, to rede so some day
> That I shal mete something for to fare
> The bet, and thus to rede I nyl nat spare.[1]

It happens—and it is of a piece with Chaucer's frequent in-determinateness that we cannot tell whether it happens by design—that these lines may be construed as holding the promise of all his later works, each of them so many poetic statements of his own maturing doctrines of love, soon to be poured into other 'olde bokes' or 'olde stories', like the Knight's Tale, or *Troilus*.

The doctrines can be separated from the poetry no more easily than the bouquet from the wine. But if we consider together the *Parlement*, the *Troilus*, and the *Tales of Marriage*—a triptych (to change metaphors) that includes all his major completed works after the early *Book of the Duchesse*—there emerges a view of the place of love in human life which is balanced, harmonious, and satisfying, yet which does not ignore the paradoxes and dilemmas that are as old as human society. The constituent features of this view are all to be discovered, in retrospect at least, in the *Parlement*. They will reappear, in different colours and combinations—sometimes in explicit 'doctrine', sometimes bathed in a new poetic light—in such places as Theseus' peroration, or the Franklin's *moralitas*, with its praise of marriage and implicit denial of the older assumptions of courtoisie.

If one now hazards the task of defining these features it is to clarify one's own meaning rather than to dogmatize about Chaucer's. Tentatively, they may be ordered thus:

1. Love is part of the divine creation, binding the uni-verse together, manifesting itself in ways innumerable, but

---

[1] ll. 697-9.

markedly in the operations of Nature as she continuates the world and human society. Inevitable as the seasons, it 'upgroweth'—as Chaucer pauses at his most serious and sublime moment to acknowledge—'with our age'. It is the basis of all happy marriage in general and of Christian marriage pre-eminently. 'Thilke love is wel at ese', as Gower says, 'which set is upon mariage.'[1] So Chaucer's happiest poems begin or end in marriage. Conversely the worst charge against the young Marquis, in Chaucer's version of the Griselda story, is not that he spent his time hawking and hunting, but that 'eek he nolde—and that was worste of alle—wedde no wyf'.[2]

2. Love plays a dominant yet mysterious part in life, its early joy being constantly attended by grief, despair, disillusion, or sad satiety. *Sub specie aeternitatis*, life remains, even to those who perceive the 'naturalness' of love, and its place in the divine scheme, a prison or a pilgrimage, as much to Theseus ('this foule prisoun of lif') as to Egeus ('a thurghfare ful of wo') or to Scipio ('a maner deth'). To overvalue one's individual experience of love, to desire *supra modum*, to build a private world entirely upon this desire, is to court sorrow and disaster. Troilus' witness confirms Lancelot's, and Abélard's.

3. Yet the stern law of Necessity (sometimes it seems to be but an aspect of the law of Kind), governs this passion, as all else. Troilus, or the tercel, or Palamon, cannot prevent himself from falling in love, any more than the horse can refuse to draw with the team. Cupid shoots his arrows unawares.

---

[1] *Confessio Amantis*, iv. 1477. In the following lines Genius, as priest of Venus, commends marriage whilst a maiden can bear the 'charge' of children 'whiche the world forbere Ne mai, but if it scholde faile'; an interesting variant of Jean de Meun's doctrine. [2] C.T.E. 83–84.

4. Love is beautiful and has its own especial 'worthinesse'; but its beauty offers no security against decay; rather, the beauty gives a harsher accent to the decay; the plight of Tristram or of Dido is the more pitiable when portrayed on the very walls of the lovely Venus' Temple, and Criseyde's acceptance of Diomede is the uglier because of what we know of her love with Troilus. Fruitful in 'charite' as love sometimes is, it can also be sterile; ennobling some men, in others (see the Miller's Tale, or the Merchant's) it is hard to distinguish from a mere lust of the blood and a permission of the will.

5. Unsatisfied love may beget sorrow, anguish, and physical distress—'the lovers maladye of hereos'; and the secret love of courtoisie contains the seeds of its own destruction; yet courtoisie fosters many commendable qualities, the practice of which prepares Youth for adult life and marriage. Thus, the faithfulness and patience that it enjoins are consonant with the 'suffraunce' and 'reverence' enjoined by the Parson on a husband; and both are implicit in Nature's injunction:

> Beth of good herte, and serveth, alle three;
> A yeer is not so longe to endure.[1]

Such patience is simply a facet of that self-control which, far from hindering Nature's progenitive purpose makes for its fulfilment. But Nature allows no place to Messagery, or Meed, or any of the other sinister concomitants of Venus-worship. She is fecund yet not wanton, lavish yet not lascivious, 'free' yet 'orderly'. Nature, or natural law, as St. Thomas would put it, brings it about that the species is propagated; but it does not (*pace* Jean de Meun) insist that

---

[1] ll. 660-1.

everyone without exception should take part in the propagation.[1]

6. The power of love personified in Venus must be seen in the context of Nature, a far greater, older and more beneficent power, directly expressive of the divine will. So the answer to the question about love lies in learning and obeying Nature's laws: they can be seen operating in bird and beast, who in their mating still preserve some of the instinctive innocence of the lost Paradise. To ignore or wilfully break these laws is, as Dante says, 'to disdain Nature and her bounty'.[2] Her basic principles are Harmony and Measure. The harmony is preserved by the voluntary subservience of one creature to another, as she prescribes it, and by their mutual dependence. This is likewise the basis of social harmony, and of any happy union between man and woman: so at, least, Chaucer seems to suggest by allowing the Franklin to dwell on the marriage of Dorigen and Arveragus:

> Here may men seen an humble wys accord;
> Thus hath she tak hir servant and hir lord,
> Servant in love, and lord in mariage.
> Than was he both in lordshipe and servage.
> Servage? Nay, but in lordshipe above,
> Sith he hath both his lady and his love:
> His lady, certes, and his wif also,
> The which that lawe of love accordeth to.

'Love is a thing as any spirit fre . . . lerneth to suffre.'[3]

---

[1] S.T. 11a, 11ae, 152, 2.　　　　　　　[2] *Inf.* xi. 48.

[3] C.T.F. 791–8, 767, 777. There is some resemblance between the Franklin's doctrine of freedom and that of Amis in *RR*: if either wife or husband is domineering or jealous, says Amis, the marriage cannot be happy or lasting: 'Amour ne peut durer ne vivre S'il n'est en cueur franc e delivre' (ll. 9941–2). Gunn, op. cit., p. 349, &c., maintains that de Meun's emphasis is on love within marriage.

Once this doctrine of love and marriage, with its emphasis on free choice, has taken root in Chaucer's mind there is
no room in it (except in somewhat the same sense and
degree that Malory has room for a Dinadan) for such
sophisticated assumptions as that conventionalized by Andreas Capellanus, in which the husband plays the part of
Le Jaloux—a part possible, indeed, only in a society based
on *mariages de convenance* (and only in such a society can
Andreas's teaching have much appeal). Emily will love
Palamon so tenderly, and he will serve her 'so gentilly'

> That never was ther no worde hem bitwene
> Of jalousie, or any other teene.

Thus this doctrine incorporates that principle of service
which courtoisie had so much insisted on, but has no room
or need for the secrecy that was an essential article of the
courtly lover's creed as it motivates (for example) Boccaccio's Troilo. The tercel confesses his love for the formel in
public, unashamedly. And when marriage is seen as an
operation of Nature's principle of Harmony, the disparities
that often produce jealousy and adultery disappear. For
love, by Nature's rule, belongs to *Juventus*, the May of life,
'our first age', as the poet of *Sir Gawain* puts it, 'the first
stage of life' as Dante has it in the *Convivio*.[1] Thus Chaucer
—though not Boccaccio—makes Pandarus say of the young
and beautiful Criseyde, after claiming that everyone is
prone to 'loves hete celestial [Venus Urania,] or elles love
of kinde [Venus Pandemos]':

> It sit hir nought to be celestial
> *As yet*, though that her liste bothe and couthe.[2]

---

[1] *Conv.* IV. xxiii ff.
[2] *Troilus and Criseyde*, i. 979–84. O.E.D. records no other ME. examples of
'celestial' used of love.

For a hoary January to behave as if he were a young squire
is, in Dante's view no less than in Chaucer's, 'wretched
and vile'. Equally, for anyone to grow besotted with love,
as Merlin did, or the Maid of Astolat, is folly—so it is for
doting not for loving that the Friar reproves Romeo. For
twin to Nature's principle of harmony is that of Measure.
It was an Aristotelian doctrine that could not be accom‑
modated with equal ease in every mansion of Christian
thought, but in the great debate about the nature of human
love it provided an invaluable resource. To love 'out of
measure' is demonstrably a form of selfishness; and in
hidden ways that are not now, or not yet, traceable, this
scholastic doctrine, commonplace as it soon became (Man‑
deville can refer to it casually in his first chapter), penetrated
to the very heart of courtoisie; so that in the Prologue to the
Legend of Good Women, after the figures of Pitee, Daunger,
Mercy, and the rest have paraded, we suddenly come upon
it, and with a scholastic reference to boot—'Vertu is the
mene', as Etik saith'.[1] It is left to Gavin Douglas to make
the application deliberate. In his Fourth Prologue (after
invoking, in terms akin to Theseus', the Chain of love),
the bishop comes to rest in the doctrine that love is 'ane
kindly passioun', fatal equally if it be defective *or* inordin‑
ate:

> Than is thy luiff inordinat, say I,
> Quhen any creatur mair than God thow luffis;[2]

[1] Prol. G, 165–6. Cf. *La Pélerinage de la Vie Humaine*, Lydgate's translation,
ll. 11868–70. S. Thomas adopts the phrase in S.T. 1a, 11ae, 58. Jessie Crosland,
M.L.R. xxi (1926), pp. 380–4, discusses the adaptation of French 'mesure' by
Chaucer, for whom 'out of mesure' is practically synonymous with 'agayn
resoun'.

[2] Prol. iv. 128–9. Dr. D. S. Brewer reminds me that 'inordinate affection'
is the A.V. equivalent to the Vulgate *libidinem* (cf. p. 41 above) at Col. iii. 5.

whilst it is defective (our cuckoo comes to mind) if you 'luff thyn awyn and gif of utheris na cuir'. Women must not, then, love out of wedlock, gallants must not pursue 'para/ mours'; but

> Ground your amouris on charite al new;
> Found you on *resoun*.[1]

The deceit and 'fals dissimulance' of illicit love—'under the cloke of luffis observaunce'—he condemns, finally, as 'contrar to Kind'. There is much of homiletic tone and specifically Scots temper here; but not many bishops, Scots or English, medieval or modern, have preached such ser/ mons (or, it may be added, taken their texts from *Aeneid* iv); and in his appeal to 'Kind' as the criterion, Douglas is at one with Chaucer.

Such, then, are some of the suggestions and designs—they never harden into dogmas—that may be discerned in Chaucer's love/poetry. If we seem to attribute to him an excessive preoccupation with the nature and effects of love, be it remembered that for him as for his predecessors and contemporaries, French and Italian, love was pre/eminently the theme of poetry, to which was dedicated intellect as well as art. More than the sixteenth/century sonneteers, or the seventeenth/century metaphysicals, they believed that to define love, to distinguish its kinds, was their supreme office. Of their sense of ultimate failure in encompassing the mystery, unfinished poems like the *Hous of Fame*, Re/ tractions like Chaucer's or de Meun's, may be taken as oblique evidence. But in their search for a meeting/place

Cf. Barberino's definition of illicit love as 'una furore inordinato', quoted by Panofsky, op. cit., p. 17, n. 69; which evidently goes back to Isidore's comment on Cupid: 'Puer pingitur quia stultus est et inrationabilis amor' (*Etym. Lib.* VIII. xi. 80).

[1] Loc. cit. 205–6.

between ethics, passion, and traditional teaching, they found new paths for the human spirit. If some of them strayed far from orthodox doctrine, some of them enlarged the boundaries of Christian thought on love and marriage; and if their paths issue in no earthly paradise, they lead—or Chaucer's do—to that special kind of *Canterbury Tales* contentment wherein, having seen all varieties of human folly and self-deception, we come to an abiding sense of the worth and purpose of human love, even though we be no whit the nearer to defining or explaining it.

APPENDIX

Natura, Nature, and Kind

THE appearances of Nature as a personified figure in Latin literature have been carefully listed by E. C. Knowlton,[1] and illuminatingly discussed by C. S. Lewis.[2] For the present purpose we need only mention that already in Cicero (who discusses the use of the word by other philosophers in *De Natura Deorum*, II. xxxii) she is *opifex callida* (ibid. lvii), endowing man with reason (*De Finibus*, II. xiv); that Statius briefly but pregnantly describes her as *princeps et creatrix* (*Thebaid*, xi. 466), suggesting that there is some

---

[1] *J.E.G.P.*, xix (1920), pp. 224 ff. ('The Goddess Nature in Early Periods').

[2] *The Allegory of Love*, pp. 54, 55, 77. Cf. E. R. Curtius, *European Literature in the Latin Middle Ages*, pp. 100 ff., and *Medium Ævum*, xxv (1956), p. 134). The subject of *Natura* in medieval literature and thought demands a monograph; this Appendix can do no more than refer to works that may have a bearing on the *Parlement*.

It is worth noting that in Lucretius Venus has the major role that later poets were to give to Nature: she is 'alma' ('increasegiving'), and 'rerum naturam sola gubernans' (i. 2, 21). He never invokes 'Natura', though the actions of Nature are treated as though they were human (e.g. ii. 17 f.); at ii. 167 he discusses the view that the gods had ordained Natura and the arts of Venus, 'ne genus occidat humanum', but only to refute it. The hypothetical personification of *rerum natura* (iii. 931 ff.) does not concern us.

Ovid's 'Hanc deus et melior litem natura diremit' (*Met.* i. 21), where God and Nature seem to be identical, has a Stoic flavour; it refers to the conflict in Chaos of hot and cold, wet and dry, soft and hard, heavy and light, for which cf. *Parlement*, l. 380.

For Pliny's description of Nature as 'parens rerum omnium' (xxvii, *ad fin.*), &c., *v.* de Lage, op. cit. below, p. 74, n. 177. Cudworth was to develop Cicero's notion of Nature as 'the manuary opificer of the Divine architectonical art' in his *True Intellectual System of the Universe* (1678), c. iii.

thing about her different from the pagan gods (ibid. xii. 566); and that Claudian has her bestow mental and physical qualities on her creatures, and gives her an habitation; she sits—'vultu longaeva decoro', like Boethius' Philosophia—at the entrance to a cave of immense age: 'Est ignota procul, nostraeque impervia genti, Vix adeunda deis . . . .'[1] In the fourth century Chalcidius personified Nature (along with Fortune and Chance) in his Commentary on the *Timaeus*, that prime source of medieval Platonism; he subordinates the three powers to the Trinity: 'His subjectas fore rationabiles animas legi obsequentes, ministras vero potestates Naturam, Fortunam, Casum et daemones inspectatores speculatoresque meritorum.'[2]

The early Christian poets Lactantius and Prudentius treat Natura as a pagan deity; and the extensive use of the word as a theological term by St. Augustine bore no fruit in poetry. Nor, directly at least, did Johannes Scotus Eriugena's division of Nature into four species: 'natura quae creat et non creatur; natura quae et creatur et creat; natura quae creatur et non creat; natura quae nec creat nec creatur.'[3] Somewhat reminiscent of these categories, though evidently independent of them, is the distinction that Averroes—or rather, his translator—draws between 'natura naturans' and 'natura naturata'; Francis Bacon used the former phrase in describing 'form'; but 'naturing Nature' occurs rarely in English between Hawes and Hardy—and in Hardy probably via Spinoza.[4] St. Thomas, insisting

---

[1] *De Consulatu Stilichonis*, ii. 424 ff. At l. 442 she runs to meet the sun as he bends his head at her threshold.

[2] *Timaeus Platonis*, ed. Wrobel, c. 138.

[3] *De Div. Nat.* I, i: cf. III, i. For a discussion of these categories *v.* F. Copleston, *History of Philosophy*, ii. 123 ff.: they give 'creating Nature' a technical sense that it has hardly lost in *Winter's Tale*, IV. iii. 87.

[4] *v. Ethics*, I, Prop. xxix. For Bacon's use *v. Novum Organon*, II. i. Michael

on immediate creation, and eschewing metaphorical language, has little place for a personified Nature—though he can say: 'Natura in sua operatione Dei operationem imitatur.'[1] It is in a much earlier philosopher, Boethius, that we should perhaps look for the origins of this figure as she is to appear in Bernardus Silvestris and Alain of Lille. Such expressions as 'Natura respuit ut contraria quaeque iungantur' (*De Cons. Phil.* ii, Pr. vi. 11), 'Quantas rerum flectat habenas natura potens' (idem, iii, m. ii) and 'dat cuique natura quod convenit' (idem, iii, Pr. xi. 13) could easily be read as though Natura was a personal power, and not simply the natural order of things; as also could a sentence like this from Macrobius:

. . . semine semel intra formandi hominis monetam locato hoc promum artifex natura molitur, ut die septimo folliculum genuinum circumdet humori . . .[2]

—a passage that Alain doubtless read, perhaps noting the image of the mint and the coin which somewhat resembles his own.[3] John of Salisbury, in his *Metalogicon* (1159), speaks of Nature's workshop (*officina*, i. 17) and calls her *parens* (i. 1; iv. 17).

In Bernardus' *De Mundi Universitate*, that fascinating amalgam of 'the Chartrain tradition, Christian piety and

Scotus distinguishes 'natura naturans' as 'divina', 'natura naturata' as 'elementaris': *Liber Introductorius* (MS. Bodl. 266, f. 2r.). Dante speaks of 'deus naturans', *Mon.* ii, c. 6. Gower uses the verb 'naturatur' in *Vox Clamantis*, v. 205–6:

O natura viri, quae naturatur eodem,
Quod vitare nequit, nec licet illud agi!

Cf. *Conf. Am.* vii. 393: 'He which natureth every kinde . . .

[1] *S. Th.* i. 66, 1. 2. He uses the phrase 'natura naturans' idem, ii. 85. 6; but very guardedly in *De Nom.* 4. 21. In the chapter on marriage cited above (*Contra Gentiles*, iii. cxxii) we have '. . . *velut* a natura praeparatum'.

[2] *Somn. Scip.* i. vi. 63. Cf. *Saturnalia*, v. i. 18, and pp. 50, 121 above.

[3] *v.* p. 95 above. Cf. Surrey's 'Give place, ye lovers,' st. 2.

natural science, the Neo-platonic cosmology and the Aristotelian dialectic',[1] Natura, after complaining to Noys about the formlessness of matter, journeys through the heavens to seek the help of Urania and Physis in creating man. With Urania she passes through the regions of the planets (including Venus), reaching at length the abode of Physis, a veritable Eden. Here Noys reappears, and ordains the creation of man the microcosm, who 'Divus erit, terrenus erit, curabit utrumque' (ii. x. 19; cf. p. 47, n. 1, above), and who is given organs of generation which 'Naturam reparant perpetuantque genus'. Thus in one work we have (besides much else) the association of Natura and a paradisal pleasaunce, the mention of Venus, and the theme of the continuation of the race. We have also—what is much more puzzling—a distinction between Physis and Natura: Natura, a goddess, being the higher power ('a personification of the general order of things, in the largest sense', suggests Mr. Lewis); Physis, who dwells on earth, being organic nature, *élan vital*; as a figure associated with the creation of life she has a long ancestry in Platonic commentators.[2] Fine as the distinction may sometimes be, it can be justified; and one feels the need of it in attempting to analyse the sense in which 'nature' is used in Middle English: Bernardus' Natura corresponding to the *O.E.D.*'s definition, s.v., iv. 11, his Physis to ii. 6, iii. 10; ME. 'kynde' seems rarely to be used in the sense of 'physis', though it is often practically interchangeable with 'nature' as defined at iv. 11 (cf. *O.E.D.*, s.v. *kind*).[3]

---

[1] Bolgar, op. cit., p. 176. Over twenty-five MSS. of the work are known. For a lucid account of the book as a whole *v. The Allegory of Love*, pp. 90–97; cf. also F. J. E. Raby, *History of Secular Latin Poetry*, ii. 8 ff.

[2] *v.* E. Gilson, *La Philosophie au Moyen Age*, pp. 117 f.; cf. also Curtius, loc. cit., n. 6.

[3] 'Law of kind', or 'kindly law' were the earliest English equivalents to

The *Anticlaudianus* of Alain of Lille follows the pattern traced by Bernardus, though it includes no discourse on propagation. The celestial voyage is now made by Pru⁄ dentia; and the planetary Venus is associated with 'Veneris pestes' (vi. 482), from which the new⁄formed soul is pre⁄ served by the unguent of Noys (baptism). To receive this soul Nature fashions a beautiful body:

> Omnes divicias forme diffundit in illo
> Nature prelarga manus; post munera pauper
> Pene fuit Natura parens que dona decoris,
> Forme thesauros vultu deponit in uno (vii. 38–41).

She lives in an evergreen garden which is walled round, as in the *Parlement*, by a forest, and watered by a fountain:

> Flore novo gaudens, folio crinita virenti,
> Non demorsa situ, non iram passa securis,
> Non deiecta solo, sparsis non devia ramis,
> Ambit silva locum, muri mentita figuram.
>
> . . . .
>
> In medio lacrimatur humus fletuque beato
> Producens lacrimas, fontem sudore perhenni
> Parturit et dulces potus singultat aquarum.
>   (i. 81–84, 97–99).[1]

But Alain reserves his most elaborate description of Nature herself for the *De Planctu Naturae*, in which he describes at length her dress 'in qua, prout oculis pictura imagina⁄ batur, animalium celebratur concilium'. Nature is the

---

lex naturae; 'lawes of nature' first occurring in Gower: *v. Conf. Am.* iii. 175, 350 ff., vii. 5375 ff. (where Gower insists that in man Reason must 'modify' these laws). 'Natural law' is first recorded from *Cursor Mundi* (*ante* 1300), but refers in its earliest uses to innate moral feeling: cf. *O.E.D.* s.vv. *natural*, I. 1; *law*, 9c; and Lydgate, *Troy Book*, v. 3239. Prologue to Deguilleville, l. 52.

[1] For other details *v.* p. 127 above; and for summaries of the whole work *v.* Lewis, op. cit., pp. 98–104, and Raby, *History of Christian⁄Latin Poetry*, ii (1927), 16 ff.

willing deputy of God: 'ejus opus sufficiens, meum opus
deficiens; ejus opus mirabile, meum opus mutabile . . .'.[1]
Alain is a theologian as well as a poet: his Natura gives
Theologia her due place; and it is as a divine agent that she
reappears in his *Contra Haereticos*:

Cum ergo Deus, mediante Natura, res procreaturus esset,
propter peccatum Adae noluit mutare legem naturae. Haec
enim fuit lex naturae ab origine, ut ex similibus similia pro-
crearentur, ut de homine homo, de rationali rationalis—[2]

where, as de Lage says, 'ce terme de "procréer" est capital
pour définir l'œuvre de la Nature'. This Nature had
in the *Planctus*, conferred on Venus, Hymenaeus (her
husband), and Cupid (her son) the regulating of love; but
Venus had abused her trust, consorted with Antigamus,
and borne him the bastard Jocus; in other words, man has
perverted nature and abused his appetites.

[1] *Ed. cit.* (T. Wright), ii. 437–55. The lists of animals on her garments—
birds on the peplum, fish on the pallium, other animals on the tunic—have
antecedents in Mathieu de Vendôme and elsewhere: cf. G. Raynaud de Lage,
Alain de Lille, Montreal and Paris, 1951, p. 79, and nn. 186, 187. The passage
describing the sun's aspect at her approach—'Phoebus etiam vultum solito
induens laetiorem in occursum virginis ostendens totas sui luminis effundebat
divitias' (p. 445)—seems to show Alain adopting Claudian (*v.* n. 1, p. 195
above).

[2] Cited by de Lage, p. 63, n. 151. The doctrine, which Alain evidently
takes from Boethius, is repeated in a typical thirteenth-century encyclopedia, the
Image du Monde: *v.* Caxton's version, ed. O. H. Prior, E.E.T.S. (E.S.), 110,
1913, pp. 46–47; and the references supplied by Prior. Note also pp. 43–44
('Nature maketh redy and habandouneth whereas God wylle . . . fourmeth
nothing in vayn', &c.). For a full discussion of the *De Planctu Naturae* and of
Alain's conception of Nature *v.* de Lage, cc. ii–iv, and H. Gelzer, *Zum
Einfluss der Scholastik auf den Afr. Roman*, Halle, 1917, pp. 30 ff.; Gelzer discusses
Alain's relation to the Chartrain philosophers, and quotes the important
article on Natura in Alain's *Distinctiones* (*P.L.* ccx. 871), which may be com-
pared with Cicero's discussion of 'quid sit ipsa natura', *De Nat. Deor.* II. xxxii.
(R. H. Green's article in *Speculum*, xxxi (1956), pp. 649 ff., came to hand
too late to be considered here.)

Klibansky has been able to claim that medieval allegory was essentially a development of the Platonism that per-meates Bernardus and Alain. It is not surprising, therefore, that the Natura who embodies so much of twelfth-century platonic doctrine should henceforth figure largely in alle-gorical poetry. Shortly after the appearance of the *Anti-claudianus*, Jean de Hanville wrote his *Archithrenius* (1185),[1] in which a youth in search of Natura passes on his way the golden palace of Venus, who is attended by a lovely damsel, and by Cupid, both of whom are described in much detail; thence proceeds to a tavern, falling a prey to gluttony; and beyond Mount Ambition comes ultimately to a Thule of eternal spring, where the discourse of philo-sophers prepares the youth for life. Suddenly looking up, he sees a beautiful woman, 'shining like a star . . . reverend yet eternally young'; it is Natura, who, after expounding natural philosophy, listens to his complaint against her (the motif recurs often in later poetry), but persuades him to wed a fair virgin identified with 'moderantia'; among other gifts she brings the girdle of Venus; the marriage is celebrated with music in the presence of birds all speaking after their own fashion (cf. p. 182 above). Here the new features that the reader of the *Parlement* will notice are the abode of Venus, the association of Nature and moderation,[2] and the speaking birds. Very different is the Natura glimpsed in an anonymous poem of about the same date,[3] in which the poet finds her living *in medio nemoris plano circumdata parvo*;

---

[1] *Satirical Poets of the Twelfth Century*, i. 240–392. For a summary *v.* Raby, op. cit. ii. 100 ff. Interesting incidental references to *Natura parens* and to her forge occur on p. 248, ed. cit. The text as Wright prints it is often puzzling.

[2] Cf. p. 191 above.

[3] Printed by Raby, op. cit. ii. 22, from B.M. MS. Burney, 305. Nature also stands in opposition to excessive curiosity in Gautier de Chatillon's *Alexandreis*; x. i ff. (*P.L.* ccix. 563).

she is *quasi nude virginis instar*, forbids him to approach, and warns him against prying into her secrets:

> Sta procul et noli mihi plus inferre pudorem.
> In mea te secreta fui vix passa venire,
> Debuerasque mihi deferre fidemque perhenni
> Custodire pie matri domineque tenore . . . .

The author may have been an Englishman; but the phrase 'secrets of Nature' is not recorded in the vernacular before the sixteenth century (*Pilgrimage of Perfection*, 1526).

Once Nature had been identified with the divine work of creation, and Alain had described her as creating the perfect body, poets were quick to give her the special role of the creator of beautiful women. Even before Bernardus had written, Hildebert of Tours could flatter Matilda, wife of Henry I of England, in these words:

> Parcius elimans alias Natura puellas,
>   Distulit in dotes esse benigna tuas.
> In te fudit opes, et opus mirabile cernens,
>   Est mirata suas hoc potuisse manus.[1]

The French poets of courtoisie popularized this rhetoric, the more easily because they linked love with spring time, celebrating it as the season in which Nature created beautiful flowers, and mated bird and beast. Thus in *La Messe des Oisiaus*, of the early fourteenth century, Venus, whilst acknowledging Nature's primacy, says:

---

[1] *P.L.*, clxxi. 1143. Cf. Hildebert's epigram on a bishop:
>   Ad decus ecclesiae cum te Natura crearet,
>   'Sis expers vitii, caetera', dixit, 'habe . . .'
(Raby, op. cit. i. 318); Dante has Nature create 'quel sommo Ippocrate . . . agli animali . . . ch'ell' ha più cari' (*Purg.* xxix. 136–9); *v.* also Geoffroi de Vinsauf, *Poetria Nova*, 563 ff. (ed. Faral, p. 214). Gelzer, op. cit., collects Old French examples (but *v.* Curtius, p. 181, n. 36).

Nature et je faisons amer
Bestes, oisiaus, poissons de mer

. . . .

. . . Nature à amer semont
Toutes creatures del mont.[1]

In Machaut's *Dit de l'Alerion* she instructs the birds[2] and
in his *Dit du Vergier* she presents to the poet her three
children Sens, Rhétorique, Musique, whilst Amours
presents Doux-Penser, Plaisance, Espérance, 'pour lui
donner matere à faire ce que Nature li a enchargié'; the
poem proper, set in a paradisal 'vergier' full of singing
birds, is primarily concerned with Amours and the poet's
mistress, the image of perfection—'Dieus et Nature l'ont
si faite'.[3] The poets often place Nature in company with,
though sometimes at odds with, Reason—the relation
between the two has never been easy to describe, even in
philosophic terms. Her physical characteristics vary, but
in *Les Échecs amoureux*, an early fourteenth-century work
the popularity of which is attested by Lydgate's version
entitled *Reson and Sensuallyte*,[4] she is indescribably beautiful, 'under god the chefe goddesse', and 'sempte by her
vysage, To be but yonge and tendir of age'; her mantle, as

---

[1] *Dits et Contes de Baudouin de Condé* (ed. A. Scheler, Bruxelles, 1866–7),
iii. 1–48, ll. 979–80, 1097–8; *v.* also ll. 1355–6, with the surprising reference
to Scripture. Most of the other appearances of Nature in Old French literature
are listed by Knowlton, *Modern Philology*, xx (1923), pp. 309 ff., though he
does not refer to the full-length allegory of Nature and Norreture in the *Roman
de Silence*, for which *v.* Gelzer, pp. 68 ff.: in this allegory Nature quotes in her
defence Gen. i. 26 (l. 6044: cf. p. 9 above).

[2] *Œuvres* (S.A.T.F.), ii. 359. The poem includes much bird-lore.

[3] *Œuvres* i. 1 ff. Miniatures showing Nature are reproduced from a MS. of
this poem (B.N. fr. 1584) in H. Martin, *La Miniature française*, figs. lxv–lxvi,
and *Manuscrits à peinture du XIIIe au XVIe siècle*, 1955 (pl. xvii). In Graunson
'Dieu, Raison et Nature' make the perfect woman: ed. cit., p. 210.

[4] Quotations are from Lydgate's version, ed. Sieper, E.E.T.S. (E.S.), 81, 84,
1901, 1903. The French text awaits an editor.

in *De Planctu Naturae*, pictures all creation, her hair shines like the sun, the seven planets are set in her crown, and she

> The elementes doth governe
> In ther werkynge ful contrayre.
> And this lady debonayre
> Doth them somwhile acorde in oon,
> And after severeth hem anoon. (286–90)

She bids the author rise from his bed where he lies in sloth whilst the birds are

> For gladnesse of the morwenynge
> Preysing god, as they best may,
> Synging ther hourys of the day; (458–60)

and she urges him to choose the path of Reason as against Sensuality. Later Venus appears, maintaining that 'by goddis ordynance' she serves Nature (in fact she resembles the apostate Venus of Alain), but Diana warns him of her perils. Deduit leads him to Amor, who (to quote Sieper's summary) represents Love as distinct from sensual pleasure; Nature, 'in wise care for the conservation of her works', knows how to unite both. Pallas, on the other hand, claims that Amor does not fulfil his office properly, and that to serve Venus is to ignore Reason and to wrong Nature. The poem, which is incomplete, probably owes something to Brunetto Latini's unfinished *Tesoretto*, in which the dreamer finds himself in the presence of Nature, an awe-inspiring figure, who as vicar of God expounds the universe; he visits the home of the virtues, and then the realm of Amor with his attendant passions; escaping at length, he resolves to turn to the higher, 'spiritual' love, which is in accord with Nature's counsels.[1] Here we have a foretaste

---

[1] *v.* Knowlton, 'Nature in Earlier Italian', *M.L.N.* xxxvi (1921), p. 330. A critical text of the *Tesoretto* is to be found in *Zeits. für roman. phil.* vii (1883), 336 ff.

of the tediosíties of Polifilo's *Hypnerotomachia*; but we also
have, as in the *Parlement*, the juxtaposition of sensual love
and Nature; and Brunetto's *Li Livres dou Trésor*, like the
Archithrenius, associates Nature with measure, concluding:
'nus ne doit aler contre Nature'. Even if Chaucer had
read Latini he could have gleaned from him little that
was new; whilst in Dante the references to 'Natura' are
almost incidental.[1]

Nature as she appears in the *Roman de la Rose*, or rather,
in Jean de Meun's part of it, derives largely from Alain.
Again she is a goddess of surpassing fairness, with a forge
of generation; again all creatures obey her save man.[2] In
Guillaume de Deguilleville's *Pélerinage de la Vie Humaine*
(1335), on the other hand, she appears as a lady 'off gret
age', with eyes 'brennynge briht as any glede'; and 'wonder
large of hir feature'; she is in a furious temper with Grace
Dieu because the latter's miraculous powers impinge on
her authority over all things below 'the cercle of the colde
moone'; having described all her operations, she adds that

> I am nat Rakel nor hasty;
> I hate, in myn opyniouns,
> Al sodeyn mutacyouns.
> My werkys be the bettre wrought,
> Bycause that I haste nought.
> I take record of dame Resoun—[3]

---

[1] e.g. *Inf.* xi. 56, 61 (Love made by Nature); xxxi. 49 ff. (*v.* p. 141, n. 2);
Purg. xvi. 79 ('miglior natura' implicitly identified with God). [For a (lost)
English MS. of *Li Livres dou Trésor v.* Benolt's Inventory, printed by A. R.
Wagner, *Heralds and Heraldry*, 1956, p. 153.]

[2] ll. 16165 ff. Robinson notes the resemblance to C.T. C. 11 ff.; but
Chaucer's application of the references to Apelles and Zeuxis is new. De Meun
calls Nature 'la deesse' at l. 16728. Illustrations of her forge occur in several
MSS. of the *Roman*, including Harl. 4425, f. 140, Douce 371, f. 40*v.*, and
Douce 195, f. 114*v.*; in this last she is shown forging beautiful birds.

[3] Quotations are from Lydgate's version (*The Pilgrimage of the Life of Man,*

which gives Grace-Dieu her opening: Nature's complaint,
she says,[1] belies her: 'You say I entered your garden without
leave; but all your power comes from me; your own clerk,
the paynim Aristotle, proved that all generation is sustained by the sun, which comes under my authority'.
Nature at once confesses her error; and a similar dialogue
between Sapience and Aristotle, who had

> seyn so many fayre thynges,
> And so many uncouth werkynges
> Withinne my scole, of gret favour, (5701-3)

has a similar outcome—at least, both Nature and Aristotle
see that they must accept what Sapience says. Thus Nature
is fitted into a firmly orthodox pattern—which includes a
discourse on Christian marriage such as Chaucer might
have written:

> They most of herte be al on,
> Tweyne in on, and on in tweyne.[1] (1928-9)

Chaucer was probably the first English poet to use
'Nature' in a clearly personified sense, following the
example of Alain and the *Roman de la Rose*.[2] In *Anelida*

E.E.T.S. (E.S.), 67, 83), ll. 3495 ff. That 'natura in operando procedit ordinate'
was a commonplace: cf. e.g., Albertus Magnus, *Opera Omnia*, xii (1952),
301. 5, and Donne, *Devotions*, ed. Sparrow, p. 111.

[1] For comments on Deguilleville's doctrine of Nature *v.* C. S. Lewis,
op. cit., pp. 266-7. His belief that the soul is buried alive in the body is of a
piece with his assertion that Nature ordained strife between them.

[2] But we should probably recognize in *Pearl*, l. 749 ('þy beaute com never
of natur') an allusion to her role that may be as early as any in Chaucer: cf. the
references to Pygmalion and Aristotle, ll. 750-1, which derive from *RR*,
16165 ff. Thus the form should probably be capitalized, as also in *Destruction of
Troy*, l. 4010; and in several of *O.E.D.*'s other quotations s.v. Nature, 9. C.T.A.
2758-9 ('ther Nature wil nat wirche, Farewel physik') recalls Hippocrates
(*Lex*, ed. Kuhn, l. 4) and Albertus, ed. cit., p. 234: 'Natura agit contra morbum
tripliciter: Materiam digerendo, dividendo, et expellendo'—cf. l. 2751; cf.
also Alain's eighth *distinctio*, cit. Gelzer, p. 31: 'Dicitur naturalis calor, unde

and Arcite, l. 80, the *Book of the Duchesse*, ll. 871, 1195, *Troilus and Criseyde*, i. 102–5, she appears as the creator of beautiful women, in the *Complaint of Venus*, l. 14 (cf. *Troilus*, iv. 1096), of handsome men.[1] In the *Book of the Duchesse*, ll. 871 ff., this 'goddesse, dame Nature', makes the woman's eyes open and close 'by mesure'; where again he is following French models. But he refers to Nature under the name of another deity when he describes the Black Knight as almost demented,

> Thogh Pan, that men clepen god of kinde,
> Were for his sorwes never so wrooth. (512–13)

This identification of Pan with Nature is likewise found in Gower's *Confessio Amantis*, where the lover, having com‑ plained in the course of his supplication, that

> Nature techeth me the weie,
> To love, and yit no certein sche compasseth
> How I schal spede,

applies to himself the tale

> Hou whilom Pan, which is the god of kinde,
> With love wrastled and was overcome;
> For ever I wrastle, and ever I am behinde—(viii. 2239–41)

where the reference is presumably to Pan's love for Syrinx, as described by Ovid (*Met.* i. 689 ff.). The early association of the pastoral god's name with πᾶς, πᾶν, had led to his being thought of as 'totius naturae deus' (Servius, Com‑

physicus dicit esse pugnam inter morbum et naturam, i.e. naturalem calorem'. Chaucer's Criseyde (but not Boccaccio's) invokes Jove as 'auctor of nature' (*Troilus and Criseyde*, iii. 1016 and 1437)—a phrase echoed by Troilus: cf. p. 125, n. 2, above; and C.T. F. 469; *Hous of Fame*, l. 584. As God's 'vicaire‑general' (C.T. C. 20) Nature resembles Dante's Fortune ('general ministra', *Inf.* vii. 78).

References in later poets to Nature as 'dame' or 'empresse' (e.g. *Book of the Howlat*, l. 32, Lindsay's *Papyngo*, 127, &c.) are as likely to be due to French as to Chaucerian influence.   [1] Cf. Usk's *Testament of Love*, ii. xii, *ad fin.*

mentary on Virgil, *Ecl.* 2. 31), and in the Orphic Hymns and a metrical inscription of the Antonine period he is linked with Physis.[1] Isidore of Seville takes over the description, and the etymology:

Pan dicunt Graeci, Latini Silvanum, deum rusticorum, quem in naturae similitudinem formaverunt; unde et Pan dictus est, id est omne. . . . Caprinas ungulas habet, ut soliditatem terrae ostendat, quem volunt rerum et totius naturae deum; unde Pan quasi omnia dicunt.[2]

Walter Map is one of several medieval Latin writers to repeat this;[3] and conceivably the use by Chalcidius and Bernardus Silvestris (*inter alios*) of *silva* as a designation of matter in its formless state[4] helped to establish Pan as a synonym for Nature, though examples in the vernacular appear to be rare.[5]

In using 'kinde' for *natura* Chaucer is following the example set by the Alfredian translator of Boethius, who regularly renders the Latin word in all its senses, including 'kind, species of a thing', as 'gecynd'; some trace of a personified sense may be present in *Hali Meiþhad*, l. 45 (*c.* 1200): 'Ichulle halde me hal þurh þe grace of godd, as cunde me maked.' *Lex naturae* becomes 'lagh o kinde' in *Cursor Mundi*, l. 28491 (where it is broken through lechery). Kind and Nature are implicitly identified in the Chaucerian *Complaynt d'Amours*: the mistress is

---

[1] Curtius, loc. cit., nn. 2 and 3.

[2] *Etym. Lib.* VIII. xi. 81–83. Macrobius has an interesting variant: 'hunc deum Arcades colunt appellantes τὸν ὕλης κύριον, non silvarum dominum, sed universae substantiae materialis dominatorem, significari volentes (*Sat.*, l. xxii. 2).

[3] *De Nugis Curialium*, Dist. ii, c. xvi, *ad fin.* Cf. Grosseteste, cit. Gilson, op. cit., p. 472.

[4] Cf. ὕλη, meaning not only '(a) wood' but 'matter as a principle of being'; e.g. Aristotle, *Metaph.* 63. 2, and Macrobius, loc. cit.

[5] In *RR* Pan appears only in conventional conjunction with Bacchus, Ceres, and Cybele.

The benignest and beste eek that Nature
Hath wrought or shal, whyl that the world may dure

(ll. 53-54);

but the lover wonders

> Why that she lefte pite so behinde?
> It was, ywis, a greet defaute in Kinde—

'God or Nature sore wolde I blame' (ll. 55 ff.).

God and Nature are frequently linked by Gower (e.g.
Confessio Amantis, i. 31; 'thing which God in lawe of
kynde Hath set');[1] *Vox Clamantis*, i. 1092, 1308 ('Quod
natura sibi vel deus ipse petit'), and in his account of the
creation of man Nature has her place: Adam raises his
head, views the stars in their courses,

> Noticiamque tamen illi Natura ministrat:
> Quod sit homo, quod sunt [*v.l.* sint] ista creata videt:
> Quod sit ad humanos usus hic conditus orbis,
> Quod sit ei proprius mundus, et ipse dei.
> Ardet in auctoris illius sensus amorem,
> Iamque recognovit quid sit amare deum.

(*Vox Clamantis*, vii. 561-6)

The sequence of thought here, traditional as it is,[2] recurs in
Piers Plowman, when Kind appears to the dreamer

And nempned me by my name and bad me nymen hede,
And thorw the wondres of this worlde wytte for to take,
And on a mountayne that mydelerd hiȝte—as me tho thouȝte—
I was fette forth by ensaumples to knowe
Thorugh eche a creature and kynde my creatoure to lovye.[3]

---

[1] But *v.* p. 197, n. 3, above; cf. viii. 2231 ff.; *v.* also vii. 794.

[2] Wickert, *Studien zu John Gower*, 1953, p. 160, compares Vincent of
Beauvais, *Spec. Morale*, I. 1, Dist. 10. Cf. also William of Conches, *cit.*
R. L. Poole, *Medieval Thought and Learning*, 2nd ed. 1920, p. 106.

[3] B. xi. 313–17: Skeat prints 'Kynde', l. 317; but Langland may be referring
not to the totality of creatures but to 'my *own* nature', 'the light of nature'.
A similar uncertainty obtains in many other passages: thus *Book of the Duchesse*,

He sees all beasts ruled and rewarded by Reason—'save man and his make'; even so had Alain and many a later writer deplored that only man was recalcitrant to the laws of Nature. Neither Kind nor Reason (who appears at xi. 326 without formal introduction) is here described. Reason is treated as masculine (361), and so is Kind in Langland's parable of the Castle of *Caro* (B. ix. 1 ff.). At the end of that parable the dreamer asks outright: 'What kynnes thyng is Kynde?' (l. 25), and Wit answers:

Kynde is a creatour of alle kynnes thinges;
Fader and fourmour of al that ever was maked;
And that is the gret god that gynnynge had nevere,
Lorde of lyf and of li3te, of lysse and of peyne . . .

Thus Nature for Langland appears under one aspect to be identifiable with God as Creator, which would be reason enough for his treating Kynde as masculine. It is Kind that knows the causes of the colours in flowers, the mysteries of breeding (cf. p. 142 above),

And kennede Adam to know his pryve membres
And tau3te hym and Eve to hylien hem with leves.[1]

For Langland as for Chaucer Nature is primarily concerned with procreation, and birds are the most appropriate examples of its operation. Kind appears later in the

ll. 16 ff., probably requires the sense 'lex naturae', C.T. A. 3007 ('nature hath nat taken his bygynning . . .') the sense 'natura rerum' (the phrase in Boethius, iii, Pr. x. 4, which Chaucer is following at this point). A typical borderline case is 'kuinde craved nou þe riht' (*English Lyrics of the XIIIth Century*, 4, l. 9); but the poet who wrote 'Where kynde cannot go ytt will crepe' (*Secular Lyrics of the XIV–XVth Centuries*, 129, l. 48) was hardly thinking of a personified Nature; nor was Lydgate in speaking of persons coupled 'againes al nature' (*Temple of Glas*, l. 181). Alain's *distinctiones*, referred to above, may profitably be kept in mind when interpreting ME. examples.

[1] B. xii. 225 ff.; once again Kynde has a touch of the ambiguity noted above, here being almost equivalent to 'instinct': cf. Alain's ninth *distinctio*: '. . . natualiter . . . id est naturali instinctu rationis'—and Tertullian, *De Anima*, 16.

poem (B. xx. 79 ff.) in response to an appeal from Conscience, and, coming out of the planets (thought of astro-
logically), sends fevers and pestilences on the followers of
Antichrist. Kind here represents the forces of nature; but
they are subject to change (*mutabile*, as Alain had put it):
for, Conscience having besought him to cease, he did so,
'to se the peple amende' (108); whereupon Fortune sent
Lechery to beguile 'al maner men wedded and unwedded'
(111)—another instance of Lechery and Nature being in
opposition. Kind eventually counsels 'what crafte is best to
lerne':

'Lerne to love', quod Kynde, 'and leve of alle othre.' (207)

Caritas, in short, is a natural instinct.[1] Langland's
treatment of Nature remains throughout free from any unorthodox tincture: his Kind never becomes that self-
existency which the Edmund of *King Lear* takes for his
goddess; and Passus xix, like Chaucer's list of cruel and
wicked birds, makes it clear that these poets were free from
naïvely optimistic views of Nature such as an uncritical
acceptance of the philosophy of plenitude might produce.
   In English fifteenth-century literature the few representations of Natura derive almost entirely from Alain;[2]
and the modern editors of the alliterative *Death and Life* have
detected a hypostasis of Alain's Natura in the Lady Life
of that poem, who is, to be sure, described in terms similar
to his: she is clad in green, and 'brighter of her blee then
was the bright sonn'; boughs bend down at her approach,
birds sing—and she 'welcometh them full winlye'; but
though her entourage includes two knights (Hope and
Love) who have equivalents in Alain's Spes and Amor,

---

[1] Cf. B. i. 140-1.

[2] Most of them have been listed by Knowlton, *J.E.G.P.* xx (1920),
pp. 186 ff.; he does not refer to *The Kingis Quair*, st. 43.

and though the scene in which she opposes Death may have been suggested by *Anticlaudianus*, viii. 218 ff., yet the climax of the poem—Life's narration of the Passion and Resurrection—brings it closer to Langland than to Alain.[1]

Lydgate has disconsolate lovers 'pitouslie on god and kynde pleyne' in his *Temple of Glas*,[2] and in his *Flour of Curtesye* the birds fly

> As they of kynde have inclinacioun
> And as Nature, emperesse and gyd,
> Of everything liste to provide. (ll. 61–63)

As this poem refers to St. Valentine's Day we should prob-ably treat the phrase 'by custome of nature' (l. 16) as a reference to the goddess; but Lydgate (who a few lines later can speak of Venus and Cypride as different divi-nities) was perhaps not very clear, and not very much concerned, about the force of the words. Elsewhere he is capable of giving to a Nature confessedly modelled on Alain's figure in the *De Planctu Naturae*, and clad 'al in flours and blosmes of a tre', the kerchef of Valence that in the *Parlement* is the sole apparel of Venus.[3]

---

[1] It was printed in *Bishop Percy's Folio Manuscript*, iii (1868), and re-edited by Hanford and Stedman, *Studies in Philology*, xv (1918).

[2] l. 224. For the association cf. e.g. *Secular Lyrics of XIV–XVth Centur es*, 181, ll. 50–52, and the sixteenth-century *Court of Love*, ll. 1160 ff., where maimed and ugly lovers, 'of nature complaining',

> . . . seide that god and kind
> Hath forged thaim to worshippen the sterre
> Venus the bright, and leften all behind
> His other werkes clene and out of mind;

here Skeat emends to 'god of kind'—though 'forged' would apply better to Nature than to God (cf. p. 196 above); in the same century Sir David Lindsay gives her a 'natural forge'.

[3] 'Horns Away', st. 3 (E.E.T.S. (o.s.) 92, p. 662). For other references to Nature in Lydgate *v. Troy Book*, Index to Bergen's edition, and Schick's note to *Reson and Sensuallyte*, ll. 203 ff.: at ll. 164 ff. of that poem he dwells on Nature's instruction of the birds in nest-building, as Langland does at B. xi. 336 ff.

Of his successors Dunbar may be taken for our present purpose as representative. To him Nature is still 'the noble quene' (*The Merle and the Nichtingaill*, l. 22). His merle argues that the nightingale who claims that 'all love is lost but upone God allone' goes expressly against the law of Kind: God puts great beauty in women in order that they should be loved:

> To luf eik natur gaif thame inclynning:
> And he of natur that wirker wes and king
> Wald no thing frustir put, na lat be sene,
> Into his creature of his awin making. (52–55)

But the nightingale replies that God put these graces and goodnesses in women so that he should be praised as their creator. In the end the merle confesses his error: 'This frustir love all is bot vanite'. If this sentiment seems to hark back to Deguilleville, the Dame Nature of *The Thrissil and the Rois* comes out of Alain. In *The Tua Mariit Wemen and the Wedo* a passage on disparate marriages which (like the four lines just quoted) owes something to de Meun, introduces Nature alongside Kind, as Lydgate might have done: 'It is agane the law of luf, of kind, and of natur' (l. 58). In the same poem she 'full nobillie annamilit, with flouris the rich verdure' (l. 31). In *The Goldyn Targe* Nature and Venus are 'quene and quene' (l. 73); but it is Nature that has the first place; she bestows on May a gown 'rich to behald, and nobil of renoune' (ll. 87–88), which she surely owes to Alain; and the birds who at the beginning of the dream thank her, 'thair quene so clair', for 'thair nobill norising', are still there when Venus, Cupid, and their Courts have taken ship and vanished, and the dreamer has awoken. Thus almost all the diverse medieval conceptions of Nature find a place in our last medieval poet.

Bibliographical Note

BIBLIOGRAPHIES of the poem will be found in Eleanor Prescott Hammond's *Chaucer, a Bibliographical Manual* (1908), pp. 387 ff., and in Dudley Dale Griffith's *Bibliography of Chaucer*, 1908–53 (1955), pp. 284 ff. Since 1953 the following articles, essays, and notes have appeared:

GARDINER STILLWELL, 'Chaucer's Eagles and their Choice on February 14', *Journal of English and Germanic Philology*, liii (1954), pp. 846–61.

DOROTHY EVERETT, 'Chaucer's Love Visions, with particular reference to the *Parlement of Foules*' (chap. iv of her *Essays on Middle English Literature*, Oxford, 1955).

MACDONALD EMSLIE, 'Codes of Love and Class Distinctions', *Essays in Criticism*, v (Jan. 1955), pp. 1–17. See also comments by Cecily Clark and D. S. Brewer, with a reply by Mr. Emslie, ibid., pp. 405–18.

CHARLES O. MACDONALD, 'An Interpretation of Chaucer's Parlement of Foules', *Speculum*, xxx (July 1955), pp. 444–57.

DOROTHY BETHURUM, 'The Center of the *Parlement of Foules*', in *Essays in Honor of Walter Clyde Curry* (Nashville, Tennessee, 1955), pp. 39–50.

ETHEL SEATON, '*The Parlement of Foules* and Lionel of Clarence', *Medium Ævum*, xxv (1956), pp. 168–74.[1]

ROBERT WORTH FRANK, JR., 'Structure and Meaning in the *Parlement of Foules*', *Publications of the Modern Language Association of America*, lxxi (1956), pp. 530–9.

THOMAS P. HARRISON, *They Tell of Birds*, University of Texas Press, 1956 [c. ii discusses birds in Chaucer].[1]

[1] Published whilst the present work was printing.

Index

PRINTED IN
GREAT BRITAIN
AT THE
UNIVERSITY PRESS
OXFORD
BY
CHARLES BATEY
PRINTER
TO THE
UNIVERSITY